Discourse
and
Lifespan
Identity

LANGUAGE AND LANGUAGE BEHAVIORS SERIES

Howard Giles
SERIES EDITOR
Department of Communication
University of California, Santa Barbara

This series is unique in its sociopsychological orientation to "language and language behaviors" and their communicative and miscommunicative consequences. Books in the series not only examine how biological, cognitive, emotional, and societal forces shape the use of language, but the ways in which language behaviors can create and continually revise understandings of our bodily states, the situations in which we find ourselves, and our identities within the social groups and events around us. Methodologically and ideologically eclectic, the edited and authored volumes are written to be accessible for advanced students in the social, linguistic, and communication sciences as well as to serve as valuable resources for seasoned researchers in these fields.

Volumes in this series

1 THE POWER OF SILENCE: *Social and Pragmatic Perspectives*
   Adam Jaworski
2. AFRICAN AMERICAN COMMUNICATION: *Ethnic Identity and Cultural Interpretation*
   Michael L. Hecht, Mary Jane Collier, and Sidney A. Ribeau
3 POWER IN LANGUAGE: *Verbal Communication and Social Influence*
   Sik Hung Ng and James J. Bradac
4. DISCOURSE AND LIFESPAN IDENTITY
   Nikolas Coupland and Jon F. Nussbaum, Editors

Volumes previously published by Multilingual Matters in the series Monographs in the Social Psychology of Language and in the series Intercommunication may be obtained through Multilingual at 8A Hill Road, Clevedon, Avon BS21 7 HH, England.

Discourse
and
Lifespan
Identity

NIKOLAS COUPLAND
JON F. NUSSBAUM

LANGUAGE
AND
LANGUAGE
BEHAVIORS
volume 4

SAGE Publications
International Educational and Professional Publisher
Newbury Park   London   New Delhi

For information address:

SAGE Publications, Inc.
2455 Teller Road
Newbury Park, California 91320

SAGE Publications Ltd.
6 Bonhill Street
London EC2A 4PU
United Kingdom

SAGE Publications India Pvt. Ltd.
M-32 Market
Greater Kailash I
New Delhi 110 048 India

Printed in the United States of America

Library of Congress Cataloging-in-Publication Data

Main entry under title:

Discourse and lifespan identity / edited by Nikolas Coupland, Jon F. Nussbaum.
    p. cm.—(Language and language behaviors ; v. 4)
    Includes bibliographical references and index.
    ISBN 0-8039-5105-1 (cl).—ISBN 0-8039-5106-X (pb)
    1. Discourse analysis—Social aspects. 2. Social interaction.
3. Life cycle, Human. I. Nussbaum, Jon F. II. Series.
P302.84.D57   1993
306.4'4—dc20   93-25530

93 94 95 96 10 9 8 7 6 5 4 3 2 1

Sage Production Editor: Astrid Virding

Contents

Acknowledgments   ix

Introduction: Discourse, Selfhood,
and the Lifespan   x
NIKOLAS COUPLAND, JON F. NUSSBAUM,
and ALAN GROSSMAN

SECTION I Discursively Formulating the Lifespan   1

1. Becoming Someone:
   Identity and Belonging   5
   JOHN SHOTTER

2. Autobiographies and
   the Shaping of Gendered Lives   28
   MARY M. GERGEN and KENNETH J. GERGEN

3. Discursively Formulating the
   Significance of Reminiscence in Later Life   55
   KEVIN BUCHANAN and DAVID J. MIDDLETON

4. Positioning and Autobiography:
   Telling Your Life   81
   LUK VAN LANGENHOVE and ROM HARRÉ

SECTION II Achieving Control, Transition,
and Continuity   101

5. Pedagogic Discourse and Interaction Orders:
   Sharing Time and Control   103
   KARIN ARONSSON and ANN-CARITA EVALDSSON

6. Contextualizing Social Control:
An Ethnomethodological Analysis of
Parental Accounts of Discipline Interactions   132
DIANE T. PRUSANK

7. Transitions Through the Student Career   154
ANN Q. STATON

8. Making Connections: Narrative as
the Expression of Continuity Between
Generations of Grandparents
and Grandchildren   173
VALERIE CRYER McKAY

SECTION III Discourse and Intergenerational
Relationships   187

9. The Construction of "Closeness"
in Mother-Daughter Relationships
Across the Lifespan   191
KAREN HENWOOD and GERALDINE COUGHLAN

10. Intergenerational Communication
in the Mother-Daughter Dyad
Regarding Caregiving Decisions   215
VICTOR G. CICIRELLI

11. Investigations of Marital Communication
and Lifespan Development   237
ALAN L. SILLARS and PAUL H. ZIETLOW

12. Couples and Change: Intervention
Through Discourse and Images   262
WILLIAM W. WILMOT and JOYCE L. HOCKER

Epilogue: Future Prospects
in Lifespan Sociolinguistics   284
NIKOLAS COUPLAND, JUSTINE COUPLAND,
and JON F. NUSSBAUM

Author Index   294

Subject Index   301

About the Contributors   304

Acknowledgments

The Fulbright USA/UK Commission has in many ways supported international cooperation in the area of Communication and the Lifespan. In 1988, they sponsored an international conference at the University of Wales Conference Centre, Gregynog, Powys, Mid Wales on the theme of "Communication, Health and the Elderly." The proceedings were published as a volume in the Fulbright Colloquia series, University of Manchester Press, 1990. For the academic session 1989/1990, they funded Nikolas Coupland as Fulbright Scholar at the Department of Communication, University of California, Santa Barbara. Reciprocally, they funded Jon F. Nussbaum as Fulbright Scholar at the Centre for Applied English Language Studies, University of Wales College of Cardiff for the 1991/1992 session. It is largely through Fulbright support, then, that this volume was conceived and produced.

Further thanks are due to the University of Macquarie, Sydney, Australia, where Nikolas Coupland was Visiting Research Fellow for October/November of 1992, allowing various aspects of the editing of this book to be completed. We also thank Mark and Carol Bergstrom for their help in the final editing of this book.

Introduction: Discourse, Selfhood, and the Lifespan

NIKOLAS COUPLAND

JON F. NUSSBAUM

ALAN GROSSMAN

One central theme underlies and unites the very diverse chapters of this book. It is that *who we are,* at the various points in our passage through the life course, bears some systematic relation to our experiences of, and our participation in, *language* and *social interaction.* At first sight, this may not seem such a challenging association of ideas. In our day-to-day lives, as well as in academic literatures, we commonly enough take age, maturity, and experience to be factors that condition different forms of talk and different degrees of language competence. The clearest academic instance is the psycholinguistic study of "language development" in childhood. Psycholinguistics presupposes that, within certain constraints, age conditions linguistic and communicative competence, and then goes on to give this association substance and detail. Generalizing very grossly about this productive tradition of research, we can say that its main contribution has been to map out the predictable and rule-governed stages through which the maturing child passes into adulthood, revealing increasingly rich and complex linguistic and communicative resources.

When attention has been paid to the other end of the lifespan (and this is far less common), some researchers have set out to demonstrate that linguistic and communicative competence, at least in some specific respects, *decline* with advancing age. At present this is a controversial area of study having produced inconclusive findings (see Coupland, Coupland, & Giles, 1991, for a review and critique of this approach). But the study of child language "development" and this approach to elderly linguistic "decrement" are built on the same underlying assumption: that age can appropriately be seen as a *determinant* of language competence and language behavior.

However, our perspective in the present book is in many ways the *converse* of the psycholinguistic one. Although we have come to think of language use as being conditioned by the developmental stage of the self, might it not also be true that our developing selves are in the thrall of language use, and *throughout our lives* rather than merely at the fringes? Can't we see the positions that we occupy in the lifespan, our changing roles and identities, at least in part as a function of our forms and practices of talk? If we adopt this alternative perspective, we need to think critically about taken-for-granted social categories such as "child" and "adult," "youth," "middle age" and "old age." Where do they come from, and what cultural assumptions sustain them as sense-making concepts in our lives and in our language? What social rituals endorse our accepted views of "coming of age," "turning 40," "entering retirement," or generally "acting our age"? What conventional forms of talk do we have for discussing life "stages," life changes, and age itself? How, where, and when does age surface as a theme in everyday talk, and when and why do we sometimes suppress age-talk and age-categorization? Most importantly, what force can we see in these and other patterns of language and discourse for defining and constituting our changing selves, and indeed for establishing stability and continuity in life circumstances that often change very rapidly?

To begin to theorize lifespan development and identity in this way takes us well beyond the traditional realm of linguistics. What we hope to illuminate here is not the changing nature of language itself, although in some ways this is an inevitable and desirable by-product. We are interested in what language may achieve in and for us. The issue, then, is not language development as much as language and discourse in the service of personal and social development. Rather than taking "age" or "life-stage" as an objectively factual departure point, we have placed "the developing self" and processes of identity formation, maintenance, and change at the center of this book's concerns. That emphasis on *process* suggests a research endeavor that involves trawling social encounters, and wider cultural discourses about age, aging, and human development, with an eye to the overt and covert developmental meanings articulated within them. Research needs to build essentially critical accounts of how we formulate the lifespan— either in general or in particular cases. This is interdisciplinary territory where contributions from social linguists and interactionists need to be set alongside those from lifespan psychologists and social theorists. And it is very much in this collaborative spirit that this book has been developed.

The general rubric of "social constructionism" fits the book's intention well. On the other hand, this label risks being read as a contemporary antitraditional dogma that might obscure the book's particular interest. The claim that all social categories and routines, attitudes and identities are constituted through discourse has been worth putting very strongly as a radical challenge to an earlier empiricist social science (see, e.g., Potter & Edwards, 1992; Potter & Wetherell, 1987). But the impetus for a discursive perspective on the lifespan is, for us, its empirical validity as well as its theoretical interest. That is, we believe that the book's general argument is (and needs to be) warranted by the *particular* discourse processes that research can offer for scrutiny, as well as by intuitively correct theorizing. Theorizing the lifespan in discursive terms can make a significant contribution to several established areas of research, including child studies, gerontology, clinical and lifespan psychology, sociolinguistics, and communication. On the other hand, we believe that this contribution will be more immediate, compelling, and useable if theoretical claims are substantiated through analyses of language and discourse *practices*. It is for this reason that we have set more theory-driven and more text-driven studies alongside each other in the chapters that follow.

A note about interpretive research in this area needs to be made early on in this book. Many (not all) of the empirical studies assembled in this volume focus on discourse data, either from naturally occurring social interactions or from open-ended interviews with people of different ages in various social contexts. On the whole, contributors have argued (or assumed) that the resulting losses, in terms of experimental control and the marshaling of descriptive statistics in the service of specific hypotheses, are outweighed by the access that is gained to *people's own* representations and formulations of lifespan processes. This sort of profit/loss assessment is intrinsic to research in the social sciences, and we are not campaigning for a qualitative cause at the expense of other causes.

On the other hand, lifespan change does not merely "happen." It is both experienced by and enacted by people, even though studies have tended to override this experiential dimension. There is no guarantee that recordings of people "doing lifespan discourse" will produce "correct" versions of individual experience, let alone "authoritative" theories or generalizations. But it is surely wrong to ignore such data, when so much of our self-positioning in relation to society is achieved through talk, and when so much of talk orients to lifespan concerns. The moral aspect of this debate is that it is appropriate to "give voice" to the different groups of people we want to study (who otherwise become objects of research, though we tend to call them "subjects"). It is then down to our interpretive sensitivities, as researchers but also as aging humans, to read contextual meanings into these texts. This may seem a modest agenda, but the issues at stake—how we constitute ourselves in relation to life change—are far from modest.

In the remainder of this Introduction, we first consider the renewed theoretical interest in identity and self-identification as a lifespan phenomenon in contemporary writings in sociology and social psychology. Then we consider how identity, and in a few instances lifespan identity, have been approached by language and discourse researchers. We shall introduce the chapters that follow and explain the organization of the volume in short Prefaces to each of the three Sections. The Epilogue chapter suggests some organizing principles and some questions for further research in this new tradition of work.

Recent Perspectives on
Lifespan Identity and Identification

Giddens's repeated use of the phrase "the reflexive project of the self" in his recent writings (1990, 1991) is itself a denial of fixity and an appeal to process in considering personal and social identity. For Giddens, "the self" must be seen as the focus of an ongoing dialogue that individuals sustain with themselves in relation to their changing lived experiences. Selfhood is a "project" in the sense that any account of "who we are" will need to respond to continuously evolving circumstances and how we align ourselves in relation to them.

> The reflexive project of the self, which consists in the sustaining of coherent, yet continuously revised, biographical narratives, takes place in the context of multiple choice as filtered through abstract systems. In modern social life, the notion of lifestyle takes on a particular significance. The more tradition loses its hold, and the more daily life is reconstituted in terms of the dialectical interplay of the local and the global, the more individuals are forced to negotiate lifestyle choices among a diversity of options. (Giddens, 1991, p. 5)

This dynamic perspective on identity establishes a very appropriate backdrop to the present volume, but it is not unique to Giddens. It can be found very explicitly, for example, in Mead's (1932) process model of identity, which assumed that the self emerges through interactional experience. A thread of social psychological theory has for some time stressed the on-the-ground negotiative nature of age-identity (Ainley & Redfoot, 1982; see also Taylor, 1989). Harré (1983) also writes of "identity projects," by which he means practical action by individuals toward "the achievement of uniqueness within a moral order" (p. 273), including various forms of self-credentialing activities. Harré further argues (1987; Van Langenhove & Harré, this volume) that we indulge in "language games through which the grammatical models of self appear as a mode of personal organisation" (1987, p. 41). Gergen too (e.g., 1987; Gergen & Gergen, this volume) has theorized the self as being made possible through our social relationships. Shotter (e.g., 1984, this volume; Shotter & Gergen, 1989) has given detailed consideration to the social processes underlying the concepts of selfhood and citizenship. But we shall continue to explore Giddens's work at this point because it makes explicit links to lifespan theorizing in ways that are not unproblematic, but crucially relevant to this volume. For Giddens, the updating of the "biographical narrative," as in the earlier quotation, is very clearly a lifelong process:

> Self-identity for us [in the late modern age] forms a *trajectory* across different institutional settings of modernity over the *duree* of what used to be called the "life cycle," a term which applies more accurately to non-modern contexts than the modern ones. Each of us not only "has," but *lives* a biography reflexively organised in terms of flows of social and psychological information about possible ways of life. Modernity is a post-traditional order, in which the question, "How shall I live?" has to be answered in day-to-day decisions about how to behave, what to wear and what to eat—and many other things—as well as interpreted within the temporal unfolding of self-identity. (Giddens, 1991, p. 14)

The lifespan, for Giddens, is specifically *not* to be equated with a fixed and orderly progression through generational stages or periods, although this has been a dominant model of lifespan development. In *The Problem of the Generations*, for example, Manheim (1952) reflected the view that for each of us, any one point in time represents a different period of our self, which can only be shared with people of our own age. Giddens argues, to the contrary, that

> The idea of the "life cycle" . . . makes very little sense once the connections between the individual life and the interchange of the generations have been broken. . . . Generational differences are essentially a mode of time-reckoning in pre-modern societies. . . . In traditional contexts, the life cycle carries strong connotations of renewal, since each generation in some substantial part rediscovers and relives modes of life of its forerunners. Renewal loses most of its meaning in the settings of high modernity where practices are repeated only in so far as they are reflexively justifiable. (1991, p. 146)

From our own perspective, it is more reasonable to pose as empirical questions *whether, for whom, where, when* and *in what respects* the lifespan in fact is or is not "freed from the externalities associated with pre-established ties to other individuals and groups" (Giddens, 1991, p. 147), rather than assume this to be the general case. There are certainly agencies and ideologies in contemporary Western life that (still?) vigorously predetermine generational and lifespan positions for individuals and constrain their potential for reflexive self-determination. These can be found not least in dominant Western assumptions about child rearing and community care for the elderly, in norms for career development, sexual and recreational practices, and in many other domains. What we can take from Giddens, then, is a new formulation of a fundamental issue to be addressed in lifespan studies: What are the social contextual forces and processes that militate against but also *for* "traditional" conceptions of life-stages and life-potentials, and how are they distributed in contemporary life? The chapters that make up the body of this book are in many ways designed to address this central issue.

The cornerstone of Giddens's theorizing is the claim that the contemporary experience of life and of selfhood, in what he calls "late" or "high modernity," is profoundly different from the "traditional" or "pre-modern" experience. His argument runs that the electronic media have altered the "situational geography" of modern social life (1991, p. 84), to the extent that our experiences of social life are more fluid, uncertain, and complex than in pre-mass-mediated life. Life strikes us as a plethora of prepackaged alternatives in relation to which we can, and do, construct highly variable self-identities: "mediated social situations construct new communalities—and differences—between preconstituted forms of social experience" (p. 84). This is an intuitively appealing insight, though again it seems to us that it is very easy to overstate the rigidity of traditional orders, and the flexibility of current ones, as far as their power to determine self-identity is concerned. And of course Giddens offers us very little justification for his claims beyond their intuitive appeal.

But, as before, whether *or not* we are persuaded to distinguish sharply between pre-modern and high-modern periods, there are many key questions that arise out of Giddens's work that a lifespan theory of self will need to consider. First, how pervasive in fact is the reflexive activity that generates selfhood? Giddens writes that, "At each moment, or at least at regular intervals, the individual is asked to conduct a self-interrogation in terms of what is happening" (1991, p. 76). The qualification at the beginning of this last quotation is potentially very significant. It seems likely that self-interrogation will be occasioned by rather specific experiential triggers—lifespan boundaries, moments of achievement or failure, births or bereavements, threats to morale or health or the passing of such threats. Research activity itself can give lifespan positioning a sharp salience when we invite people to reflect on their lives and their intergenerational relationships (e.g., Henwood & Coughlan, McKay, Prusank, Staton, this volume). Wilmot and Hocker (this volume) give ample evidence of how couple identities are actively reconstructed by mediators through subtle discourse interventions.

Giddens does refer to "fateful moments" that are "threatening for the protective cocoon which defends the individual's ontological security, because the 'business as usual' attitude that is so important to that cocoon is inevitably broken through" (1991, p. 114). Once again, we clearly need a contextually sensitive account—both of how and when "fateful moments" arise, and of how we recognize them as fateful *for us*. But we also need an account of how and when we *resist* reflexive reappraising our selves. That is, a theory of lifespan identity also needs to account for how some *consistency* of the self is achieved. And in fact, Schutz and Luckmann (1973) argue that people do, as a general rule and for most practical purposes, *suspend* their doubts and work with their provisional understandings of events. A key quality of personal life narratives may be to impose a relatively enduring "configurational structure" (Ricouer, 1981) or frame (Goffman, 1974) upon personal experiences and their consequences for the self, as a means of defusing the threat of instability and pressures toward realignment. Sillars and Zietlow (this volume) find evidence that older couples are generally more passive in their relationships than younger ones, but also more satisfied and less conflict oriented.

Gubrium too (1976) writes about the growth of *stability* under some conditions during aging and into late life:

> It might be argued . . . that as one grows older, social investment becomes an increasingly important dimension of self-validation. Over the life cycle, a person learns to trust other specific individuals to support and lend credibility to his [or her] actions. With age, these others are likely to become relatively stable. Likewise, a person's routine expectations of himself [or herself] become increasingly stable. The extensive social investments accumulated in others over time provide the ground for personal confidence when they remain secure, and can cause disintegration when they become shaken. (pp. 180-181)

The specific case that Gubrium then goes on to consider is elderly unmarrieds, who he feels have some distinct identity advantages by comparison with the vast majority of their peers who lose their spouses and whose stability is therefore predictably shaken. Elderly singles, as Gubrium's data suggest, are isolates but not desolates. But Gubrium's central claim that advancing adulthood is associated with increasing stability of the self, if it is generally correct, is a very significant qualification of Giddens's general thesis. Other researchers, however, do indeed argue that old age is a time of radical uncertainty for many elderly people. Featherstone and Hepworth (1989) take up the theme of there being a far wider range of identity alternatives for older people, as for all generations, during postmodernity. They speculate about Western societies possibly becoming "uni-age," just as they have become, in certain respects, "uni-sex" (see also Coupland & Coupland, in press).

A more differentiated account, then, would need to ask whether *all* individuals, at all ages, are equally prone to reflexivity? Giddens writes:

> The individual appropriates his [or her] past by sifting through it in the light of what is anticipated for an (organised) future. The trajectory of the self has a coherence that derives from cognitive awareness of the various phases of the lifespan. The lifespan, rather than events in the outside world, becomes the dominant "foreground figure" in the *Gestalt* sense. (1991, pp. 75-76)

There is again a contextual vagueness in this claim. It seems to us that the quotation most naturally characterizes the reflexivity of the mid-life, affluent Westerner, committed to his or her individualism, outside of a long-term relationship that would itself condition identity, with an adequately long and differentiated past to sift, and with adequate resources (emotional, material, temporal) to organize a significant future from alternative possibilities.

Several of the data-contexts that arise in later chapters take us into domains where few of these characteristics are likely to be found—for example, in childhood and again in late life. The socialization of young children (Aronsson & Evaldsson, and Prusank, both this volume) may be the inculcation of assumptions and norms that are powerfully reproduced *because* children are less likely to have a fully reflexive apparatus in place. In late life, a dominant outcome of reflexive reappraisal, for some people, may be the frustration that desired realignments seem out of reach. (Cicirelli, this volume, argues strongly for a "threshold" model of late life after which adaptation to the environment is far less feasible.) But research on mid-life has also produced highly ambiguous theories of individual and social development. Harwood and Giles (in press) show that literatures fall into two traditions, developing accounts of either "crisis" or "stability" as the key characteristics of the self in the middle years of life.

Above all, what Giddens's approach necessarily fails to elucidate is the discursive *means* by which identity formations are achieved across the lifespan. Most of the chapters of this volume focus on precisely this question, exploring the many social contexts in which versions of selves or relationships are achieved, either in reflective interviews or in face-to-face interaction. Henwood and Coughlan, for example, examine how mothers and daughters themselves construct definitions of *closeness* in their talk, and how this semantic captures key aspects of their adjudged relationships. Wilmot and Hocker show how extended metaphors can be powerful means of interpreting, and so of changing, couple relationships. Staton finds that students give very predictable discursive accounts of their various positions within the academic system, and so on. These sociolinguistic data are where we find our best evidence of a rhetoric of self-identification.

Despite the reservations voiced above, what we find in Giddens and other contemporary interdisciplinary theorizing about selfhood is a vigorous commitment to dynamic and process-based formulations. These necessarily focus analytic attention upon social relationships and social interaction as the breeding grounds for versions of self. In another sense, this realignment of perspective takes much of the theoretical load off the concept of selfhood itself, because "the self" ceases to be a consolidated, explanatory entity in social science. Rather, as in Giddens's interpretation, it is a pervasive but contingent and ongoing "project"—a focus for many of our day-to-day activities and encounters, but never finally achieved or fully formed. Most important for this book, contemporary perspectives on identity are also dynamic in seeing the self as in some sense a *narrative* project. Identity is inherently a lifespan concern, so that studies of language and discourse within a lifespan frame are arguably the primary means by which to carry forward the analysis of personal and social identity. Autobiographical narratives feature strongly in the book (Gergen & Gergen, McKay, Shotter, Van Langenhove & Harré, Wilmot & Hocker) as well as social discourses *about* autobiographical reminiscence (Buchanan & Middleton).

If we now turn to the language, communication, and social interaction literatures, we can see how a confluence of research interests is being achieved from that direction, too.

Language, Discourse, and Lifespan Identity

The U.S. tradition of research on communication and the lifespan (Nussbaum, 1989; Nussbaum, Thompson, & Robinson, 1989) has established an important empirical basis for the chapters in this book, and for the studies we hope will follow from it (see the Epilogue). Methodologically very diverse projects have increased our understanding of how social relationships develop and change over the lifespan, of intergenerational communication, and of interactions involving specific age-populations in everyday and institutional settings. This enterprise is certainly too broad and too diverse for us to try to review it here (but see Nussbaum & Coupland, in press, for a detailed overview and integration). On the whole, however, this literature has not conceptualized language and interaction as *constitutive* of lifespan experiences and identity, as is generally true of linguistic and sociolinguistic literatures.

On the other hand, sociolinguists and communication researchers have regularly appealed to "identity" as part of a functional explanation for language behavior, mainly in relation to ethnic or community allegiances. For example, it is widely assumed that the most powerful explanations for language maintenance and shift (e.g., Fishman, 1971) and for distributional patterns of accent and dialect (e.g., Ryan & Giles, 1982) are to be found in the symbolic and indexical social identifying properties of these varieties. Within the social psychology of language (see Giles & Coupland, 1991), identity has been explicitly modeled and researched in very many respects. One central example is Giles's ethnolinguistic identity theory (again see Giles & Coupland, 1991, for a review), which accounts for changing patterns of minority and majority language usage. The related paradigm referred to as communication accommodation theory (Giles, Coupland, & Coupland, 1991) explains how the desire to mark an individual's or a group's uniqueness can result in the strategy of "divergence" from an interlocutor, for example reducing speech or other communicative similarities.

Within research on communicator goals—for example—it is common to interpret social actors as responding to three broadly characterized constellations of goals—instrumental, relational, and identity goals (Tracy & Coupland, 1991). Within linguistics, on the other hand, identity considerations have, arguably, been much underplayed. For example, functional models of language (in particular, work inspired by Halliday, e.g., 1978) have assumed that networks of semantic options through which speakers generate textual meanings operate in three "macrofunctional" domains— ideational, interpersonal, and textual. Identity functions are not specified. To an extent similarly, within sociolinguistics, communicative purposes are often mapped out as occupying two principal dimensions, the referential (or ideational) and the relational (e.g., Holmes, 1990). Issues to do with personal and social identity *do* arise within the relational domain (a good example is Brown & Levinson's [1987] influential model of facework and politeness), but sociolinguistics does tend to locate its interpretations of variation and discourse phenomena at the level of the relationship (principally through notions of power and solidarity) rather than at the level of self-identity.

It is ironic that sociolinguistic and communication research should have endorsed, on the whole, a *static* conception of identity, when, for many social scientists, language and interaction are achieved *above all* as dynamic and processual events in shifting social contexts. So, what precursors are there to the discursive analysis of identity within language and communication research?

As Hadden and Lester (1978) point out, it has been left principally to sociologists, particularly those working in the traditions that are now labeled ethnomethodology and conversation analysis, to develop process-oriented accounts of self-identification through talk and social interaction. Goffman (e.g., 1959) has made probably the most enduring contributions to this approach. But it is to the public presentations of self, rather than to implications for what Giddens calls self-identity, that Goffman's readings of interaction contribute. Again, Cicourel (e.g., 1974) and Sacks (e.g., 1972) have both made important contributions to our understanding of identifying and categorization practices in ongoing interaction generally.

One central contribution that a sociolinguistic and interactional approach can achieve is precisely to fill out the contextual account (necessarily missing in the work of Giddens and other theorists) of where and how self-identification does and does not operate. In Hadden and Lester's (1978) exploratory study of the text of magazine interviews with musicians, a simple but significant observation is that "in many interactions, relatively exhaustive 'coverage' of self is not a purpose at hand" (p. 342). Although self-identification, through the indexical properties of our voices, stances, and appearances, may be a pervasive and inevitable feature of all interaction, the point is that "doing self- and other-identifying," when it *is* constituted as the business in hand, deserves special consideration. So, as Hadden and Lester show, a sociolinguistic account needs to be specific about domains in which, as well as the interactional means by which, identification can be achieved.

In their analysis, Hadden and Lester (1978) in fact identify three main processes. First (and principally), *locating*, through which speakers can display a socially recognizable status or role. The defining characteristics of locating are then said to be *contexting* (locating self or other as a member or coparticipant of some network or aggregate of people), and *differentiating* (depicting unique features of a self or projecting a self as specifically not belonging or corresponding to a recognized social network or group). The second process is *retrospecting*, where a person "produces an account of autobiographical particulars which offers an interpretive scheme . . . for 'making sense' of previous locating" (p. 350). Third, *prospecting*, where "an anticipated or aspired-to identity is forged" (p. 352). In ongoing interaction we need to expect these processes to interconnect in complex ways, so the schema cannot be interpreted as a category system for classifying speech acts or utterances. Its value, as Hadden and Lester themselves indicate, is that it begins the task of specifying the discursive means by which social actors *selectively* display and detect identifying information at a local level.

This exploratory work on self- and other-identification and categorization in discourse has only rarely, however, been taken specifically into *lifespan* domains. Recent work of our own has addressed processes of age-identity marking in elderly/young adult discourse. The main elements of this schema are produced below. Discussions of it, and related detailed studies of discourses of age-telling and painful self-disclosure, are available in Coupland, Coupland, Giles, and Henwood (1990) and Coupland, Coupland, and Giles (1991, chap. 3-6).

We identify six broad strategies through which an "elderly" identity can be made salient, either by an older speaker or by her or his conversation partner. We organize these under two general headings. As (A) *Age-categorization processes* we consider (i) *Disclosure of chronological age.* The telling of age proves to be unevenly distributed across age-groups, far more frequent by older than by younger speakers. But in our data, age-telling is mainly of interest because of its interconnectedness, discursively, with issues of health-in-aging. For example, age is commonly told as an *account* for ill-health or frailty. (ii) *Age-related category or role reference* subsumes the wide range of means by which speakers locate themselves or their conversational partners within specific age-groups or generations. For example, young adults may align themselves with the succeeding generation to an elderly co-speaker; elderly speakers may distance themselves in generational terms from people who are apparently their peers (e.g., "My friend who's getting on in years . . . "). (iii) *Age-identity in relation to health, decrement, and death* refers to how discourses of frailty can themselves thematize old age (cf. Taylor, 1989). In the sources cited above, we have developed a rather detailed sequential model of elderly "troubles-telling" sequences, and given particular attention to how these sequences can be initiated, supported, and terminated by troubles-talk recipients (cf. Goodwin, 1984; Ochs, Smith, & Taylor, 1989 on recipient-participation in interaction).

As a second major category, we consider (B) *Temporal framing processes.* Within this, our data showed instances of (iv) *Adding time-past perspective to current or recent-past states or topics.* Related to this, Boden and Bielby (1983, 1986) have shown that talk about the past commonly functions among elderly speakers as a topic-resource for the organization of current experiences (e.g., "I've been a widow now 30 years . . . "). (v) *Self-association with the past* constructs elderly identity by appealing to cohort-experiences, associating with earlier periods, knowledge, and values (e.g., "I wouldn't recognize the city nowadays . . . "). Relatedly, (vi) *Recognizing historical, cultural, or social change* establishes elderliness through commenting on general (non-cohort-specific) change, such as "In those days you had to work hard to make ends meet. . . ."

Studies of child language development, as we noted at the beginning of the chapter, have mainly followed a psycholinguistic tradition. An important alternative, however, that could inform future *socio*linguistically oriented lifespan research, has grown from a base in anthropological linguistics. Ochs and Schieffelin (Ochs, 1988; Schieffelin & Ochs, 1986) have contributed a very influential and challenging account of at least one domain of lifespan development—the role of language in the socialization of children across cultures. *Social identity* is not a keyword in Ochs and Schieffelin's work, though *culture* is; and Ochs explicitly assumes a definition of culture, allied to that of Geertz (1973), as social knowledge and understanding that is created, negotiated, and refined by people. And Ochs and Schieffelin's central thesis is that cultural knowledge and cultural norms both inform and are informed by language use.

> Given that meanings and functions are to a large extent socioculturally organized, linguistic knowledge is embedded in sociocultural

knowledge. On the other hand, understandings of the social organization of everyday life, cultural ideologies, moral values, beliefs, and structures of knowledge and interpretation are to a large extent acquired through the medium of language. (Ochs, 1988, p. 14)

Schieffelin and Ochs give the name *language socialization* to these reciprocal processes of influence.

As Ochs points out (1988, p. 16), this position is entirely consistent with Bourdieu's (1977) sociological stance, seeing the predispositions and motivating assumptions of a social group as generating *and* in turn being reproduced by what he terms its "habitus" (its habitual behaviors). It is a short step from here to Giddens's specification of the relationship between self-identity and social encounters, *except that* Ochs and Schieffelin have given their empirical attention exclusively to the socialization of the child. But there is no reason why language socialization should not be seen as a lifelong process. Indeed, Ochs makes this very point: "Throughout our lives, we are socializing and being socialized by those we encounter" (1988, p. 6). The only limiting aspect of her theory, from our perspective, is to equate socialization with the "acquisition" of linguistic and sociocultural "competence," with these terms' strong implications of finitude.

Adapting the language socialization perspective in some respects, then, in this book we are trying to encourage a perspective that respects and explores, theoretically and empirically, the continuous socializing potential of language and discourse throughout lived lives. As we age, we confront an ever-changing *cultural* panoply in relation to which we must, as an ongoing project, at least attempt to establish a tolerable sense of self and of belonging. The hedges built into such a formulation are important, because, in Gergen's words, "people frequently lack objective information with which to evaluate their various capacities and attributes. As a result, they often compare themselves with others to reach an adequate self-definition" (Gergen, 1987, p. 58). The everyday rhetorical format for articulating this experience is "I'm not too bad considering . . . " or "I'm getting along as well as can be expected" (Coupland, Coupland, & Robinson, 1992).

That is, we must expect people to be often uncertain—and perhaps in a profound sense—about where they stand developmentally, and perhaps to be discontented with the outcomes of their provisional self-positioning attempts. Lifespan discourse may above all be the locus of partial and unsuccessful attempts at "adaptation" to age—at locating our own and others' selves within, or against the grain of, socially normative categories and roles. "Will I be able to/was I able to carry off that youthful/mature self-projection?"; "Should I act/was I acting in an age-appropriate manner?"; "Is this aging body truly 'me'?"; "Am I necessarily circumscribed by being a Baby-Boomer, a product of Hippy Culture, an Eighties Yuppy, or by some other cohort designation?"; "What does turning 18/retirement mean for how I should comport myself, and am I now "adult"/"old"? However assiduously the mass media, social institutions, and our own routines of talk may try to package us into age-appropriate positions, there is likely to be continuous dialogue about "how I am" in relation to "how I should be" at my age, itself mediated by our perceptions of others' responses to us (Coupland, in press).

Language socialization throughout life cannot be said to achieve any single target or status as would be implied by the notion of a cultural "competence," although lifelong maturation may well be characterized as the achievement of certain domain-specific understandings and competences. Given the way in which the individual's own "internal" lifespan socialization needs to be mapped against simultaneous shifts in cultural and social norms over time (see the Epilogue), there is never an absolute and final goal. For this reason, "development" is a far better formulation than "acquisition," even though the positivity of the term *development* might not always be matched by the felt experience of social aging. Indeed, the ways in which *ageism* (Butler, 1969, 1975; Coupland & Coupland, in press), social prejudice, and discrimination against the elderly, motivate discourses of the lifespan need to be more systematically explored.

References

Ainley, S. C., & Redfoot, D. L. (1982). Ageing and identity-in-the-world: A phenomenological analysis. *International Journal of Ageing and Human Development, 15*, 1-15.

Boden, D., & Bielby, D. (1983). The past as resource: A conversational analysis of elderly talk. *Human Development, 26,* 308-319.

Boden, D., & Bielby, D. (1986). The way it was: Topical organisation in elderly conversation. *Language and Communication, 6,* 73-89.

Bourdieu, P. (1977). *Outline of a theory of practice.* Cambridge: Cambridge University Press.

Brown, P., & Levinson, S. (1987). *Politeness: Some universals in language usage.* Cambridge: Cambridge University Press.

Butler, R. N. (1969). Age-ism: Another form of bigotry. *The Gerontologist, 9,* 243-246.

Butler, R. N. (1975). *Why survive? Being old in America.* New York: Harper & Row.

Cicourel, A. (1974). *Cognitive sociology.* New York: Free Press.

Coupland, J., Coupland, N., Giles, H., & Henwood, K. (1991). Formulating age: The management of age identity in elderly talk. *Discourse Processes, 141,* 87-106.

Coupland, J., Coupland, N., & Robinson, J. (1992). "How are *you*?": Negotiating phatic communion. *Language in Society, 21,* 207-230.

Coupland, N. (Ed.). (in press). *Discourse, institutions and the elderly.* Special issue of *Journal of Aging Studies.*

Coupland, N., & Coupland, J. (in press). Age-identity and health-identity in geriatric medical discourse. In *Health Care Encounters and Culture* [Proceedings of the 1992 Summer University of Stockholm Seminar, Botkyrka, Sweden].

Coupland, N., & Coupland, J. (in press). Discourses of ageism. *Journal of Aging Studies.*

Coupland, N., Coupland, J., & Giles, H. (1991). *Language, society and the elderly.* Oxford: Basil Blackwell.

Featherstone, M., & Hepworth, M. (1989). Ageing and old age: Reflections on the postmodern life course. In B. Bytheway, T. Keil, P. Allatt, & A. Bryman (Eds.), *Becoming and being old: Sociological approaches to later life* (pp. 133-157). London: Sage.

Fishman, J. A. (1971). *Sociolinguistics: A brief introduction.* Rowley, MA: Newbury House.

Geertz, C. (1973). *The interpretation of cultures.* New York: Basic Books.

Gergen, K. J. (1987). Towards self as relationship. In K. Yardley & T. Honess (Eds.), *Self and identity: Psychosocial perspectives* (pp. 53-63). Chichester, UK: John Wiley.

Giddens, A. (1990). *The consequences of modernity.* Cambridge: Polity Press (in association with Basil Blackwell).

Giddens, A. (1991). *Modernity and self-identity: Self and society in the late modern age.* Cambridge: Polity Press (in association with Basil Blackwell).

Giles, H., Coupland, J., & Coupland, N. (Eds.). (1991). *Contexts of accommodation developments in applied sociolinguistics.* Cambridge: Cambridge University Press.

Giles, H., & Coupland, N. (1991). *Language: Contexts and consequences.* London: Open University Press.

Goffman, E. (1959). *The presentation of self in everyday life.* Garden City, NY: Doubleday.

Goffman, E. (1974). *Frame analysis: An essay on the organization of experience.* New York: Harper & Row.

Goodwin, C. (1984). Notes on story structure and the organization of participation. In M. Atkinson & J. Heritage (Eds.), *Structures of social action* (pp. 225-246). Cambridge: Cambridge University Press.

Gubrium, J. F. (Ed.). (1976). *Time, roles and self in old age*. New York: Human Sciences Press.

Hadden, S. C., & Lester, M. (1978). Talking identity: The production of "self" in interaction. *Human Studies, 1*, 331-355.

Halliday, M. A. K. (1978). *Language as social semiotic*. London: Edward Arnold.

Harré, R. (1983). *Personal being: A theory for individual psychology*. Oxford: Basil Blackwell.

Harré, R. (1987). The social construction of selves. In K. Yardley & T. Honess (Eds.), *Self and identity: Psychosocial perspectives* (pp. 41-52). Chichester, UK: John Wiley.

Harwood, J., & Giles, H. (in press). Creating intergenerational distance: Language, communication and middle-age. *Language Sciences*.

Holmes, J. (1990). Politeness strategies in New Zealand women's speech. In A. Bell & J. Holmes (Eds.), *New Zealand ways of speaking English* (pp. 252-275). Clevedon, UK: Multilingual Matters.

Manheim, K. (1952). *The problem of the generations* (P. Kecskemet, Trans.). New York: Oxford University Press.

Mead, G. H. (1932). *Philosophy of the present*. LaSalle, IL: Open Court.

Nussbaum, J. F. (Ed.). (1989). *Life-span communication: Normative processes*. Hillsdale, NJ: Lawrence Erlbaum.

Nussbaum, J. F., & Coupland, J. (Eds.). (in press). *Handbook of communication and aging research*. Hillsdale, NJ: Lawrence Erlbaum.

Nussbaum, J. F., Thompson, T., & Robinson, J. D. (1989). *Communication and aging*. New York: Harper & Row.

Ochs, E. (1988). *Culture and language development*. Cambridge: Cambridge University Press.

Ochs, E., Smith, R., & Taylor, C. (1989). Detective stories at dinnertime: Problem-solving through co-narration. *Cultural Dynamics, 2*, 238-257.

Potter, J., & Edwards, J. (1992). *Discursive psychology*. London: Sage.

Potter, J., & Wetherell, M. (1987). *Discourse and social psychology*. London: Sage.

Ricouer, P. (1981). *Hermeneutics and the human sciences*. Cambridge: Cambridge University Press.

Ryan, E. B., & Giles, H. (Eds.). (1982). *Attitudes towards language variation: Social and applied contexts*. London: Edward Arnold.

Sacks, H. (1972). An initial investigation of the usability of conversational data for doing sociology. In D. Sudnow (Ed.), *Studies in social interaction* (pp. 31-74). Englewood Cliffs, NJ: Prentice-Hall.

Schieffelin, B. B., & Ochs, E. (Eds.). (1986). *Language socialization across cultures*. Cambridge: Cambridge University Press.

Schutz, A., & Luckmann, T. (1973). *The structures of the life-world* (R. M. Zaner & H. T. Engelhardt, Jr., Trans.). Evanston, IL: Northwestern University Press.

Shotter, J. (1984). *Social accountability and selfhood*. Oxford: Basil Blackwell.

Shotter, J., & Gergen, K. J. (Eds.). (1989). *Texts of identity*. London: Sage.

Taylor, C. (1989). *Sources of the self: The making of the modern identity*. Cambridge, MA: Harvard University Press.

Tracy, K., & Coupland, N. (Eds.). (1991). *Multiple goals in discourse*. Clevedon, UK: Multilingual Matters.

SECTION I

Discursively Formulating the Lifespan

First within this section, Shotter establishes the need for a social constructivist vision of lifespan identity. Our unique selves, he argues, are a matter of our own crafting, and particularly in the modern world where traditional constraints of time and space exert far less control over who we *can* be. This far, the chapter echoes and elaborates on the theoretical work of Giddens we discussed in the Introduction. But beyond this, Shotter gives a highly dynamic and moral account of the process of crafting selfhood. To be our social selves, to be individuals functioning within social and political communities, we need to *voice* our identities and so participate in the active reproduction of these communities. The community and the individual therefore enter into a complex, interdependent relationship.

Shotter's chapter sets the tone for the volume in his claim that "the primary human reality is face-to-face conversation." This is a position he defends through a wide-ranging, integrative review of texts on language, meaning, ideology, and selfhood (Wittgenstein, Gergen, Harré, Billig, Bakhtin, Taylor, Giddens, and others). A key point is that, Shotter writes, we need to escape from "the illusion of the self-contained self." Like other aspects of meaning, our identities are shaped only in relation to the contexts onto which they are projected and through the interpretive responses of others. For lifespan research, Shotter argues that this requires a dramatic shift away from theories and research methods that have taken an individualistic position and assumed life stages to be so predictable as to be an adequate baseline for empirical inquiry.

Shotter ends with a powerful and personal retrospective on "the politics of personhood" and a call for a new program of action through which "what used to be called the social sciences" can *implement* their own theorizing. The agenda must be to create new discourse resources to *engender* the social conditions we value for selves and for groups.

Building on many of the central assumptions in Shotter's chapter, Van Langenhove and Harré take up the issue of consistency and multiplicity of selfhood. How does recognizing the diversity of selves that we are able to project in social interaction square with the need to accept at least some continuity of self—across social situations and across time? They overview central elements of Harré's theory of *positioning,* which allows us to conceptualize how social actors orient to the story-lines, autobiographical or biographical, that they regularly produce in face-to-face talk. Van Langenhove and Harré argue that it is through the precise positioning of self and other in oral biographical talk that personal identity achieves its continuity.

Gergen and Gergen's chapter considers representations of selves in written autobiographies. Their approach is to deconstruct the cultural practice of writing in this genre. Arguing (along with de Man and others) that autobiography is part of an interpretive, sense-making textual process, they review how the genre is built on very different presuppositions in the cases of women's versus men's autobiographies. What they emphasize is that women's life experiences are in many ways at odds with the established forms and contents of the popular autobiographical "monomyth."

The specific focus is on autobiographers' accounts of their *bodies,* drawing data from 16 popular works recently published in the United States. From this informal but suggestive sample, it emerges, for example, that male autobiographers are in many ways less deeply embodied in their narratives, even distancing themselves from their bodies in their accounts of adult lives. Women autobiographers, on the other hand, articulate their experiences very much in terms of and through their bodies. In later life, male writers do present themselves as embodied, at least in recognizing their physical limitations. Females' texts suggest a continuing investment of self in physical experiences and in aspects of lived lives that connect intimately to the body. As Gergen and Gergen indicate in their closing pages, these are issues that deserve to be taken up also outside the autobiographical domain.

Buchanan and Middleton's chapter (whose title we have adapted for this first section of the book) concerns the social practice of reminiscence work—an increasingly common element of care-provision for older people. Reminiscence sessions appear to offer the same general opportunities for lifespan recall, or more likely reconstitution, as written autobiographies. In parallel with Gergen and Gergen, Buchanan and Middleton are concerned to locate reminiscence as a socially constituted activity, rather than exploring it in (the more traditional) functional terms. Here, they work not with texts of people reminiscing but with texts of care workers talking about their work. By these means they are able to assess aspects of the cultural and practical significance of "doing reminiscing," embedded in received assumptions about aging and the lifespan generally.

What they find is highly diverse implicit and explicit accounts, expressed in dialogical forms—defending positions on the value of reminiscence designed to counter or subsume competing positions. Arguments in defense of reminiscence, for example, can be framed as moral arguments against social ageism; on the other hand, carers can suggest reminiscence as a "last resort" for confused elderly people, or even as a risky alienation from the reality of the present. These everyday understandings reflect the day-to-day contexts in which reminiscence work is actually carried on, whatever their relation to academic theories.

CHAPTER ONE

Becoming Someone: Identity and Belonging

JOHN SHOTTER

Between the late 1960s early 1970s and now, the 1990s, times have changed. In terms of the analytic-discursive vocabulary that I want to introduce into lifespan developmental research, what has changed are the narrative resources available to people in making sense of their lives; the resources have increased, thus expanding the genres available. A best-selling book of the 1970s was Gail Sheehy's (1976) *Passages,* a popularized report on scientific research claiming to solve the mysteries of the "life cycle." Now, we have Mary Catherine Bateson's (1990) *Composing a Life*—a "blurred genre" (Geertz, 1983), part autobiography, part biography, reflexively illuminated by many of the literary and social scientific commonplaces (*topoi,* see below) currently shared amongst college educated people[1]—in which the idea that the proper living of a life involves the following of a "cycle" has disappeared, and one's task has become instead "an improvisatory art"—where "adjusting to discontinuity is not an idiosyncratic problem of my own," she says (p. 14), "but the emerging problem of our time." For now, as Giddens (1991) sees it, instead of a "sense of place"[2]—a place in which one was surrounded by traces of the past and intimations of the future, and in which the idea of "stages" in a life thus made sense—"self-identity for us forms a *trajectory* across the different institutional settings of modernity over the *durée* of what used to be called the 'life cycle' " (p. 14). Currently, as Gergen (1991) has

5

described in detail, due to the way that our technologies of communication and travel have advanced, there is a quantum leap in our exposure to each other; we have become "saturated" with the voices of others. We have become embroiled in (what Giddens, 1991, calls) the dialectic of the local and the global: Events distant from us in both space *and time*, transmitted to us through communication media, play an intimate part in who we feel we want or ought to be. No wonder that *identity* has become the watchword of the times; for it provides the much needed vocabulary in terms of which we now define our loyalties and our commitments.

Should we have shown our solidarity with the students in Tiananmen Square? How should we stand in relation to the Serbs and Croats—or the Kurds? Ought we to grieve over Gorbachev being deposed and replaced by Yeltsin? Applaud Bush's "environmental presidency," and Quayle's concern with "family values"? What about taking a new job away from one's home town—but how will that promote the return to community values one fears are being lost? Perhaps one should return to school to retrain as a doctor, genetic engineering having lost its charm in these polluted times? Worries over global issues feed into more local concerns. It is in these new times that social constructionism becomes relevant to lifespan developmental psychology. For central to it is the following claim: that in creating and negotiating the complex and detailed time-space relations between ourselves and others, we also craft our own unique selves. In other words, we become and are ourselves only in relation to others. In such a (relational) view as this—in which we all soak up, and float in, so to speak, the (to an extent) same sea of creative interrelational activity—what makes me as a person unique, in relation to everyone else in the extensive social "seascape"[3] around me, are the places or positions I and only I occupy within it, and the degree to which I am, or can become, answerable or responsible to others for them (Shotter, 1984). But that seascape is, as I said above, only "to an extent" the same for us all: Some of us have a more easy passage into certain regions of it than others. What elsewhere I have called "a political economy of developmental opportunities" (Shotter, 1984) is at work within it, limiting who or what we can become. We cannot just position ourselves as we please; we face differential invitations and barriers to all the "movements" (actions and utterances) we might try to make.

Having a Voice

Below, as a contribution to the recontexualization of lifespan research and its embedding in a discursive context, I want to explore a particular variant of social constructionism: what I shall call a rhetorical-responsive version of it. I call it that because it takes the living utterances of particular individuals, voiced in concrete social contexts, addressed to particular audiences, as its analytic or investigatory unit. Where, an "analytic unit" here is not a "theoretical" unit in the sense of accurately representing an actual state of affairs in the world (as in realist approaches), but is, in Wittgenstein's (1953, no. 122) sense, a "perspicuous representation," that is, a metaphorical resource that helps in producing "just that understanding which consists in 'seeing connections.' " Like a telescope or microscope, the metaphor functions as a device or conceptual instrument "through" which to "see"[4] details of processes that otherwise would remain rationally invisible to us, that is, unamenable to mutually intelligible discussion (see the section on rational-invisibility below). Such a (situated) unit, in being "shaped" in different ways by different speakers, is revealing (in that "shaping" process) of many of the important influences making people who they are. And it is through the concept of what it is "to have a voice," and how that "voice" is revealing of our identity, that I want to relate my rhetorical-responsive version of social constructionism to lifespan developmental psychology.

Indeed, what I shall want to argue is that, if one is to grow up and to qualify as a self-determining, autonomous person with one's own identity—to feel that one has grown up to be "someone," someone who "counts" in one's society—then, although one must grow up as a human being within that society, that in itself is not enough. For even as a participating member of it, one can still remain either dependent upon other members of it in some way or under their domination in some other way. To be a person and to qualify for certain rights as a free, autonomous individual, one must also be able to show in one's actions certain social competencies, that is, to fulfill certain duties and to be *accountable* to others in the sense of being able to justify one's actions to them, when challenged, in relation to the "social reality" of the society of which one is a member (Shotter, 1984). Being someone in this sense is a rhetorical achievement.

But this is still not enough to provide one with a "sense of belonging," with a sense of "being at home" in the reality that one's actions help to reproduce. To live within a community that one senses as being one's own, as "mine" as well as "yours," as "ours" rather than "theirs," a community for which one feels able to be answerable, one must be more than just a routine reproducer of it; one must in a real sense also play a part in its creative reproduction and sustenance as a "living" tradition. As MacIntyre (1981) puts it, "a living tradition . . . is an historically extended, socially embodied argument, and an argument precisely in part about the goods which constitute that tradition" (p. 207). In other words, a living tradition contains what one might call second-order arguments, that is, arguments about what should be argued about, and why. And one of the major arguments embedded in our current forms of social life, as both Gergen (1991) and Taylor (1989) point out, is that between romanticism (subjectivism and agent as a creative source) and modernism (objectivism and the determinism of the external world)—a dilemmatic theme we shall return to below. This idea of a "living" tradition is, of course, a very different idea from what we are used to thinking of as a tradition: of it as a hierarchically structured, organized, unitary *system* of already accepted knowledge that is supposed to provide members with ready-made solutions to the problem of how to be proper members of their group.

A living tradition, rather than supplying ready-made solutions, supplies only the resources (the "tools" and "materials")—what, as we shall see, Bakhtin (1986) and Volosinov (1973) call the relevant "speech and behavioral genres" (to which below I shall add "career genres," e.g., the resources relevant to being someone in business, an academic, a soldier, a layabout, etc.)—in terms of which one can fashion one's own "position" within the tradition (the "argument"), in relation to the positions of the others around one. These are what are *real* in a social constructionist approach.[5] Indeed, it is one of the delusions of a liberal society that the totally free individual exists in a state of nature and is deserving of rights and respect merely by "social contract." For, it is in the form of their myriad daily contacts that the "atomistic" individuals of the West reproduce the illusion of the self-contained self (Sampson, 1988). To be a *responsible* member of such a society, in which one is a "free individual," is *already* to have an obligation to sustain the society making such an identity possible; one must not just draw upon its resources, one must also contribute to their critical evaluation and creative reproduction, to their renewal by participating in the second-order arguments mentioned above. However, for one to feel able to play a proper part in such arguments, to feel that one's formulations, whether ultimately accepted or not, will at least be at first welcomed and listened to seriously, one must feel able to speak without having to struggle to have one's voice heard. One must feel that an "invitation to speak" already exists in virtue of who one is. In other words, the question: "Who *is* that person? Is he or she one of us?" will not first be asked before one is given permission to speak. One must not first have to *prove* oneself "qualified" before one can join the communal discourse.

To live under terms set only by others is always to feel not just different, but inadequate in relation to the others around one. That is, one must not feel one's own views inadequate in the sense of having to more fully justify voicing them, than do those who already seem to possess a lifetime's unconditional membership of the community. Part of a sense of "belonging," of a sense of being "at home" in one's own community, is that one has an automatic right of initial access to the community simply by virtue of having contributed, in developing oneself, to the development of *its* ways of making sense. In other words, to the extent that we all participate equally, "we" are the authors, not only of our "selves," but of *our* "realities"; they will be as much mine as yours. This does not mean that one will unthinkingly feel a sense of total harmony with those around one. Indeed, it means that one must live within a number of conflicting and competing "forms of life" with their associated "language games" (to use Wittgenstein's terms). But it does mean not having a sense of being an intrusive alien, of being able to realize one's true self in the world (rather than only in one's dreams). That is, I think, a sickness or a tiredness in having continually to live a life not of one's own: thus a part of what many people in the West now want, in wanting to be *citizens* of one or another community, is to have a voice, and to be listened to seriously *as of right*, thus to make their community's form of life *their* form of life too. And it is this issue—of what it is to have a voice, in the right genre, in the fashioning of one's own affairs— that we shall explore in detail below. But first we must set the scene in a more general fashion.

Social Constructionism

To this end, let me first turn to the nature of the social constructionist movement itself. Common to all the versions of it known to me is the central assumption that—instead of the study of the inner dynamics of the individual psyche (romanticism and subjectivism), or the already determined characteristics of the external world (modernism and objectivism), the two polarities[6] in terms of which we have thought about ourselves in recent times (Gergen, 1991; Taylor, 1989)—it is the contingent flow of continuous communicative interaction between human beings that becomes the central focus of concern. A dimension I shall call the *self-other dimension* of interaction. Until recently, this flow of diffuse (sensuous or feelingful[7]) activity has remained in the background as the unordered hurly-burly or bustle of everyday social life, awaiting elucidation in terms of either supposed principles of mind or world. But it is from within this flow of relational activities and practices, constructionists maintain, that all the other socially significant dimensions of interpersonal interaction—with their associated modes of being: either subjective or objective—originate and are formed.[8] This activity is formative, for instance, not only of the special ways in which, as scientists, say, we interact with the different worlds of only theoretically identified entities, but also of the routine ways in which as ordinary persons we function in the different "realities" we occupy in our everyday social lives. The ways of "being ordinary" available to us in our society are just as much sociohistorical constructions as our ways of being a scientist. In other words, not only do we constitute (make) and reconstitute (remake) our own social worlds, but we are also ourselves made and remade by them in the process. It is this dialectical emphasis upon *both* the contingency *and* the creativity of human interaction—on our making of, and being made by, our social realities that is, I think, common to social constructionism in all its versions.

These, then, are some of the more general issues raised and the changes that would occur in what one could be said to be "doing" in doing lifespan research, if one were to switch to a *social construc-tionist* context of research (away from the *realist* stance implicit in almost all current social scientific work). However, the focus upon that third possible category of events I mentioned above—the sphere in which the sociohistorical processes responsible for the shaping and the changing of our commonsense ways of thinking, perceiving, talking, and acting take place—requires an appropri-ate analytic unit in terms of which to explore and characterize events. Without such a unit, there is no way of identifying our own role in such processes; we have to treat them yet again either as due to "individuals of character" (romanticism), or as "naturally" (modernist) occurring phenomena. Elsewhere, I have called this flow of interactive activity in general, "joint action" (Shotter, 1980, 1984) and talked of it as taking place within what might be called a "zone of uncertainty" (between Culture and Nature). Here I want to be more specific and to endorse Harré's (1983, 1990) view, that the primary human reality is face-to-face conversation.

Although many may disagree and feel that many other (more nonverbal) spheres of human interaction are more basic,[9] here I shall take it as primary in the following (judgmental) sense: As human realities do not endure through the physical rigidity of their structures (indeed, it makes no sense even to talk of them in this way), to repeat the by now familiar theme, they must be sustained in existence by being continually remade in people's everyday social activities. In such processes, however, people mutually judge and correct both each other and themselves as to the "fittingness" of their actions to what they take their reality to be. As Wittgenstein (1953, no. 242) insists, "if language is to be a means of communication there must be agreement not only in

definitions but also (queer as this may sound) in judgments."
Utterances are judged, then, not solely or primarily in terms of
their grammatical form, but are evaluated in terms of the "count-
less" (Wittgenstein, 1953, no. 23) uses they can have in relation to
the social reality in which they occur. And conversation is the
ultimate sphere in which all such judging and evaluating takes
place, and in which such assessments are negotiated and shared
agreements are reached. This emphasis upon the judgmental process in conversation, upon the normative pressures at work con-
straining acceptable speech, however, should not detract from the
possibility of it also being *creative:* it simply means that one cannot
just be creative as one pleases. Indeed, when we turn to talk of
biographies and careers, it appears that they too like ways of
speaking fall into genres, and that what seems desirable or required at one point in history is quite different from the desirable
or required at another.

A Rhetorical-Responsive Version

The scene is now set for the turn to my rhetorical-responsive
version of social constructionism. Besides the reasons I mentioned
above, I have chosen to give it a distinctive title because, in
treating the phenomena of voice and genre, I want to pick up on
the work of two people: (1) the turn to rhetoric in the recent work
in social psychology by Billig (1987, 1991; Billig et al., 1988); and
also, as I have already mentioned, (2) to call upon the "dialogical"
work of Bakhtin (1981, 1984, 1986; and Volosinov, 197310). Of immediate relevance to us here are two central points in Billig's approach:
(a) One is his claim that all our behavior, even our own thought
about ourselves, is conducted in an ongoing argumentive context
of criticism and justification, where every argumentive "move" is
formulated in response to previous moves; (b) the other, is that (in
accord with MacIntyre's (1981) views quoted above) what we
have in common with each other in our society's traditions, is not
a set of agreements about meanings, beliefs, or values, but a set of
intrinsically two-sided "topics" [Gr: *topoi* = "places"] or dilemmatic themes, the "commonplaces" from which we may draw the

two sides of an argument. I mention these points here, because what makes the version of social constructionism I want to pursue distinctive is its recognition of the irresolvable, dilemmatic nature of our commonsense knowledge. Thus, along with both Billig (1991, pp. 5-9) and Bakhtin (1984), I shall not attempt to impose a theoretical resolution upon this dialectic.[11] Indeed, I shall take it that it is its existence—the fact that every way of speaking embodies a different evaluative stance, a different way of being or position in the world—that keeps everyone in permanent dialogue with everyone else, and gives the processes of interest to us their intrinsic dynamic. Thus, I shall suggest that, instead of attempting to capture the nature of communicative activity in a unified, systematic theory, we must analytically display its dilemmatic character. And *through* the analytic unit of the utterance, study the different ways in which people *in practice,* at different times, in different contexts, resolve the dilemmas they face, and formulate the lines of action they pursue.

Thus within this view, a social practice is, as Billig et al. (1988) term it, a "living ideology": it is a set of institutionalized ways of talking, thinking, perceiving, and acting that, in their performance, sustain a form of social life (with its associated social reality) in existence—to the benefit of some members of the group over others, we must add. To this extent, a living ideology is the equivalent to what Bakhtin (1984, p. 97) calls a "genre," which, as Morson and Emerson (1990) say, when

> understood as a way of seeing, is best described neither as a "form" (in the usual sense) nor as an ideology (which could be phrased as a set of tenets) but as a "form-shaping ideology"[12]—a special kind of creative activity embodying a specific sense of experience. (p. 282)

The tendencies that shape people's behavior *ideologically* can be seen at work "in" the social practice, as influencing the formulations one voices in attempting to claim one or another position for oneself. In this respect Billig and Bakhtin are in close agreement: the (contrary) themes made available within a living ideology are "the *seeds,* not *flowers* of arguments" (Billig et al., 1988, p. 16, quoting Bacon, 1858, p. 492).

> The very existence of these opposing images, words, evaluations, maxims and so on is crucial, in that they permit the possibility not just of social dilemmas but of social thinking itself. (Billig et al., 1988, p. 17)

They do not just constrain thought, but both motivate and enable it. Unless we express ourselves within the right genre at the right time, what we say will not be heard aright—likely, it will not be understood at all. Genres, although constituting the sites, or the architectonic resources, for creative work, can also exert an influence upon what is considered normatively possible.

Indeed, the disputes involved are deeper than just to do with matters of the proper use of language, for often they are not about what already exists at all. They are to do with, so some of us would claim, attempting to make new forms of human being *possible*—for "to imagine a language is to imagine a form of life" (Wittgenstein, 1953, no. 19). Thus, in revealing new possibilities for human being and in instituting new forms of human relationship, the attempt to introduce a new genre can involve a genuine political struggle, to do with bringing a new form of social life into existence. We can see how a new genre, a new way of talking can exert a normative influence as follows: The "practical" view taken above suggests that all our actions, and all our utterances, must, in the course of their performance, involve essentially a "developmental" process of a negotiatory kind. That is, in practice, the voicing of an utterance is not simply a mechanical matter of putting an (inner) idea or theory into (outer) practice, according to a set of preestablished rules, but involves a moment-by-moment process of adjustment by the speakers to the ever-changing context into which they must "fit" their speech—a context that is itself responsive to their utterances in the course of their uttering. Thus, just as a carpenter wields a chisel, continuously varying its direction and the pressure upon it, to shape a piece of wood according to his or her desire, he or she is limited by what the grain and hardness of a piece of wood will afford, permit, or allow, so also, an utterance "in" its temporal shaping will express a speaker's desire, but only within the possibilities afforded or permitted by the context.

Such a view of language as this is, of course, a very different one from the classical Saussurian/Chomsky view in which it is the job of linguistic communication to duplicate in the head of a receiver, an idea originating in the head of a sender. "The fact is that," says Bakhtin (1986, p. 68),

> when the listener perceives and understands the meaning (the language meaning) of speech, he simultaneously takes an active, responsive attitude toward it. He either agrees or disagrees with it (completely or partially), augments it, applies it, prepares for its execution, and so on. And the listener adopts this responsive attitude for the entire duration of the process of listening and understanding.[13]

This we might call a "responsive" rather than referential[14] account of understanding and meaning; indeed, a "referential response" can be seen as a special case within it.

Writing, Rational-Invisibility, and Exclusion

Such an account of meaning has many important consequences, but there is one in particular that I want to explore here: to do with the very different view it implies of what it is one is doing in the *writing* of social constructionist texts. Typically, in social scientific writing it is claimed—in lifespan psychology, for instance—that one is depicting and explaining the *causes* of lifespan development in a yet more accurate way by the presentation of a *unified theory*. Indeed, theories in the strict sense of unified deductive systems of interlocking propositions (as well as the search simply for causal determinants) must be abandoned—along with Enlightenment urges for unity, harmony, and system. For the very nature of the social constructionist movement—in requiring one to be reflexively self-aware of the rhetorical "moves" made and "devices" used in one's textual productions (e.g., Bazeman, 1988; Stam, 1987)—precludes such a project. Indeed, as "deconstructive" analysis has shown (Derrida, 1976), the two-sided tendencies at work in all human affairs mentioned by Billig are also at work in the supposed *systematic* texts in which we present our theories: We now realize, for example, that the concept of "Man" (Foucault, 1970), which has been at the heart of all such systematic theories—

the idea of a self-controlled, self-contained subjectivity at the center of the individual person—entails the "othering" of a whole class of subordinated or colonized subjects who, in not "belonging" to the category, are politically excluded and marginalized.

Thus, as I have already intimated above in discussing the explicit acceptance of the dilemmatic nature of our communicative activities, instead of a systematic theory, I shall try to provide what might be called an adequate analytic and specificatory *vocabulary*. This will consist of a set of terms that will work in instructive ways to inform both our perceptions and action: (a) through which we can see the possible significances of certain circumstances in people's lives: as well as (b) through which we can judge how we might best respond to such perceptions. I emphasize the issue of adequacy, as many (e.g., Billig, 1991; Gergen, 1989; Giddens, 1991; Shotter, 1984; Taylor, 1989) would maintain that current social scientific research, to the extent that it draws upon a whole network of assumptions both implicit in modernity itself and explicit in modern philosophy, draws upon an extremely impoverished existential and moral vocabulary. Indeed, it is in its very insistence that properly rational discussion must be orderly and systematic, that much of importance in making sense of the dilemmatic nature of ordinary social life is rendered "rationally invisible" (Shotter, 1987); that is, it is rendered unavailable for rational discussion as a commonplace feature of our everyday social lives together—either the sociohistorical context disappears in psychology, or, the thinking individual disappears in sociology.

Or, to put it another way: As I mentioned above, we study either (a) the inner dynamics of the individual psyche, or (b) the already determined characteristics of the external world, but not (c) the contingent flow of continuous communicative interaction between people. In our concern, as first-person subjectivities with only a third-person objective world, this whole third category of events, in which the responsibility for an outcome is shared between a "you" and "I," disappears (Shotter, 1989)—like the other disappearances noted above. As scientists, we have lacked an intelligible vocabulary in terms of which to make any sense of it. For us, the gap between the subjective and the objective, and the illusion of the self-contained self, has been a part of our lived ideology. And it is this that has made it difficult for us to fashion a set of stable, agreed terms, in which to discuss this third category of events, which are neither subjective nor objective. They have been excluded. Only by the "political" act of writing in a nonscientific, "blurred" genre (often considered by others to be a "philosophical" genre), have I been able to approach their nature.

Authorship in Life and in Texts

In their biography of Bakhtin, Clark and Holquist (1984) discuss a number of early, incomplete texts of Bakhtin's—written between 1918 and 1924—to which they assign the title *The Architectonics of Answerability*. In these early texts, Bakhtin outlined a concern with the ethics of everyday life activities, that is, with activities within that third category of events, within which it is impossible to decide ahead of time who is responsible for what: His concern was not with the end product of an action, its outcome, but with the "ethical deed in its making" (p. 63). For given the indeterminacy of such situations, what one can make of oneself depends upon what one can draw upon from the others around one; it depends upon how one is answerable to others, within and during the very activity of authoring itself. Thus what it is that makes me who I am is not just the unique place or position I now occupy in existence, but *how* I came to occupy it. As Clark and Holquist (1984) put it:

> What the self is answerable to is the social environment; what the self is answerable for is the authorship of its responses. The self creates itself in crafting an architectonic relation between the unique locus of life activity and the constantly changing natural and social environment which surrounds it. (pp. 67-68)

In other words, one's social identity is structured like a language, to parody Lacan. Where, the "architectonic" relationship between oneself and one's surroundings is not one of a fully formed, finalized kind, but one in which one assembles around one possible "architectural" materials, resources, for use as circumstances require.

To examine the nature of the ethical deed in its making, the process of the practical authorship of oneself, we must turn to an examination in detail of what is involved in our acts of speaking—in the formulation of an utterance—and to the nature of the architectonic resources available to us for use in our current social contexts. In discussing their nature, both Billig and Bakhtin insist upon their paradoxical and unfinalizable nature: Not only do our words make us as much as we make them; but we never succeed in finally saying anything. For, even as we complete an utterance, feeling that at that moment it expresses everything we wish to say, it always occasions a response from another. From their position, things are always different. Thus, as Bakhtin (1986, p. 76) says, "The first and foremost criterion for the finalization of an utterance is *the possibility of responding to it* or, more precisely and broadly, of assuming a responsive attitude to it (for example, executing an order)." Further, as Billig and Bakhtin see it, as one's words are always also another's words, the paradox of ideology—that we both shape and are shaped by it—is a variant of the general paradox of language, that is (to use Bakhtin's words!):

> A word (or in general any sign) is interindividual. . . . The word cannot be assigned to a single speaker. The author (speaker) has his own inalienable right to the word, but the listener has his rights, and those whose voices are heard in the word before the author comes upon it also have their rights (after all, there are no words that belong to no one). (Bakhtin, 1986, pp. 121-122)

A word only becomes "one's own" as one actively makes use of it in a context (or not, because one feels unable to, as the case may be), inflecting it with one's own tone, for one's own purposes, according to whom it is addressed. Thus, although there is much that is constant already in the word (to do with the "taste"[15] of all its past usages), what is its living use is not something that was already there in virtue of its constant aspects. It is as a speaker adapts it to his or her own use that it becomes in-formed with the speaker's own viewpoint; but not simply and completely, but in relation to the moment-by-moment, changing conditions surrounding its utterance. Hence the necessity, if one is properly to responsively understand an another's utterance, of being jointly immersed with them in the speech situation.

To understand the import of this for what has so far been written about lifespan development in the context of scientific psychology, we must examine the ideological context within which it has, so far, functioned. That is, we must examine what at the time it was deemed sensible (and legitimate) to say about how people ought to be. For me, its individualistic ideology is best captured in expressions of what I would call "the John DeLorean complex": when accused in the early 1980s of drug dealing, his wife in defending him in court said, "John has done nothing wrong. He has always believed in the American dream, that you can be anyone you want to be, if you want to be it *enough*." In other words, much of recent lifespan developmental psychology has emerged within a context in which individuals have felt themselves to be wholly responsible for what they become, and that their lives and those of others are freely chosen. It is also within this context that the idea of the lifespan as being made up of a distinct set of stages has flourished, for although the "impulses" toward each stage of change were always meant to come from within a person's "deep interior" (Gergen, 1991), the causes of people's (predictable—Sheehy, 1976) identity crises were to be found in their failure properly to "manage" crucial events in their surrounding circumstances.

However, in fostering a belief in rational control and autonomy, even in those situations in which it is impossible, the ideology of individualism is now, it would seem, uttering its last gasps. Times have changed; its constituency has withered; people seem not only not to be having "mid-life crises" any longer, but their mood has changed. A "culture of [me-first] narcissism" (Lasch, 1979) has given way to a "culture of survivalism" (Lasch, 1985), in which respect is sought for a "minimalist" or a "privatized" self, in a set of extremely restricted circumstances. Those who still embody the ideology of individualism, feel beleaguered and embattled, for as Giddens (1991) points out, the world of modernity has turned out to be much more risky than it was at first hoped or imagined. That third category of events I discussed above, outside of the power of individuals to control ahead of time, by the putting of abstract theories into practice (*fortuna* as it was called in medieval times—Giddens, 1991), has reclaimed a central position for itself in human affairs.[16] But what has happened also, which Giddens (1991) fails properly to analyze, is that those "othered" and "silenced" in modernity have, in this postmodern age, begun to benefit from its pervasive reflexive awareness; they have begun to find their voices, and to talk back. And it is this phenomenon and its relation to the concept of citizenship that I would like to discuss in the little space remaining to me.

Whose Genre Is It, Anyway?

As Hall and Held (1989) point out, the current upsurge of interest in the "politics of citizenship"—as distinct from the old politics of class—is due to an expansion of claims to rights in a whole host of new areas: national liberation movements both in (what was) the communist world and in other regions, victim to "external" hegemonies; questions of community membership posed not only by feminism, black and other ethnic movements, ecology (including the moral claims of other species including Nature itself), and other vulnerable minorities like children and the aged; but also by the problems posed in a genuine recognition of the importance of differences rather than similarities. In short, they are due to the demand for a unique individuality rather than the atomistic individualism afforded by liberal individualism or state socialism. As Gergen (1991) has described it, we are all now the "beneficiaries"—willing or unwilling—of the "multiphrenia" arising out of the diverse ways in which one must participate in a modern, pluralistic, multiethnic, multiontological (varied life-style) society. And in this new "politics of identity," what is at issue is not the possession of property as such, but opportunities to give shape and form to one's own life; for, as I called it above, a political economy of access to developmental opportunities is at work.

So, although the new politics of identity is, as I have also already mentioned, to do with the terms in which we now define our loyalties and our commitments, when social identities are structured like a language, more than just our loyalties and commitments are at stake. As black writers like Hall (1982) and Mercer (1990) have pointed out, a shift from being called a member of an "ethnic minority" by others to calling *oneself* "black," is a shift in one's political identity, for it shifts one's "position" in a political discourse. Instead of being silently defined as an object by those already with a voice in a racialist discourse, one moves toward reconstituting oneself as a subject of social, cultural, and political change, as a voice in the discourse, actively making history—albeit, not under circumstances of one's own choosing. But there is even more at stake here than a struggle over the meaning of single words, for as Volosinov (1973, p. 23) makes clear, words are in themselves "multiaccented"[17]—thus rather than as already having a meaning, they are best thought of as a *means* in the making of a meaning. Their meaning only becomes clear within particular ways of speaking, that is, *within a genre*. Thus what is at issue here, to repeat, is not so much the gaining of a position in an ongoing political discourse, as contributing a new genre to political speech in general, a new way of talking, a new way of being in the world. For new ways of talking "about" social relations, new forms of debate, work to constitute and to establish the very relations to which the words uttered within those ways seem to refer.

Thus one of the tasks in the new "politics of citizenship" is to articulate a new analytic-discursive vocabulary of terms, a new set of formative-relational commonplaces (*topoi*), that all the new and diverse groups within civil society can use in expressing their (ontological) needs—their feelings of anger and despair, their dreams and expectations, their need for respect and for civil relations with others, if one is to be one's own self while still "belonging," along with others, to one's society—while still participating in the debate, while still playing one's part *in the invention of citizenship*. For at the moment, we have something of a standoff: Those with a respect for the being of others fear claiming solidarity with them; they fear claiming to recognize and understand *their* "position." For, within a referential theory of meaning, any difference, any lack of correspondence between what their circumstances are said to be and what they themselves feel them to be, means: "You don't understand; I'm not like that; its not like that!" Within a rhetorical-responsive perspective, however, solidarity with others does not mean everyone thinking and feeling the same. It simply means that, in realizing the degree to which one relies upon one's responsive relations with others in being oneself, one cares about establishing a common ground with them *when required*. Without a common set of terms in which to share disagreements and criticisms openly, as Mercer (1990) points out, the improvising of alliances and coalitions with others, when required, is inhibited—people are paralysed by the fear of being seen as insensitive, as not "politically correct" or as not "ideologically right on."

Lacking the required arena of collective or public creativity, debates about freedom and democracy are currently carried on in the language of "the market." For the market, as Milton Friedman (1962, p. 200) has described it, "is one of the strongest most creative forces known to man—the attempt by millions of individuals to promote their own interests." But it is clear that the existing social conditions of the market do not "afford" the conditions of possibility required for the invention of citizenship. Indeed, in assigning us all either to the role of producers or consumers, it would seem to reproduce those very forms of exclusion and closure (classes)—that particular lack of a sense of belonging—that the idea of citizenship was originally concerned to address. As a genre, market economics is inadequate to our tasks. A new, as yet to be fashioned genre is required. Thus the politics of citizenship is not something to be instituted in society at large through a top-down system of power relations. It cannot be passed down, once the concept of citizenship has been first clarified, and an appropriate genre for its discussion has been fashioned, by a philosophical and social scientific vanguard. The Party in that sense is over.

This is where those of us concerned with the "politics of personhood" in the 1960s failed: then, we did not grasp the *formative* and *relational* power of language—its "social function of co-ordinating diverse social actions" (Mills, 1940, p. 439). Operating within a hierarchical model of power, we thought the emancipatory task was one of protest, of making those in power see the wrong of their mechanistic, inhuman ways. As R. D. Laing (1967, p. 11) then put it: "Humanity is estranged from its authentic possibilities, we are strangers to our true selves." Then we thought correct theories would give us access to our "true" selves, to the actual conditions required for authentic human being. We did not realize then the power of our talk, the "political" nature of genres Laing used in his writings, the fact that new ways of talking, new forms of debate, work to produce, to invent, rather than simply to reflect the entities we talked about. Thus now we realize that if everyone is to participate in that process of invention, citizenship cannot simply be instituted as a new ideology in a top-down power play by an elite group. It must emerge as a "living ideology," a new "tradition of argumentation," consisting in a whole diversity of interdependent arenas in which, and between which, argument over "precisely . . . the goods which constitute that tradition" (to repeat MacIntyre's formulation) can take place.

And the emergence of that debate becomes a possibility if the linguistic resources adequate to the task (the "goods" in question, above) become available to everyone. The resources for the debate about citizenship are, I think, now being fashioned by many within the social constructionist, discursive tradition of argumentation now growing up upon the boundaries of what used to be called the social sciences. But now their worth must be evaluated in debates of quite different kind to those we engaged in in the past. Now, it cannot be a matter of the empirical correctness or accuracy of a theoretical claim by an external observer, but a matter of us fashioning images or metaphors of a revealing kind—ones afforded or permitted by the resources actually (or potentially) available both to us and to the people we aim to help. Indeed, to fashion both our claims and their justifications, we must use the self-same (set of intrinsically two-sided) resources or "commonplaces" in the tradition of argumentation we share with them. Where, of course, other versions, formulated in terms of other images, will be put forward to contest ours. Hence, we must offer *good reasons*—some of it of an evidential kind gathered in empirical investigations, no doubt in favor of the claims we make. In this respect, I hope this chapter can be seen as offering some good reasons for preferring debates of this kind to those in this area conducted in the past.

Notes

1. But clearly on their way out toward the whole populace at large. Such books these days are not so much "about" social processes as materials for use by people in their constitution.

2. See also Meyrowitz's (1985) account of how the "situational geography" of social life—the communicative activity within which we have our psychological being—has become disconnected from the physical geography in which we live.

3. I say *seascape* rather than *landscape* for, as we shall see, one of our tasks in lifespan psychology is to develop a more "fluid" way of imagining the future (Gergen, 1991).

4. Wittgenstein (1953) uses the notion of "language-game" (reflexively, as it happens) in the same way (Edwards, 1985): to reveal aspects of our use of language that would otherwise remain unnoticed. Such metaphors can be "seen as" instruments, or paradigms, in our language games; they function as a *means* of representation, something with which comparison is made.

5. Although what might be called a "convergent realism" (Harré, 1990), in which successive theories are thought of as better and better approximations to a perfect representation of a partially unknown world, is incompatible with social constructionism, what Harré calls a "policy realism"—or I will here call a "situated realism"—is not.

6. To talk like this is, of course, to oversimplify, for these two polarities play into each other and borrow from each other to such an extent that all theories in psychology contain aspects of both tendencies.

7. Here I have in mind Marx's first thesis on Feuerbach, that "the chief defect of all hitherto existing materialism (that of Feuerbach included) is that the thing, reality, sensuousness, is conceived only in the form of the *object of contemplation*, but not as *sensuous human activity, practice,* not subjectively." (Marx & Engels, 1970, p. 121).

8. I shall call these secondary or derived dimensions, *person-world dimensions* of interaction. If we think of the main self-other dimension as a horizontal dimension, the person-world dimension can be thought of as being orthogonal to it. Where what one is as a self includes the whole of one's diffuse, embodied being, while what one is as a person includes just those aspects of one's self for which one is able to be responsible, and to answer for.

9. My focus in this chapter is methodological not ontological, that is, I am trying to find, if not an already fixed *basis* in terms of which to "root" or to "ground" analytic or instructive claims, at least to identify the "place" or "sphere of activity" within which the judging of such claims can be properly located, that is, to claim that the "grounds" for settling arguments are to be found within arguments themselves, not outside them. This is not to say, however, that it is in the sphere of verbal interaction that we should seek the *developmental origins* of all our verbal formulations.

10. Until recently it has been customary to treat Volosinov as a "voice" through which Bakhtin spoke, or ventriloquated. Morson and Emerson (1990) give good

reasons for not taking this view. I shall still "recruit" certain statements of Volosinov's, however, to Bakhtin's cause.

11. Although I cannot argue the point here, it is in the very nature of many of the *topoi* at the heart of a living tradition, that they can never be resolved in principle, ahead of time; they have the character of "essentially contested concepts" (Gallie, 1955-1956; also see Shotter, 1990).

12. A term Bakhtin (1984, p. 97) uses to describe the worldview used by Dostoyevsky in giving shape to his novels.

13. It is worth adding to this what Volosinov (1973) has to say:

> Understanding is to utterance as one line of a dialogue is to the next. Understanding strives to match the speaker's word with a *counter word*. Only in understanding a word in a foreign tongue is the attempt made to match it with the "same" word in one's own language. (p. 102)

14. About what I have called referential understanding Bakhtin (1986) says that

> the speaker does not expect passive understanding that, so to speak, only duplicates his or her own idea in someone else's mind (as in Saussure's model of linguistic communication . . .). Rather, the speaker talks with an expectation of a response, agreement, sympathy, objection, execution. (p. 69)

15. See Bakhtin (1981, p. 293).

16. Especially with the failure of centralized planning in socialist and communist states.

17. And he adds, "this inner dialectic quality of the sign comes out fully into the open only in times of social crises or revolutionary change" (Volosinov, 1973, p. 23)—and this is related to what Bakhtin (see Note 15) says about the "taste" of past usages being still present in a word.

References

Bakhtin, M. M. (1981). *The dialogical imagination* (M. Holquist, Ed.; C. Emerson & M. Holquist, Trans.). Austin: University of Texas Press.

Bakhtin, M. M. (1984). *Problems of Dostoyevsky's poetics* (C. Emerson, Ed. & Trans.). Minneapolis: University of Minnesota Press.

Bakhtin, M. M. (1986). *Speech genres and other late essays* (V. W. McGee, Trans.). Austin: University of Texas Press.

Bateson, M. C. (1990). *Composing a life.* New York: (Plume) Penguin.

Bazeman, C. (1988). *The shaping of written knowledge: The genre and activity of the experimental article in science.* Madison: University of Wisconsin Press.

Billig, M. (1987). *Arguing and thinking: A rhetorical approach to social psychology.* Cambridge: Cambridge University Press.

Billig, M. (1991). *Ideology, rhetoric and opinions.* London: Sage.

Billig, M., Condor, S., Edwards, D., Gane, M., Middleton, D., & Radley, R. (1988). *Ideological dilemmas.* London: Sage.

Clark, K., & Holquist, M. (1984). *Mikhail Bakhtin.* Cambridge, MA: Harvard University Press.

Derrida, J. (1976). *Of grammatology* (G. Spivak, Trans.). Baltimore, MD: Johns Hopkins University Press.

Edwards, J. C. (1985). *Ethics without philosophy: Wittgenstein and the moral life.* Tampa: University Presses of Florida.

Foucault, M. (1970). *The order of things: An archaeology of the human sciences.* London: Tavistock.

Friedman, M. (1962). *Capitalism and freedom.* Chicago: University of Chicago Press.

Gallie, W. B. (1955-1956). Essentially contested concepts. *Proceedings of the Aristotelian Society, 56,* 167-198.

Geertz, C. (1983). *Local knowledge: Further essays in interpretative anthropology.* New York: Basic Books.

Gergen, K. J. (1989). Warranting voice and the elaboration of self. In J. Shotter & K. J. Gergen (Eds.), *Texts of identity* (pp. 70-81). London: Sage.

Gergen, K. J. (1991). *The saturated self: Dilemmas of identity in contemporary life.* New York: Basic Books.

Giddens, A. (1991). *Modernity and self-identity: Self and society in the late modern age.* Stanford, CA: Stanford University Press.

Hall, S. (1982). The return of the repressed in media studies. In M. Gurevitch, T. Bennett, J. Curran, & S. Woolacott (Eds.), *Culture, society and the media.* London: Methuen.

Hall, S., & Held, D. (1989). Citizens and citizenship. In S. Hall & M. Jacques (Eds.), *New times: The changing face of politics in the 1990's* (pp. 173-188). London: Lawrence & Wishart.

Harré, R. (1983). *Personal being: A theory for individual psychology.* Oxford: Basil Blackwell.

Harré, R. (1990). Exploring the human Umwelt. In R. Bhaskar (Ed.), *Harré and his critics: Essays in honour of Rom Harré with his commentary on them* (pp. 297-364). Oxford: Basil Blackwell.

Laing, R. D. (1967). *Politics of experience and the bird of paradise.* Harmondsworth, UK: Penguin.

Lasch, C. (1979). *The culture of narcissism: American life in an age of diminishing expectations.* New York: Norton.

Lasch, C. (1985). *The minimalist self.* New York: Norton.

MacIntyre, A. (1981). *After virtue.* London: Duckworth.

Marx, K., & Engels, F. (1970). *The German ideology.* London: Lawrence & Wishart.

Mercer, K. (1990). Welcome to the jungle: Identity and diversity in postmodern politics. In J. Rutherford (Ed.), *Identity: Community, culture, difference.* London: Lawrence & Wishart.

Meyrowitz, J. (1985). *No sense of place: The impact of electronic media on social behavior.* New York: Oxford University Press.

Mills, C. W. (1940). Situated actions and vocabularies of motive. *American Sociological Review, 5,* 904-913.

Morson, G. S., & Emerson, C. (1990). *Mikhail Bakhtin: Creation of a prosaics.* Stanford, CA: Stanford University Press.

Sampson, E. E. (1988). The debate on individualism: Indigenous psychologies of the individual and their role in personal and societal functioning. *American Psychologist, 43,* 1203-1211.

Sheehy, G. (1976). *Passages: Predictable crises of adult life.* New York: Dutton.

Shotter, J. (1980). Action, joint action, and intentionality. In M. Brenner (Ed.), *The structure of action* (pp. 28-65). Oxford: Basil Blackwell.

Shotter, J. (1984). *Social accountability and selfhood.* Oxford: Basil Blackwell.

Shotter, J. (1987). The rhetoric of theory in psychology. In W. J. Baker, M. E. Hyland, H. V. Rappard, & A. W. Staats (Eds.), *Current issues in theoretical psychology.* Proceedings of the First International Conference of the Society for Theoretical Psychology. Amsterdam: North Holland.

Shotter, J. (1989). Social accountability and the social construction of "you." In J. Shotter & K. J. Gergen (Eds.), *Texts of identity* (pp. 133-151). London: Sage.

Shotter, J. (1990). Social individuality versus possessive individualism. In I. Parker & J. Shotter (Eds.), *Deconstructing social psychology* (pp. 155-169). London: Routledge & Kegan Paul.

Stam, H. (1987). The psychology of control: A textual critique. In H. J. Stam, T. B. Rogers, & K. J. Gergen (Eds.), *The analysis of psychological theory: Metapsychological perspectives.* New York: Hemisphere.

Taylor, C. (1989). *Sources of the self: The making of the modern identity.* Cambridge, MA: Harvard University Press.

Volosinov, V. N. (1973). *Marxism and the philosophy of language* (L. Matejka & I. R. Titunik, Trans.). Cambridge, MA: Harvard University Press.

Wittgenstein, L. (1953). *Philosophical investigations.* Oxford: Basil Blackwell.

CHAPTER TWO

Autobiographies and the Shaping of Gendered Lives

MARY M. GERGEN

KENNETH J. GERGEN

The biological differences between men and women seem to be among the most immutable and important in everyday life. These differences between males and females are accompanied by differing expectations about life choices and involve differing trajectories across the lifespan. Almost always people identify themselves in the most profound ways as either male or female, and become acutely aware of the manner in which their bodies change as they age. Yet, how we understand our gendered lives is subject to multiple interpretations. It is frequently presumed that facts about gender distinctions, along with those regarding human development and change more generally, are (or should be) derived from systematic observation of what is the case. What we believe about gender development is, from this perspective, ideally a reflection of actual differences across the lifespan (cf. reviews of sex difference research in Maccoby & Jacklin, 1974; Money & Ehrhardt, 1972). Scientific knowledge, on this account, acquires

AUTHORS' NOTE: This chapter is a revised version of Mary M. Gergen and Kenneth J. Gergen, "Narratives of the Gendered Body in Popular Autobiography," in Ruthellen Josselson & Amia Lieblich (Eds.), *The Narrative Study of Lives, vol. 1* (1993, Sage).

special status over folk psychology because scientific observation is more systematic and rigorous and its conclusions thereby more trustworthy than everyday language.

Although this view is commonplace, it is also problematic. A growing body of scholarship now contends that understanding, itself, may itself produce formative effects on sexual differentiations. That is, what we take to be knowledge of gender and development over the lifespan is not an objective reflection of the world as it is; rather, our presumptions about the world and selves serve as interpretive networks through which we make sense of what there is (Morss, in press; Walkerdine, 1990). Further, these presumptions enter reflexively into daily affairs to shape the contours of cultural life. Thus, if boys are presumed to be more biologically suited for mathematics than girls, then it is not surprising that so few women get Ph.D.s in mathematics. And, as people live out their lives, engaging in various courses of action, these characteristics serve to support the matrix of preexisting meanings attached to various physical characteristics. In a broad sense, one is thus born into a culture composed of interlocking patterns of meaning and action (Bruner, 1986). These meanings give specific significance to various biological characteristics, rendering them socially visible or insignificant, deeming them valuable or debilitating. In this sense, we follow *social* clocks that pattern our movements along gendered role paths. The result of this cultural construction of meaning is a deep sense of the natural unfolding differences between men and women as they develop and age.

From the social constructionist perspective, meanings are not private and subjective events, but public and shared.[1] Meanings are generated through the discursive practices of the culture, transmitted from adults to children within various cultural contexts. Because such practices are inherently fragile and subject to continuous alteration, various significations can become foregrounded in one cultural enclave while obscured in another. Cultural patterns of speaking and acting at any time may be viewed as a patchwork of discourses, each with its own history and context of usage.[2] In carrying out relationships it is thus necessary to borrow from various repositories of discourse to achieve mutual coordination of action (Jouve, 1991). At the same time, most recognizable cultures also contain a body of more or less interdependent, enduring, and mutually supportive discourses. Thus, for example, in the United States, discourses on freedom contain many assumptions common to conceptions of jurisprudence, theories of economic behavior, gender relations, and so on. Each domain thus lends mutual support to the lived realities of the others.

In the present offering we explore a small repository of discourse within the culture; although relatively insignificant in the literary landscape, this body of writing provides significant bearings for negotiating the life course. Our particular interest is in narrative construction, and most focally, the stories people tell about their lives. In our view, the narrative is the central means by which people endow their lives with meaning across time.[3] Thus, as people are exposed to the popular narratives within the culture, they learn how to regard themselves, how to make themselves intelligible to each other, and how to fashion their conduct. In Paul de Man's (1979) words, "We assume that life produces the autobiography . . . , but can we not suggest, with equal justice, that the autobiographical project itself may produce and determine life?" (p. 920).

To the extent that narratives are gendered, furnishing different structures of meaning for men as opposed to women, so do they contribute to cultural patterns that differentiate between the genders and prescribe what is both likely and unlikely during a lifetime. Thus as men and women tell the stories of their bodies— what they mean and how they should be considered—so do these stories affect the course of their relationships with others, their career potentials, and their life satisfactions.

Autobiography and the Fashioning of the Life Course

One of the most accessible forms of narrative available to contemporary North American readers is the popular autobiography. These autobiographies are often written so as to allow celebrities, often abetted by professional writers, to tell their life stories in a revealing and engrossing way. Despite their mass appeal, we believe the popular autobiography is far more than a mode of public entertainment. Rather, such works operate much like secularized primers for the "good life." They provide an idealized model of the life course—furnishing direction, sanctioning deviation, and providing benchmarks against which common persons can measure and judge their development. Autobiographies such as these are not, of course, the only sources for rendering the life course meaningful. However, because they bear an intertextual relationship with other popular sources of narrative—television documentaries, Hollywood films, magazine stories, as well as other fictional fare—their significance is noteworthy.

The function of the autobiography as a life course model is revealed in the narrator's positioning of self vis-à-vis the reader. As Eakin (1985) points out, the autobiographer typically takes "the stance of the wise and fatherly elder addressing the reader as son or niece" (p. 29). The principal form of the autobiographical relationship is expert to novice, elder to younger, master to apprentice, or powerful to powerless. The edifying principle behind autobiographies is also revealed in their central themes and the personages selected to write about themselves. Classical autobiographies almost exclusively delineate the life of cultural heroes—those who have achieved greatness through their accomplishments (Jelinek, 1980; Olney, 1980). Readers benefit by being able to fantasize about the pleasures of escaping their humdrum circumstances and learning the ways and means to a notable life.

Autobiography as the Hero's Tale

What kind of image of the lifespan does the popular autobiography present? There has been no systematic study of this question, but the answers can be ascertained, in part, by reference to the historical development of the autobiographical form itself. Although the history of autobiography is in its infancy, scholars suggest that its particular form took shape with the rise of the bourgeoisie, and the accompanying concept of the self-made man (Lejeune, 1975; Pascal, 1960). Similarly, Weintraub (1978) argues that the development of autobiography is closely linked in Western culture with the emerging value of the unique and independent individual. "The fascination with individual specificity leads to deep intrigue with life stories" (Eakin, 1985, p. 204). In this view, autobiographical figures represent a culturally and historically situate model of an ideal self.

With the emphasis on individual achievement, autobiographies tend to follow the classical lines of the "monomyth," a form that Joseph Campbell (1949/1956) has designated as the most fundamental in Western civilization. In its clearest form, the monomyth is the saga of a hero who undertakes a profound quest. When applied to the lifespan, the monomyth shapes the narrative form of the heroic trajectory. It thus tends to recognize youth as a preparatory period; early and middle adulthood as induction and struggle to attain one's goals; and mature adulthood and old age as full achievement and the consolidation and appreciation of one's successes. The form of the heroic lifespan is indeed like a skewed arc, with the apex at the climactic moment of highest attainment. In the autobiography, the form of the story is singular, linear, and progressive to the penultimate climax, and usually stable thereafter.

Yet, it is also clear that this account of the autobiography is most relevant to—if not the unique provenance of—prominent public figures. The chief features of the monomythic tale speak most directly to the lifespan of a man, not a woman (Gergen, 1992). As Mary Mason has written, "The self presented as the stage for a battle of opposing forces and where a climactic victory for one force—spirit defeating flesh— . . . simply does not accord with the deepest realities of women's experience and so is inappropriate as a model for women's life-writing" (1980, p. 210). Women do feature as characters in the monomyth, of course. Yet, of the several women's roles in the monomyth, none is considered heroic, rather their parts are defined as stable, passive, or service oriented. Women are thematized as fair maidens to be wooed and won, mothers and wives, witches and sorcerers.[4] They are objects of a quest, or forces that impede the hero in pursuit of his goals.

Earlier work on gendered forms of autobiography (Brodzki & Schenck, 1988; M. Gergen, 1992, in press) indicates that in contrast to men's accounts, women's story lines are multiple, intermingled, ambivalent as to valence, and recursive. Though men's stories concentrate on the pursuit of single goals, most often career oriented, women's are more complex. Women's stories usually weave together themes of achievement along with themes of family obligations, personal development, love lives, children's welfare, and friendship. Though men's stories are rarely revealing about emotional experiences, traumas, self-deprecation, self-doubt, and self-destructiveness, women's stories often express these aspects. Because of these multiple themes and self-expressions, the tone or movement of women's stories are never unidirectional, focused, or contained. Thus the content and the form of men's and women's autobiographies are distinct. The men's stories, however, exhibit the cardinal characteristics of the idealized form of autobiography. Women's forms are deviant.

Gendered Narratives of the Embodied Self

Although there are substantial differences in the narrative forms located in male as opposed to female autobiographies, our special interest is in a specific form of content, namely embodiment. As reasoned above, the body doesn't "speak for itself." Rather, as a culture, we invest it with meaning—giving it importance (or not), treating its changes as significant (or not), and elaborating these meanings in such a way that life satisfactions blossom or are obliterated. The question, then, is how these culturally acclaimed authors embody themselves over the lifespan. How do they define, elaborate, and give significance to their physical being? How do males and females differ in the model they provide for the experience and treatment of one's body through the life course?

To explore these issues we shall consider how famous men and women account for their bodies from their youth, through adulthood and old age. A sample of autobiographies of 16 men and women published in the United States in the last 7 years will serve as the basis for this discussion. These books were chosen to reflect the range of autobiographies available in the popular market. This selection includes people who have accomplished noteworthy activities, and are not merely associated with or related to famous people. The authors of this sample do vary in age, primarily because many of them—in particular the athletes and performers—have become famous in their youth. The male autobiographies include those of: Ansel Adams, John Paul Getty, Lee Iacocca, T. Boone Pickens, Ahmad Rashad, Donald Trump, Jr., Thomas Watson, Jr., and Chuck Yeager. The female autobiographers are Joan Baez, Sidney Biddle Barrows, Nien Cheng, Linda Ellerbee, Gelsey Kirkland, Martina Navratilova, Joan Rivers, and Beverly Sills. Although the full complexity of these accounts cannot be conveyed in this chapter, illustrative quotations will allow dominant themes to become apparent.

Bodily Inscription From Childhood to Adolescence

Men and women account for their bodies in very different ways, beginning with their earliest reminiscences of childhood. Two aspects of this difference bear notice. First, men are almost silent about their physical beings, except to note how effective their bodies were in attaining their goals, which were mostly athletic. A typical example is T. Boone Pickens's (1987) comment:

> I was small boy, and I clearly remember playing football on the corner lot with the kids on my block. . . . They were bigger than we were, but our brains and spunk usually combined to carry the day.

Second, men display little emotion when making these descriptions. Perhaps the time lag between event and reportage has stifled any sense of connectedness that once may have existed for the author, and/or the inclusion of any emotional reactions might seem inappropriate. In any case, the body is virtually an absent figure in their reminiscences. Women's stories tend to be far more embodied. Beginning with the early years, women include greater detail in the descriptions of the body, and they are often emotional in describing their embodied lives.

A rather poignant account to the reader, but apparently not to the owner, is photographer Ansel Adams's (1985) description of how he acquired his misshapen nose:

On the day of the San Francisco earthquake [April 17, 1906] . . . I was exploring in the garden when my mother called me to breakfast and I came trotting. At that moment a severe aftershock hit and threw me off balance. I tumbled against a low brick garden wall, my nose making violent contact with quite a bloody effect. The nosebleed stopped after an hour, but my beauty was marred forever—the septum was thoroughly broken. When the family doctor could be reached, he advised that my nose be left alone until I matured; it could then be repaired with greater aesthetic quality. Apparently I never matured, as I have yet to see a surgeon about it. (pp. 7-8)

For Adams, the contorted nose that punctuated his face [and the cover of his autobiography] simply became irrelevant to his life.

For women, the physical tribulations of childhood are often felt strongly and deeply, sometimes for many years. Feelings of present-day self-worth seem strongly conditioned by the physical nature of the person they were. For example, comedienne Joan Rivers (1986), now a plastic surgeon's dream, has made a career out of comic references to her misbegotten self. As she describes a family photograph,

When I make jokes . . . about being fat, people often think it is just my neurotic imagination. Well, on the right, with her mother and sister during a vacation trip to Williamsburg, Virginia, is the thirteen year-old fat pig, wishing she could teach her arms and hips to inhale and hold their breath. (p. 183)

Fat also plagued the prima ballerina, Gelsey Kirkland (1986). She describes her dancing debut at camp as a form of self-defense for *her* misshapen body:

The other children taunted me about the disproportions of my body. I never let them know how much I was stung by their disparagements . . . I turned my abdominal bulge to advantage by performing a belly dance to amuse those in my cabin. (p. 10)

Tennis star Martina Navratilova (1985) had the reverse problem: being too small.

> I was tiny, not an ounce of fat on me—nothing but muscle and bone—just sheer energy. In school I was kind of embarrassed about being so small, but on the tennis court it didn't really matter that much. (p. 24)

In terms of development over the lifespan, the impact of physiognomy for both boys and girls often turns on the extent to which its effects are intensified or altered in puberty. For men in contemporary Western culture, the adolescent challenge largely takes place within the arena of athletics. The body's abilities to measure up to the competition are all-important in athletics particularly. For these males, it is in this period that body and identity are more closely linked than at any other time in the lifespan. Chuck Yeager (1985), the man with the "right stuff," looks back with pleasure:

> By the time I reached high school, I excelled at anything that demanded dexterity. . . . In sports, I was terrific at pool and pingpong, good in basketball and football. (p. 11)

Having an athletic body also helped ease a racially tense social scene for footballer Amad Rashad (1988), as well as contributing to his self-esteem.

> If you lived in my neighborhood, . . . you tended not to go to Eastside— they would kick your ass over there. Because of my brother and my athletic ability, the law of the street didn't apply to me. (p. 47)

T. Boone Pickens, Jr., the billionaire "take-over" tycoon describes himself:

> Fortunately, I was well coordinated. . . . Only five feet nine inches tall, . . . but a basketball player. (p. 17)

In effect, being short was a threat to adolescent identity; being coordinated was a fortunate compensation. Donald Trump (1986), New York's bad-boy builder, avoids any physical description of himself as a youth, except to relate that he was physically aggressive, to the point of giving a music teacher a black eye when he was in second grade "because he didn't know anything" (p. 71).

Lee Iacocca (1984) turned the story of his youthful illness into gains in the realms of gambling and sex.

> Although I lost about forty pounds and stayed in bed for six months, I eventually made a full recovery. (p. 16)

While convalescing, he started playing poker and reading books.

> All I could remember about the book [*Appointment in Samarra*] was that it got me interested in sex. (pp. 16-17)

An exception to the bravado and self-assuredness of the vast majority of autobiographers, Thomas J. Watson, Jr. (1990), former head of IBM, portrays himself as unathletic.

> While I was skinny and taller than most other kids, I was no athlete. My eye-hand coordination was terrible, so I hated baseball.

A theme of overcoming his bodily and psychological defects is a stronger undercurrent in his book than in the others. His success in mastering himself is illustrated, however.

For the adolescent girl, character is not made so much on the playing fields as in private chambers. Because girls seem more fully identified with their bodies, bodily changes at puberty become an enormous issue for identity formation. It is as if the body, which seemed a reasonably stable and controllable aspect of the girlhood self, begins to undo one's identity in adolescence. Spontaneously, it can make one hideous or desirable, both of which are problematic shifts in identity. Unlike men, it is a rare woman whose personal narrative is not concentrated on the unsettlement of adolescent transformation. As Navratilova comments,

> The girls started to fill out in the sixth or seventh grade, but I didn't wear a brassiere until I was fourteen—and God knows I didn't need one then. I was more than a little upset about developing so late. (p. 24)

Later she gains in stature:

My new weight gave me some curves I never thought I'd have, and they gave me the idea that I was a full-grown woman at seventeen. (p. 122)

Joan Baez (1987) described her entry into junior high school as marked by rejection, which stemmed from her physical appearance. Without much pathos she recounted her image:

Joanie Boney, an awkward stringbean, fifteen pounds underweight, my hair a bunch of black straw whacked off just below my ears, the hated cowlick on my hairline forcing a lock of bangs straight up over my right eye. (p. 30)

In high school her self-evaluation echoed a degree of self confidence, mixed with doubt:

On the one hand I thought I was pretty hot stuff, but on the other, I was still terribly self-conscious about my extremely flat chest and dark skin. (p. 43)

Beverly Sills (1987), the great opera singer and director of the New York City Opera, describes her anguish:

I developed breasts earlier than any of my classmates, and that was a great source of anguish for me. I was already feeling tall and gawky, and when it became obvious in gym class that I was the only girl who needed a bra, I didn't just become miserable, I became *hysterical*. I was so unhappy with the sheer size of me that my mother bought me a garter belt, which was about seven inches wide, and I wore it around my chest. (p. 17)

As a more general surmise, through the period of childhood and adolescence, boys and girls develop dramatically different interpretations of their body. Boys describe their bodies as separated from self, and as more or less useful instruments to attain their will. Although the male's identity is alienated from physical form, females tend to define themselves in terms of their body. This tendency is congenial to the views of many object relations theorists who hold that daughters are much more strongly linked to their mothers' identities through the similarities of their bodies, while sons are taught that they are distinct and separate from their mothers (cf. Chodorow, 1978; Dinnerstein, 1977). To elaborate in the context of autobiography, it is possible that the distinctiveness that men acquire to regard themselves as separate from mother becomes fulfilled in their alienation from their own bodies. That is, they echo their mother's actions in regarding their bodies as "other." In support of this complex relationship, theorist Jane Flax speculates that men desire the unity with the mothering figure that characterizes girl-mother relationships, and their rejection of the "female" in themselves and others [including their embodied natures] is a constant discipline required "to avoid memories of, longing for, suppressed identification with, or terror of the powerful mother of infancy." She cites "a long line of philosophic strategies motivated by a need to evade, deny, or repress the importance of . . . mother-child relationships" (1990, p. 232).

The Adult Years: Living Within and Beyond Embodiment

In their adult lives, the tendency for men to distance themselves from their bodies is intensified. The major theme in the plot of the adult male autobiographies is on career development; careers, however, are typically defined independently from the body. The discourse of career tends toward the transcendent—emphasizing ideals, goals, values, and aspirations as opposed to organicity. Donald Trump describing his first big deal:

> I saw potential, but I also recognized a downside. . . . I tried to keep my risk to an absolute minimum, and financially, I succeeded. . . . I kept investing more time and more energy, and the stakes rose for reasons unrelated to money. I could talk big for only so long. Eventually I had to prove—to the real estate community, to the press, to my father—that I could deliver the goods. (p. 121)

For most of one's activities the body is simply taken for granted; it seems not to be a matter of particular interest or concern. Metaphorically, the body is considered a machine possession, and like one's automobile, its normal operation should enable one to get on with the real business of life. Only on occasion does the body enter the register of meaning, and that is when it serves as an asset or a liability to ends that lie beyond. Thus, as Yeager describes his early days as a pilot,

> Being in our early twenties, we were in good physical shape and at the height of our recuperative powers—which we had to be to survive those nights. That was our Golden Age of flying and fun. By the time we reached thirty, our bodies forced moderation on us. (p. 180)

In effect, one simply goes on until the machine begins to break down.

At times the male autobiographer is surprised to find the body makes a difference. Donald Trump, commenting on his early efforts to join a prestigious Manhattan club (with a lack of modesty about his body that is not found in women's autobiographies), is shocked to find his body is a consideration:

> Because I was young and good-looking, and because some of the older members of the club were married to beautiful young women, [the officer of the club] was worried that I might be tempted to try to steal their wives. (p. 96)

Having a good body can thus be a career impediment. It can also cause other troubles, especially for the man who takes too much pride in his athletic abilities. Consider J. P. Getty's (1986) attempt to pass himself off as a boxer. Enticing his friend, Jack Dempsey, to spar with him, he finds himself in difficulty in order to impress some young ladies:

> A few moments after we began to spar, I realized that Jack was pulling his punches. My *macho* was taking all the punishment, for there were two or three very attractive young women friends watching at ringside. I wanted not only to test my ability as a boxer but also to prove myself . . . "Damn it, Jack, treat me just as you would any professional sparring partner." . . . I swung my lefts and rights as hard as I could. Jack . . . moved back a pace or two.

> "Okay, Paul," he said, "If you insist . . . "
> The first punch was hard. Jack swung again—and connected. That was that . . . I picked myself up off the canvas, fully and finally convinced that I would thenceforth stick to the oil business. (pp. 276-277)

One might also note from this little tale that Getty was willing to subject his body to abuse in order to satisfy his "macho" needs.

Because the body as an asset is taken for granted—much like the beating of a heart—it is only its potential for failure that must be confronted. The male reaction is expressed in two major ways: *anxiety* and *denial*. Among autobiographers, overtly expressed fear of dysfunction is largely reserved to men whose career success is closely linked to physical condition. Thus Rashad comments,

> Injuries are the ultimate reality for a pro athlete—they throw a shadow over your days. . . . Football is like the army in that you know that a third of your men will become casualties. You just hope it isn't you that gets hit. Football is not just a job, it's an adventure—until it comes time to get killed. (pp. 118-119)

However, by far the more common reaction to the threat of dysfunction is denial. Again consider Rashad:

> On a pass play early in the game, Ferguson threw to me. . . . As I caught the ball, cornerback Jimmy Marsalis undercut me, rolling with his full body weight on my left knee.
> The pain was excruciating, but the invulnerable Keed did the natural thing: I bounced up off the turf, pretending nothing was wrong. I didn't want to be hurt, and I insisted on walking it off. That provided the next real sign that something was wrong: I couldn't put my foot down. . . . As the trainers came out, I insisted to them, "Nah, it ain't too bad. It'll be all right. There's nothing wrong with this baby." (1988, p. 179)

A more dramatic illustration of defensiveness at work comes from Chuck Yeager's account of his emergency exit from a crashing plane. Yeager's parachute caught on fire as he ejected himself from the cockpit. Upon hitting the ground, he wanders toward a passerby who has seen him land.

> My face was charred meat. I asked him if he had a knife. He took out a small penknife, . . . and handed it to me. I said to him, "I've gotta do something about my hand. I can't stand it anymore." I used his knife to cut the rubber lined glove, and part of two burned fingers came out with it. The guy got sick. (p. 360)

Yeager himself registers no reaction.

Women's accounts of embodiment in the adult years stand in marked contrast to men's. The woman's sense of identity remains closely tied to her physical condition. It is not so much that the body is used instrumentally—as a means to some other end outside the body. Rather, to be in a certain bodily condition is to "be oneself." Consider the detail in which Joan Baez describes her bodily being as she readies herself for a major performance:

> I am in my room by two o'clock, tired, wired, and thinking about what to wear. . . . By three o'clock I have finally ironed a yellow parachute skirt and cobalt blue blouse, dug out the belt with the big silver circles and the necklace made of spoon ladles linked together, and the nineteen-dollar black sandals bedecked with rhine-stones. . . . They escort me to the green room. All the saliva in my mouth evaporates on the way. I have to go to the bathroom desperately, but it's too far and won't do any good anyway, so I sit tight, sip water, and ask Mary not to let anyone talk to me. (pp. 355-357)

This is not to say that women do not speak of using their bodies as instruments of achievement. For women, appearance constitutes an integral part of every story they tell and they are often keenly aware of shaping their bodies for ulterior ends. In the dramatic tale of survival in a Chinese detention prison during the era of the Cultural Revolution, Nien Cheng (1986) described the day her long ordeal with the Red Guard began. Two men from her company arrive unannounced at her home to take her to her "trial." She delayed going downstairs to have more time to think what she should do to preserve herself in this tense situation. She strives to create an impression of herself through her appearance.

> I put on a white cotton shirt, a pair of gray slacks, and black sandals, the clothes Chinese women wore in public places to avoid being

conspicuous. . . . I walked slowly, deliberately creating the impression of composure. (p. 8)

Effects of appearance on career goals continues to be especially relevant to women in the public eye. Comments by Linda Ellerbee (1986), a television journalist, are telling:

> I was told to lose weight if I wished ever to anchor again at NBC News. I wonder if anyone's ever said that to Charles Kuralt. . . . Regarding my hair—I have lots of hair—I've paid attention to commands to tie it back, bring it forward, put it up, take it down, cut it, let it grow, curl it, straighten it, tame it—and I stopped doing so before someone asked me to shave it off. . . . Maybe I'd just gotten older, not mellower, or maybe I'd had it up to here with men telling me to do something about my hair. (p. 119)

Because women describe themselves as deeply embodied, they are more often candid than men about the discomforts and threats to their bodies. A typical example is furnished by Beverly Sills (1987), as she describes her bout with ovarian cancer at the age of 45:

> I was lucky. I had a tumor the size of a grapefruit, but the doctor removed it entirely. . . . After my operation, I probably weighed about 125 pounds. I don't think I'd weighed 125 pounds since I was four years old. (p. 264)

Returning to the stage very quickly, she mentions the pain she suffered.

> To be blunt about it, I was in agony . . . the pain was almost unbelievable

but she did it anyway.

> The plain truth is that if I had canceled, I would have worried that I was dying. (p. 267)

After her arrest and imprisonment, Nien Cheng minutely describes her experiences in prison as embodied ones of privation. Her description is rich with details of her bodily states, her illnesses, and her deteriorating condition:

> After some time, hunger became a permanent state, no longer a sensation but an ever present hollowness. The flesh on my body slowly melted away, my eyesight deteriorated, and simple activities such as washing clothes exhausted my strength. (p. 185)

Given women's close identification with their bodies, it is also possible to appreciate why violations of the body are so unsettling for the woman: They represent invasive negations of one's identity. Consider Sidney Biddle Barrows's (1986) account of how nude photos were taken of her, and published in national newspapers. With a boyfriend in Amsterdam:

> We went to the houseboat and sampled our new friend's excellent hashish. After a while, [the friend] tactfully disappeared, leaving us together in the shimmering afternoon sun. . . . I was delighted to have him snap some shots of me in my skimpy summer clothes. Pretty soon, he started flattering me: I looked so terrific, the light was just right, so why didn't I take off my clothes and let him shoot some nude photographs? (p. 22)

Later when Barrows was arrested for running a high-class escort service, her former boyfriend sold the photos to the *New York Post:*

> I was devastated. I could live with being called the Mayflower Madam, and I could even tolerate having my real name known. But now nude photographs of me were being splashed across two of the largest newspapers in the country! I couldn't believe that Rozansky had so shamelessly betrayed me, and I was disgusted that I had ever given him the time of day. (p. 290)

Other intimacies of the body were shared by Linda Ellerbee, who describes her illegal abortion.

> I'd been one of those women . . . who'd gotten pregnant, then gotten the name of someone through a friend of a friend, paid six hundred dollars cash, and waited, terrified, at my apartment until midnight

when a pimply-faced man showed up, exchanged code words with me, and came in, bringing cutting tools, bandages and Sodium Pentothol—but no medical license I could see. I was lucky. I did not bleed uncontrollably. I did not die. I recovered. I was no longer pregnant. But I wasn't the same, either. No woman is. (p. 96)

From the standpoint of the unity of mind and body, it is also possible to understand why women's stories—and seldom men's—often contain instances of bodily alteration, mutilation, or destruction. When a woman is unhappy with her identity—feeling like a failure, wishing for a change in identity—the frequent result is some form of bodily obliteration. Ballerina Gelsey Kirkland described a period of despair:

I wanted to lose my identity. . . . [at night, sleeping] I was able to dream my way into somebody else's body. I was no longer Gelsey. (p. 205)

At another point, when she has lost her boyfriend,

I went through another round of cosmetic surgery. I had my earlobes snipped off. I had silicone injected into my ankles and lips. (p. 126)

Joan Rivers turned such events into comedy:

That winter, in fact, suicide become one of my options; a way to strike back at all the people who did not appreciate me, a way to make them pay attention and be sorry. . . . I wanted to do something terrible to myself, expend my powerless rage on my body, so I went into the bathroom and with a pair of scissors crudely chopped off my hair. (p. 249)

Summing up the narratives of embodiment for the adult years, we find that the man's bodily self fades even more into the background as career interests expand. The career is typically tied to ideas and ideals, power and prestige, and not to corporality. In contrast, women typically remain wedded to their bodies regardless of their career interests and abilities. In their identification with their bodies, self and bodily activities are one.

Embodiment in the Latter Years

Because popular autobiographies tend to embrace the traditional criteria of the well-formed narrative,[5] their endings are extensions of that which proceeds. Especially for the male, the story line is a coherent one, with the writer describing early events in such a way that later outcomes are almost necessitated. Thus, in accounting for the body in the later years, much of the groundwork has already been laid. For the younger male autobiographer, the life account will be notable for its absence of body talk. Discursively, career success serves almost as an epiphany, enabling the male to achieve a state of the pure ideal. For males who do write from a more elderly position, however, matters are more complex. For here there are pervasive signs of what the culture defines as bodily deterioration. Issues of embodiment, then, begin to break through the seamless narrative of career advancement.

Three primary reactions tend to dominate the male autobiography. First, there is a *self-congratulatory* theme. If one's body has remained in reasonably good health, one may offer it (as separated from "I, myself") some form of adulation. Like a motor car that has outlasted those of one's friends, one may feel proud to be the owner of the machine. This orientation flavors Getty's commentary on aging:

> I am eighty-three. Cold, damp winters do bring on attacks of bronchitis . . . I can't lift weights or swim for hours or walk five miles at the brisk pace I did ten years ago. . . . Luckily, I can afford the best medical care available. (p. 275)

With a "touch" of the "chronic," Getty appears to revert to the earlier defensive posture.

Among those writers who are not so fortunate as Getty, two other orientations are taken toward the body. One is *begrudging admission* that one has a body, and that it must be given its due. This approach is taken by Chuck Yeager:

> My concession to aging is to take better care of myself than I did when I was younger. . . . Nowadays, I hunt as much for the exer-

cise . . . as for the sport. . . . I'm definitely not a rocking-chair type. I can't just sit around, watch television, drink beer, get fat, and fade out. (pp. 422-423)

The interruption of the heroic narrative is more dramatically illustrated in Ansel Adams's revelations of his chronic and increasingly disabling problems:

As I cleared the decks for future projects, I found an ever-present complicating factor: Health. My mind is as active as ever, but my body was falling farther and farther behind. (1985, p. 365) (The reader may note that the "real" Adams is the mental form, and the body is a recalcitrant fellow-traveler who is lagging behind.)

Adams describes his heart surgery (a triple bypass and valve replacement).

Without surgery I was fast reaching an embarrassing state of inactivity; I could not walk a hundred feet without the crippling symptoms of chest pains and shortness of breath. (1985, p. 366)

Yet, the sense of bodily infringement on the idealized masculine narrative is revealed in Adams's description of recovery:

My only complaint was a pestiferous vertigo . . . In two months the vertigo vanished and I was able to drive the late Congressman Philip Burton to Big Sur for his first view of that marvelous region; he soon became one of the leaders in the fight for its preservation. (1985, p. 366)

Back to business as usual. The body can take a back seat again to the "real" action of political life.

A third orientation to the aging body is often encountered in the male autobiography, essentially a trauma *of broken defenses*. Because of the threats to the body in the later years, the picture of the self during the middle years—detached from biological anchors—can no longer be maintained. With the disruptive sense of being the victim of "a dirty trick," the male at last confronts the possibility of finitude. Watson's (1990) description of his heart attack is illustrative:

> In mid-November, I was in my office and Jane Cahill, my executive
> assistant, started to come in the door. Then she stopped cold, because
> I had my head down on the desk, "Are you all right?" she asked.
>   I'm fine. I'm tired. . . .
>   That night I woke up with a pain in my chest. It wasn't very in-
> tense but it wouldn't go away. Olive was in the Caribbean with
> friends, so I drove myself to the emergency room at Greenwich Hos-
> pital . . . having a heart attack. (p. 392)

Employing the metaphor of the body as the serviceable machine,
Watson also reveals his sense of vulnerability.

> When you have a heart attack, you realize how fragile your body is.
> I felt that mine had let me down, damn near entirely, and for several
> months I had very volatile reactions to insignificant things. (p. 394)

It would be useful to make broad comparisons between older
male autobiographies and those written by older women. Unfortunately, however, few women write popular autobiographies
when they are past sixty. For this genre of literature, women's
reputations tend to result from achievements of the early years.
Lifetimes that culminate in professional heroics are much less
likely to be written. For those older women who do contribute to
the genre, the body continues to figure importantly in two ways.
First, although one might anticipate a drawing away from bodily
identification as it become more problematic, this does not seem
to be the case with women. Instead, the writers continue to "live
their bodies," in spite of the body's transformation. Beverly Sills's
account of her body's reaction to her chores in the management of
the opera company after her retirement as a diva is illustrative:

> I was working like a horse, my blood pressure was way up, and I
> was eating six meals a day. . . . I came into my job as general director
> weighing 150 pounds; on June 16, 1984 when I visited the endocri-
> nologist, I weighed 220 pounds. (p. 345)

There is a second theme located in the accounts of women,
including those in later years, which is far more subtle in its
manifestation, but pervasive and profound. Because the woman's

body is so closely identified with the self, one's bodily relations with others essentially extend the self. In the same way that violations of the body are defacements of identity, so are investments of the body in others, modes of enhancing the self. Thus, in pondering the preceding years and the meaning of one's life, women are more given to thinking about their children, lovers, and parents—those with whom the body has been intimately shared—and others, such as friends, who are now part of oneself. Nien Cheng's autobiography is a continuous knitting of her life to her daughter, who was killed by the Red Guard. She describes a night without sleep.

> Lying in the darkened room, I remembered the years that had gone by, and I saw my daughter in various stages of her growth from a chubby-cheeked baby . . . to a beautiful young woman in Shanghai. . . . I blamed myself for her death because I had brought her back to Shanghai in 1949. (p. 495)

This recounting of significant connection is not wholly reserved for old age, however. Even when the younger women think back on their lives, their ruminations tend to center on those related through extensions of the body. When Navratilova won the Wimbledon Championship, she expressed her first thoughts on winning as:

> For the first time I was a Wimbledon champion, fulfilling the dream of my father many years before. . . . I felt I was on top of the world. (p. 190)

Joan Baez writes an epilogue in which she describes her family and friends, those who have been important in her life. In the final pages she talks of going to a party in Paris with her son. When she returns home,

> Mom will have a fire going in the kitchen and perhaps a Brahms trio on the stereo. Gabe will fall into bed, and I will sit in front of the fire, dressed like a Spanish princess, telling Mom how the sun rose, piercing through the mist over the lake . . . and how there was peace all around as the castle finally slept. (pp. 377-378)

For men, rumination about the significance of intimates plays but a minor role in their stories. When one is on the grand highway of monomyth, it is important to travel light. Thus Yeager and Getty, for example, speak only in passing of deaths and illnesses within the family; Trump describes himself, his family members, and his then wife, Ivana, as "rocks." The major exception to this general disregard is the father's death, which often receives considerable attention. The importance of the father's death can be traced to the threat it symbolizes to the male portrayal of invulnerability. Because one can see within the father's death the possibility of one's own finitude, added attention is needed to keep the defenses strong. There is no male autobiographer who could write as Nien Cheng, who is an old woman when she is finally allowed to leave China.

> While I watched the coastline of China receding . . . I felt guilty for being the one who was alive. I wished it were Meiping standing on the deck of this ship, going away to make a new life for herself. (pp. 534-535)

Contrasting Embodied Selves Over the Lifespan

The popular autobiography is both a repository of cultural meanings and a model for future lives. As the present analysis indicates, autobiographical stories differ dramatically in the meanings they impart to the male as opposed to the female body over the lifespan. The male autobiographer suggests that the man should be "above bodily concerns," more invested in culture than nature, in rationalities and values as opposed to the corporal.[6] To be fixed on one's body would be unmanly, narcissistic, and perhaps effeminate. To put matters of corporality aside is also highly functional for the male in terms of career. More hours can be devoted to achievement, and with fewer complaints. It is only in the later years that the male autobiographer admits an important relationship between self and body, and it is often an admission of shock, fear, and sorrow. The grand story is being brought to a close by a secret villain, and that villain dwells within.

Female autobiographers present a life story in which body and self are more unified. To be a woman is to be embodied; to fail in attending to one's corporality would be to ignore the cultural codes of being. Bodies serve a more central role in women's lives and consciousness than men's seem to. As Adrienne Rich (1977) has put it: "I know no woman—virgin, mother, lesbian, married, celibate—whether she earns her keep as a housewife, a cocktail waitress, or a scanner of brain waves—for whom her body is not a fundamental problem" (p. 14). This embodiment lends itself to a far greater sense of unity with others—particularly with those who have shared the flesh. To be embodied in this way is thus to be in significant relationship with others. At the same time, the discourse of embodiment sets the stage for deep unsettlement during puberty, for self-mutilation during periods of disappointment, and for a more profound sense of aging in the later years.

Inevitably an analysis such as this raises questions of the cultural good. For if one lives the life course within frameworks of meaning, and these meanings invite and constrain, celebrate and suppress, then one may ask whether it might be otherwise. If we could alter the forms of meaning—whether in autobiography or elsewhere—should we do so? From the female standpoint, there is much to reject in the male version of life and the practices that they favor. The male life course seems a strange "out of body" experience, one that devalues potentially significant aspects of human life. For the male, the female's mode of indexing life seems often irrelevant to the tasks at hand, and lends itself to emotional instability. However, rather than conceptualizing themselves as distinct, unchangeable creatures, perhaps both genders might benefit from new strategies of meaning-making that would expand life story options for all. At the same time, however, further attention is needed to the cultural patterns in which these discourses are embedded (Bordo, 1990). So long as the power relationships between men and women appear to favor the male version of reality and value, so long as the workplace makes little allowance for embodied selves, relationships are treated in a utilitarian manner, and identity is framed as a "within skin" subjectivity, new stories might not be able to survive. Yet, one might hope that within dialogues, through reciprocal and reflexive endeavors, and via political and social changes, new stories might encourage new practices and prospects—and we might hope that embodied stories would be available to all.

Notes

1. For further discussion of meaning as discursive rather than psychological, see Gergen (1991); also, Shotter, this volume.
2. See Bakhtin's (1981) concept of *heteroglossia*.
3. See also Bruss (1980), Rabuzzi (1988), Russ (1972), and Sprinker (1980).
4. See Frye (1957), and Rich (1977).
5. See Gergen and Gergen (1983, 1988) for further discussion of these criteria.
6. It should be emphasized that the subject of concern here is how embodiment is described in autobiographies. It is possible that in private spheres, men express their embodiment involvements much as women do in print. At times this distinction becomes muted, perhaps, because the alienation apparent in the texts seems so pervasive to us.

References

Adams, Ansel, with Mary Street Alinder. (1985). *Ansel Adams. An autobiography.* Boston: Little, Brown.
Baez, Joan. (1987). *And a voice to sing with: A memoir.* New York: New American Library.
Barrows, Sydney Biddle, with William Novak. (1986). *Mayflower madam.* New York: Arbor House; London: MacDonald.
Cheng, Nien. (1986). *Life and death in Shanghai.* New York: Penguin.
Ellerbee, Linda. (1986). *And so it goes: Adventures in television.* New York: Berkley Books.
Getty, J. Paul. (1986). *As I see it: An autobiography of J. Paul Getty.* New York: Berkley. (Originally published 1976)
Iacocca, Lee, with William Novak. (1984). *Iacocca. An autobiography.* New York: Bantam.
Kirkland, Gelsey, with Greg Lawrence. (1986). *Dancing on my grave.* Garden City, NY: Doubleday.
Navratilova, Martina, with George Vecsey. (1985). *Martina.* New York: Fawcett Crest.
Pickens, T. Boone, Jr. (1987). *Boone.* Boston: Houghton Mifflin.
Rashad, Ahmad, with Peter Bodo. (1988). *Rashad.* New York: Penguin.
Rivers, Joan, with Richard Meryman (1986). *Enter talking.* New York: Delacorte.
Sills, Beverly, & Lawrence Linderman. (1987). *Beverly.* New York: Bantam.

Trump, Donald, with Tony Schwartz. (1987). *Trump: The art of the deal.* New York: Warner Books.

Watson, Thomas J., Jr., & Peter Petre. (1990). *Father son & co.: My life at IBM and beyond.* New York: Bantam.

Yeager, General Chuck, & Leo James. (1985). *Yeager: An autobiography.* New York: Bantam.

General References

Bakhtin, Mikhail. (1981). *The dialogical imagination: Four essays* (Michael Holquist, Ed.). Austin: University of Texas Press.

Bordo, Susan. (1990). Feminism, postmodernism, and gender skepticism. In L. Nicholson (Ed.), *Feminism/postmodernism* (pp. 133-156). London: Routledge & Kegan Paul.

Brodzki, Bella, & Schenck, Celeste. (1988). *Life/lines: Theorizing women's autobiography.* Ithaca, NY: Cornell University Press.

Bruner, Jerome. (1986). *Actual minds, possible worlds.* Cambridge, MA: Harvard University Press.

Bruss, Elizabeth W. (1980). Eye for I: Making and unmaking autobiography in film. In J. Olney (Ed.), *Autobiography: Essays theoretical and critical* (pp. 296-320). Princeton, NJ: Princeton University Press.

Campbell, Joseph. (1956). *Hero with a thousand faces.* New York: Bollingen. (Originally published 1949)

Chodorow, Nancy. (1978). *The reproduction of mothering: Psychoanalysis and the sociology of gender.* Berkeley: University of California Press.

de Man, Paul. (1979). Autobiography as de-facement. *Modern Language Notes, 94,* 920.

Dinnerstein, Dorothy. (1976). *The mermaid and the minotaur: Sexual arrangements and the human malaise.* New York: Harper & Row.

Eakin, Paul John. (1985). *Fictions in autobiography: Studies in the art of self-invention.* Princeton, NJ: Princeton University Press.

Flax, Jane. (1990). *Thinking fragments.* Berkeley: University of California Press.

Frye, Northrup. (1957). *Anatomy of criticism: Four essays.* Princeton, NJ: Princeton University Press.

Gergen, Kenneth J. (1991). *The saturated self.* New York: Basic Books.

Gergen, Kenneth J., & Gergen, Mary M. (1983). Narrative of the self. In T. Sarbin & K. Schiebe (Eds.), *Studies in social identity* (pp. 254-273). New York: Praeger.

Gergen, Kenneth J., & Gergen, Mary M. (1988). Narrative and the self as relationship. In L. Berkowitz (Ed.), *Advances in experimental social psychology* (Vol. 21, pp. 17-56). San Diego, CA: Academic Press.

Gergen, Mary M. (1992). Life stories: Pieces of a dream. In G. Rosenwald & R. Ochberg (Eds.), *Storied lives* (pp. 127-144). New Haven, CT: Yale University Press.

Gergen, Mary M. (in press). The social construction of personal histories: Gendered lives in popular autobiographies. In T. Sarbin & J. Kitsuke (Eds.), *Constructing the social*. London: Sage.

Jelinek, Estelle C. (1980). *Women's autobiography: Essays in criticism*. Bloomington: Indiana University Press.

Jouve, Nicole Ward. (1991). *White woman speaks with forked tongue: Criticism as autobiography*. London: Routledge & Kegan Paul.

Lejeune, Philippe. (1975). *Le pacte autobiographique*. Paris: Seuil.

Maccoby, Eleanor, & Jacklin, Carol. (1974). *The psychology of sex differences*. Stanford, CA: Stanford University Press.

Mason, Mary G. (1980). Autobiographies of women writers. In J. Olney (Ed.), *Autobiography: Essays theoretical and critical* (pp. 207-235). Princeton, NJ: Princeton University Press.

Money, John, & Ehrhardt, A. A. (1972). *Man & woman. Boy & girl*. Baltimore, MD: Johns Hopkins University Press.

Morss, John. (in press). *Lifestories: Towards an anti-developmental psychology*. London: Routledge & Kegan Paul.

Olney, James. (1980). *Autobiography: Essays theoretical and critical*. Princeton, NJ: Princeton University Press.

Pascal, Roy. (1960). *Design and truth in autobiography*. Cambridge, MA: Harvard University Press.

Rabuzzi, Kathryn Allen. (1988). *Motherself: A mythic analysis of motherhood*. Bloomington: Indiana University Press.

Rich, Adrienne. (1977). *Of woman born: Motherhood as experience and institution*. New York: Norton.

Russ, Joanna. (1972). What can a heroine do? Or why women can't write. In S. Koppelman Cornillon (Ed.), *Images of women in fiction* (pp. 3-20). Bowling Green, OH: University Popular Press.

Sprinker, Michael. (1980). Fictions of the self: The end of autobiography. In J. Olney (Ed.), *Autobiography: Essays theoretical and critical* (pp. 321-342). Princeton, NJ: Princeton University Press.

Walkerdine, Valerie. (1990). *Schoolgirl fictions*. London: Verso.

Weintraub, Karl J. (1978). *The value of the individual: Self and circumstance in autobiography*. New York: Random House.

CHAPTER THREE

Discursively Formulating the Significance of Reminiscence in Later Life

KEVIN BUCHANAN

DAVID J. MIDDLETON

Reminiscence groups have become a ubiquitous feature of care and recreation for the elderly in the United Kingdom. They provide a forum in which older people are encouraged to talk with each other about the events and experiences of their lives. Discussions tend to be thematically structured—schooldays, work, domestic life, the wars, and so on—and a small industry has grown up supplying pictures, sounds, and artifacts from the first half of this century as prompts for reminiscing (e.g., Age Exchange, 1988; Help the Aged, 1981; Winslow Press, 1989). The growing use of reminiscence work in the care of older people is just one strand of a wider concern to provide resources for cultural engagement, embracing such activities as oral history, adult education, and community publishing. Such is the popularity and burgeoning growth of reminiscence work that some have characterized it as a "social movement," with an agenda that is as much political as it

AUTHORS' NOTE: The written comments of the editors (Nikolas Coupland and Jon F. Nussbaum) and Jonathan Potter, in addition to the constructive critical discussion of Malcolm Ashmore, Michael Billig, Derek Edwards, and Caroline Dryden of the Discourse and Rhetoric Group at Loughborough University, were most helpful in the preparation of this chapter.

is therapeutic or recreational (Bornat, 1989). Alongside these developments there has been a corresponding growth of a research and practice literature examining the efficacy of, and offering guidance on, reminiscence work (e.g., Butler, 1963; Coleman, 1974, 1986; Gibson, 1989; Kiernat, 1979; Lesser, Lazarus, Frankel, & Havasy, 1981; Lewis, 1971; McMahon & Rhudick, 1964; Norris, 1986, 1989; Norris & Abu El Eileh, 1982; Ryden, 1981).

A common assumption informing reminiscence work is that the activity of "reminiscing" is in some way beneficial for people in the later stages of life. Establishing the grounds of this beneficiality beyond apparent self-evidency has, however, proved difficult (Bornat, 1989). The majority of studies examining issues of evaluation have adopted "before and after" conventions, measuring indices such as "depression and self esteem" (Perrotta & Meacham, 1981), "mood" (Fallot, 1980), "cognitive functioning" (Baines, Saxby, & Ehlert, 1987; Bender, Cooper, & Howe, 1983), "life satisfaction" (Hobbs, 1983), and "social behavior" (Baines et al., 1987; Bender et al., 1983; Kiernat, 1979). Such research work, focused as it is on the "measurement" of operationalized concepts displaced from the actual terms of conversational engagement within reminiscence sessions, omits direct analysis of the social pragmatics of talk. In previous work we aimed to demonstrate that the rhetorical organization of reminiscence talk has important implications for understanding the consequences of participation in reminiscence sessions. We argued that reminiscence groups can be seen to afford varieties of interactional work pertinent to the situation of the elderly, such as the maintenance and reestablishment of identities and membership ("re-membering"), accounting for potential and actual frailties associated with "aging", and dealing with dislocation and loss (Buchanan & Middleton, 1990; Middleton & Buchanan 1991; Middleton, Buchanan, & Suurmond, 1991).

We have also argued in this work that to treat the talk that takes place in reminiscence groups as one instance of a generic activity reminiscing is to ignore the diversity of conversational acts that might be so named. In addition, to account for the value of reminiscence work within a framework of theory associating the generic activity "reminiscing" with "old age," is also to ignore the particular set of social relations and practices within which reminiscence groups are brought into being. This is not to say that the theorizing of the association between reminiscence and aging is of no import. It is rather to point out that this theorizing does not stand outside the realm of social action. As such, it makes up a domain of discursive action whose pragmatic orientation and constructive effects are analyzable. In other work, we have also considered how gerontological accounts of reminiscence and aging have worked to argue for the "social repositioning" of older people (Buchanan & Middleton, in press). In this chapter we turn our attention to the ways in which care workers involved in reminiscence work formulate the association between reminiscence and old age in talking about their work. Our aim is to demonstrate the role of these formulations in the organization of care practices. Such formulations can be seen as constituting a "community of discursive understanding," in that they serve as a resource for practitioners in making sense of and accounting for their work, and are thus integral to the ongoing constitution of reminiscence work as an arena of practice.

The consequence of this and previous analyses is to decouple the representation of reminiscence from a developmental-functionalist framework, in which it is represented as a generic activity of specific relevance to a particular stage of lifespan development (e.g., Butler, 1963; Lewis, 1971; Lieberman & Tobin, 1983; McMahon & Rhudick, 1964). Instead, we locate the formulation (or theorizing) of the association between "reminiscence" and "old age" in the sphere of social action.

Reminiscence and Later Life

That reminiscence has a special significance in later life is an assumption common to most accounts of reminiscence practice and research. The majority of texts discussing reminiscence and reminiscence work contain, at some point and in some form, the following narrative:

> Reminiscence was once considered to be an undesirable, or even pathological activity as far as older people were concerned. It was thought to be a symptom or cause of mental deterioration, and was

thus actively discouraged, at least in care settings. Then, in 1963, the American psychiatrist and gerontologist Robert Butler published an article in which he claimed reminiscence was a psychologically healthy activity for old people, that it contributed to the vital process of "life review," and that it should therefore be permitted, respected, and even encouraged. Following Butler, people have come to realize that reminiscence is (or may be) especially beneficial for (at least some) older people.

Very often, accounts go on to document other seminal works that have identified other possible and plausible "functions" of reminiscence. Common candidates here are papers suggesting that reminiscence may be a "defence mechanism" triggered by the losses of aging (Lewis, 1971), or that reminiscence might represent the performance of a "social role" specific to older people (McMahon & Rhudick, 1964).

These seminal writings on reminiscence and old age have served to "naturalize" reminiscence as a "mechanism," "function," or "process" within the larger "natural" process of aging. Reminiscence is considered in functional terms to be an "adaptive response" to old age (McMahon & Rhudick, 1964), and is often said to be associated with "successful" aging. Although such accounts are by no means the only basis for the existence of reminiscence work as an arena of practice, the frequent appearance of this narrative in the practitioner literature attests to their importance in this regard (e.g., Gibson, 1989, p. 9; Kiernat, 1979, p. 306; Lesser et al., 1981, p. 292; Mortimer, 1982, p. 59; Norris, 1986; Ryden, 1981, p. 461). By the same token, its presence in the contemporary research literature serves to justify a continuing concern with identifying the precise function of reminiscence in the later stages of life.

However, the assumptions embodied in this narrative, and in the research enterprise it endorses, have been called into question by a wide range of work in what might be broadly termed the social constructionist tradition. In relation to aging, this work has called into question the notion of lifespan development as a "natural" process, and/or a series of universal stages, and to reveal the socially constructed, historically specific nature of such notions (see, e.g., Featherstone & Hepworth, 1989; Freeman, 1984; Gergen & Gergen, this volume). More generally, work in discourse analysis and rhetoric has demonstrated linguistic representation to be inseparable from the pragmatics of communication, showing that natural language accounts inevitably construct versions of the world that are designed to achieve particular effects or have consequences for the trajectory of an interaction (e.g., Edwards & Potter, 1992; Heritage, 1984; Potter & Wetherell, 1987).

Taking this perspective on accounts of reminiscence and its significance in later life radically alters the kinds of research questions we might ask. It directs our attention to the "cultural embeddedness" of such accounts—how they embody common-place understandings of the nature of the past and its relation to the present, and of the nature of aging and being "old." Moreover, it directs us to examine how such accounts are formulated, used, and elaborated in the unfolding of social action. To study reminiscence, then, we cannot take the categories "reminiscence" or "old age" as given. We have to address the way people formulate these categories variably and resourcefully. From a developmental-functionalist perspective this variability might be handled in terms of a variety of candidate hypotheses regarding the function of reminiscence in later life. If, as we argue, this is no longer a viable option, how else can we account for the diverse formulations of the association between "reminiscence" and "old age" that we find in practitioners' discourse? It is our intention in the following analysis to present an alternative account.

Data and Analytical Resources

The data we examine are segments of transcribed talk recorded in interviews with three care workers involved in reminiscence work with older people. The three interviewees work in different locations and were interviewed separately. In the interviews, they were asked to talk about the purpose and value of reminiscence work in general and their own work in particular. Rather than approaching "reminiscence" as a unitary object of talk, we are interested in identifying different and distinct *versions* of "reminiscence-and-aging" in their talk. This is achieved through a consideration of the various metaphors, analogies, and figures of speech used by speakers to characterize reminiscence and old age. In addition, we examine the detail of how particular versions are built up in conversation, and consider aspects of the discursive and practical context in which they are formulated. Our interest here is in how different versions lend themselves to the accomplishment of different actions, and how they are formulated in such a way as to take into account other, potentially contradictory versions of "reminiscence and aging."

"I Don't Like to Keep These Away From Today"

Extract 1 consists of three segments taken from an interview with Mary,[1] an employee of a national charity for older people. Her job is to care for a group of physically frail old people who are brought to a day center one day a week. At the center, they are given lunch, take part in a variety of organized games, and chat among themselves. Reminiscence is among the range of activities provided in the charity's day centers (according to a typewritten information sheet), and Mary's supervisor had identified this group as particularly suited to our expressed purpose of tape-recording reminiscence groups. In the extract, Mary and the interviewer are discussing her use of reminiscence with the group.[2]

Extract 1

Segment (i)

    Mary: y'see (.) with <u>these</u> [Mary's group] they're up to date (.) they know what went off yesterday and they know what's going on in the world

              (2)

      Int: right (.) yeah

    Mary: and I think with <u>these</u> (.) it's best to keep 'em- (.) it's alright to go back now and again they'll go back in their own anyway sometimes (.) just back on their own (.) but very

often they talk about (.) things now (.) which I think's a good
thing to keep them up with the everyday goings on

Int: d'y- d'you reckon it could be: like (.) not a good idea then
to talk too much about the past to <u>encourage</u> it

Mary: not <u>all</u> the time no (.) not all the time not not with your
mentally alert

Int: no

Mary: I was gonna say these are well up with everything that's
going on I mean he'll (indicates elderly man in room) discuss things he's seen on the TV the news and- (.) and I think
when you go back into the war days I think it depresses
them <u>enough</u> (.) with what they're hearing today without
taking them back (.) to war days

Int: right right (.) but you still do it (.) now and then

Mary: I still do it now and then (.) and sometimes they'll take
theirselves back (.) they'll take theirselves back

Segment (ii)

Mary: I think mine [Mary's group] are up to date so you gotta keep
em up to date

Int: yeah (laughing)

Mary: you know you can't keep throwing them back because
they're already here and in it y'know what I mean

Segment (iii)

Mary: I don't like to keep these [Mary's group] away from today

To start with, consider the nature of "reminiscence" and its
value in old age, as it is formulated by Mary in these segments.
Reminiscence is presented here as a kind of time travel—to reminisce is to *"go back,"* to be *"away from today."* The past and the
present (*"they're already here and in it"*) are construed as places, and
talking about the past is construed as displacement from the
present. There is an implication that such displacement might be
harmful if indulged in too often, at least for those older people
who are *"mentally alert"* and in touch with the present—*"I think
mine are up to date so you gotta keep 'em up to date"*; *"not all the time*

no not with your mentally alert." Reminiscence is contrasted with keeping up with the present, keeping "*up to date.*" The use of the verb phrase "*go back*" suggests not only physical displacement, but also regression. In this account, there is a hint of an association between reminiscence and mental deterioration in older people. Take people "*back*" too much, the argument suggests, and they might stay there, finding it impossible to "*keep up*" with contemporary circumstances and events. This version of the value of reminiscence in later life is in turn predicated on a particular version of aging, one that construes old age as a time when "keeping up" becomes difficult, when decline and disengagement from the present (and thus from the concerns of the rest of society) are an ever-present threat.

It is not our intention to pass judgment on this account of the value of reminiscence in later life. Instead, we can look at what it accomplishes and how it is constructed. Mary has been asked (before the tape was started) to talk about her use of reminiscence. In the extract (and in most of the interview), she is clearly mounting an argument for *not* doing reminiscence work, and in the process is saying that she herself is reluctant to do it. The interviewer himself takes up this issue, as shown by his statement "*but you still do it now and then*" at the end of Segment (i). This "*now and then*" is repeated by Mary in her next turn ("*I still do it now and then*"), as a description of the frequency with which she runs reminiscence groups. In this extract, Mary can be seen as accounting for her sparing use of reminiscence work. The version of reminiscence that she uses to do this is of such a form as to make her reportedly infrequent use of reminiscence eminently plausible, and indeed desirable. The argument runs along the following lines: If reminiscence involves displacement into the past, and if older people are anyway in danger of not keeping up with the present, then such displacement should not happen too often, because it would reduce their chances of keeping up, being up to date, living in the present. It is therefore prudent to engage sparingly in such an activity. In this sense then, Mary's version of "reminiscence and aging" accomplishes the interactional task of accounting for her own care practices. Although there are other equally plausible ways of construing the value of reminiscence for older people, they might not have suited this task so well. This version accounts precisely for Mary's sparing use of reminiscence.

We can turn now to an analysis of the conversational resources used by Mary to build her account. In particular, we want to draw attention to its conditional form. Mary uses a number of devices to qualify her representation of reminiscence and its value for older people. One way she does this is to *particularize* her account, explicitly applying it to her own group—using qualifying phrases like *"with these"* and *"mine"* (cf. Billig, 1985; Middleton, in press). Another way she does this is to construct her account so as to make available the inference that reminiscence might not be a good thing to do, rather than making an explicit statement to that effect. For example, she refers to talking about the present as a *"good thing"*—*"they talk about things now which I think's a good thing to keep them up with everyday goings on"*—the implicit contrast being that talking about the past might not be such a good thing. Moreover, even in making this comparison she is guarded. In Segment (i) she begins to say *"I think it's best to keep em"* and then cuts off this statement to offer a qualification of it, before producing what appears to be an attenuated version of her original beginning—*"which I think's a good thing to keep them up with everyday goings on"*—where *"best"* has been replaced by *"good things,"* a construction that avoids a direct evaluative comparison between reminiscence and talking about the present.

What does this organization of Mary's account achieve? As we have noted, an important feature of her argument is that reminiscence is not good for older people who are mentally alert (*"no not with your mentally alert"*), and thus her account implicitly marks reminiscence as associated with mental deterioration. As such it can be read as endorsing a view of reminiscence that, as we mentioned earlier, is routinely and explicitly refuted in the reminiscence literature (e.g., Butler, 1963; Coleman, 1974, 1986; Gibson, 1989; Kiernat, 1979; Lesser et al., 1981; Lewis, 1971; McMahon & Rhudick, 1964; Mortimer, 1982; Norris, 1986; Ryden, 1981). Moreover, this explicit refutation of an association between reminiscence and mental deterioration is only part of a wider collection of practices predicated on the beneficiality of reminiscence, some of which impinge directly on Mary's own work—the provision and promotion of reminiscence by her employer, and the attentions of the interviewer in front of her, who clearly considers reminiscence valuable enough to do research into, and on whose behalf she has previously set up and orchestrated reminiscence sessions. Mary is presenting what might be termed an "unorthodox" version of reminiscence and its value for older people that is explicitly *not* espoused in the literature, but can still be found in practitioners' talk. Her indirect formulation of this version, by means of the conversational devices described above, can be seen as indicating its status as a "dispreferred" version.[3] Just as Mary's account is rhetorically organized to account for her way of working, so too is it organized to take account of, and preempt direct contradiction of (or by), other possible versions of reminiscence.

However, there is more going on in this talk than the delicately handled defense of an unorthodox position. To characterize Mary's account merely as taking the "unorthodox" position is only half the story. It would be more accurate to say that it involves a movement *between* contrary positions, a dialogue or argument about the nature and value of reminiscence. As we have already suggested, this dialogicality is an important feature of Mary's argument, in that the plausibility of her argument rests on its inclusion of the view opposite to the one being argued for. To say that reminiscence is *always* a bad thing, for *everyone*, would not merely be unorthodox, it would invite immediate disagreement. Indeed, such "extreme case formulations" (Pomerantz, 1986) are commonly used rhetorical devices, and operate on this very basis. Mary herself uses such a formulation when, in response to the interviewer's question as to whether it is a good idea to talk about the past, she replies *"not all the time no."*[4] By discounting the extreme case, this formulation works to elicit agreement, in that no one would agree that reminiscing *"all the time"* is a good idea. Thus it has the effect of advancing the case against doing reminiscence work.

The point here then is that this inclusion of the opposing view is not just a consequence of the speaker's attempt to preempt other arguments. It is also a consequence of the recognition that there is some truth in those arguments. It is the apparent nonrecognition of this truth, the stating of the "extreme" case, that invites disagreement. The dialogical form of Mary's account handles contradictory "truths" about reminiscence and later life.

"You've Got to Remember Your Past 'Cos That's Part of You"

Extract 2 is taken from an interview with Anne, a staff nurse in a geriatric day hospital attached to a large psychiatric hospital. As part of her work, she runs twice-weekly reminiscence groups for clinically depressed and confused older people. Immediately previous to the extract, the discussion has turned to common criticisms directed at reminiscence work.

Extract 2

> Int:what about the other criticism of reminiscing erm (.) that
> it's (.) it's just an encouragement for people to live in the
> past and and not face up- no
>
>   [

Anne: no I don't agree (.) I don't agree with that <u>at all</u> (.) no (.) no
(.) cos I think you've got to: (.) remember your past cos that's
part of you (.) your past and how (.) and how you've lived
(.) and that can help you deal with what's happening today
or tomorrow (.) so no I don't agree with that at all (.) I think
it's a good thing to reminisce and remember

> Int:mmm (.) it is something we all do anyway isn't it
>
>   [

Donna: mmm (.) that's right (.) it's not just the elderly

In her reply to the interviewer's question at the start of the extract, Anne offers a version of the value of reminiscence that constructs it as oriented to present circumstances, and unequivocally beneficial. This version emphasizes the intimate relation between memory and self, biography and identity (*"you've got to: (.) remember your past cos that's part of you"*), and the importance of past experience as a guide for action in the present and future ("*that can help you deal with what's happening today or tomorrow*").

In presenting this version, Anne is countering the interviewer's formulation of reminiscence as "*an encouragement (.) for people to live in the past.*" To the extent that this latter version is congruent with Mary's version of reminiscence as displacement from the present, Anne's version might be seen as an argument against the position taken by Mary in Extract 1. We want to go on to make some analytical points about this contrast between Anne's and Mary's accounts.

First, the contrast between the two accounts is in part a consequence of the different kinds of rhetorical work being done with them. Whereas Mary's version accounts for her reportedly sporadic use of reminiscence, Anne can be seen as countering a version of reminiscence that calls into question the value of her own reportedly regular practice of reminiscence work, and presenting an alternative version that accounts for this practice. Formulating the value of reminiscence in terms of the maintenance of identity and as a resource for dealing with present and future circumstances renders its regular use unproblematic—in fact one could perhaps say "the more the better," given the nature of the benefits implied.

There are, however, further interesting differences between Mary's and Anne's versions of the value of reminiscence, besides the obvious one of past orientation versus present orientation. In making her claim that reminiscence is not so good for the "*mentally alert,*" Mary makes a distinction between "*mentally alert*" older people and others that are presumably not so "*mentally alert.*" Anne, however, makes no such distinction. Now, it could be argued here, from the developmental-functionalist point of view referred to earlier, that these two versions of reminiscence differ because they relate to different populations—that reminiscence is good for the confused and depressed older people in Anne's care, but not so good for Mary's "mentally alert" group. We would suggest instead that such distinctions are deployed rhetorically. In Mary's case, this distinction is a central feature of her argument. In Anne's case, however, her position is strengthened by *not* making such a distinction, by claiming the relevance of the past to the present and future for people in general, using the generic "you" throughout her account. The interviewer's response *"it is something we all do anyway"* can be seen as orienting to the generality of her claim. At this point, Anne makes this generality explicit by stating *"it's not just the elderly."* Here, then, in the course of constructing a plausible argument for the value of reminiscence, not only does Anne *not* distinguish between different elderly client groups, she explicitly rejects a distinction between older people and other people. Thus the different accounts of the value of reminiscence in Extracts 1 and 2 are not based on distinctions between populations; rather, they differ in whether or not they use the distinction between populations as part of their argument. Such distinctions can be seen as rhetorically occasioned, in that they can be invoked or ignored in line with the particular case being made.

A further contrast between Mary's and Anne's accounts can be seen in the relative directness of their formulation. In contrast to Mary's tentative "dispreferred" version (see Note 3), Anne's version is much more directly formulated. She states her disagreement explicitly and repeatedly (*"I don't agree (.) I don't agree with that* at all *(.) no (.) no"*) and adds the unequivocal assertion that *"it's a good thing to reminisce and remember."* In taking the position she does, she is aligning herself with arguments that are routinely and widely used to justify the practice of reminiscence work—that reminiscence is indeed a beneficial activity for older people. The directness with which her account is formulated, then, can be seen as marking it as a "preferred" version of reminiscence, as against Mary's "dispreferred" version.

As in Extract 1, though, there is more to Anne's account than the marking of an "orthodox" position. Her unequivocal disagreement can also be seen as a consequence of the extreme case put to her by the interviewer. To suggest that reminiscence is *"just an encouragement to live in the past"* is to rule out of court, with that *"just,"* all other possible accounts of the value of reminiscence. Thus Anne can be seen as responding to this extreme case formulation in equivalent terms, stating the opposite case unequivocally. Here again, then, we have a dialogue of versions, this time as actual dialogue between two speakers. The movement between extremes that is evident in the first two turns of Extract 2 is echoed in Mary's attempts to take account of both positions—to argue that reminiscence is not *just* one thing, nor is it *just* the other.

Again, then, it would be a gross characterization of the data to say merely that Mary and Anne take opposing positions in relation to the value of reminiscence. We might even argue the opposite—that there is some agreement between them, in that Mary, like Anne, takes some pains to say that reminiscence is *not* just an encouragement to live in the past, although it may be so for her group. In an important sense, then, Anne and the interviewer are having the same argument with each other, in the first two turns of Extract 2, that Mary is having "with herself" in Extract 1.

"All They've Got to Give Is Their Memories"

Extract 3 is taken from an interview with a medical nurse, Jane, working with elderly patients who attend a day hospital attached to a large general hospital. Most of the patients are suffering from the effects of arthritis or recent strokes, and attend the day hospital for various kinds of therapy, medical checkups, and a cooked lunch. Each morning, before lunch, selected patients are gathered in the "group room," where Jane orchestrates discussion groups that are partly reminiscence based. Immediately previous to the extract, Jane has been talking at length about how she attempts to keep her clients up to date with what's going on in the world—men's use of makeup, the price of gasoline, changing sexual mores, the expansion of air travel—and how this "stimulates their thinking." This account is followed by the interviewer's question, at the start of the extract, about the place of reminiscence in the group sessions.

Extract 3

Int: so I mean we're going way beyond reminiscence here really (.) reminiscence seems to be a component in this-

Jane: reminiscence is part (.) I mean sometimes they just sit and chat about the old days (.) that's fine cos reminiscence is valuable (.) it helps them feel that they've got (.) something to offer (.) people (.) as I explain to the learner nurses (.) if you've got (.) on your ward a care for the elderly ward you'll hear people say (.) ooh he's telling me that story <u>again</u> about when he was in the war or (.) when he had- was shot

> or (.) something (.) and as I say to the learners (.) that's *all*
> these people the elderly people have to give in return (.) I
> said (.) look we're doing for them physically by (.) looking
> after them looking after their physical needs (.) taking them
> to the toilet (.) pulling their knickers down for them (.)
> sitting them on the toilet (.) even wiping their bottoms and
> pulling their knickers up (.) they want to say thank you in
> some way all they've got to give is their memories (.) and
> that's why you find old people are always going on about
> the past (.) because that's all they've got to give to say thank
> you (.) and if anybody is wise enough that people should
> be (.) if somebody starts talking about the past instead of
> thinking (.) oh gawd here we go again (.) they should think
> (cough) make the time to listen <u>because</u> (.) someone of the
> younger generation I'm 32 but I feel very honoured that I
> can learn so much about the past (.) just through talking to
> them they are walking encyclopedias (.) make the most of
> the elderly listen to them listen to what they've got to say
> (.) because once you've got a knowledge about (.) the past
> about earlier this century about what they can tell you (.) it
> gives you a great deal of insight for the future (.) I always
> say the past gives you the wisdom for the future

In this extract, we find further versions of reminiscence and its
value in later life. These versions are structured in various ways
around the theme of social exchange, emphasizing the role of
others in the activity of reminiscing, as well as that of the reminiscer. Jane begins by accounting for the value of reminiscence for
her elderly patients, and for their acts of reminiscing, in terms of
reciprocation for the ministrations of their carers—"*it helps them
feel that they've got (.) something to offer (.) people*"; "*that's all they've
got to give to say thank you.*" In this version, the value of reminiscence (for both reminiscer and audience) inheres in the fact that it
is offered as reciprocation, rather than in any intrinsic value it
might have. This version is then followed by a second version,
which constructs reminiscence as the transmission of culturally
and personally valuable knowledge ("*I feel very honoured that I can
learn so much about the past (.) just through talking to them they are
walking encyclopedias*"; "*once you've got a knowledge about the past
about earlier this century about what they can tell you (.) it gives you a
great deal of insight for the future*"). Here, in contrast to the first

version, reminiscence is presented as having high intrinsic value, independent of its status as a means of reciprocation.

These contrasting versions of reminiscence can in turn be seen as predicated on contrasting versions of aging. The first construes aging in terms of decrement and loss, involving the concomitant diminution of "resources" for engaging in social exchange. The second construes aging in terms of maturation and the accretion of experience, recruiting the common association between old age and wisdom.

These two versions of the value of reminiscence in later life serve, in Jane's account, as the basis for a moral exhortation to learner nurses (*"as I explain to the learner nurses"; "as I say to the learners"*), urging them to listen to their elderly patients (*"make the time to listen"; "make the most of the elderly listen to them listen to what they've got to say"*). In fact, much of the extract is formulated as an account of how Jane describes reminiscence to student nurses.

In the service of accomplishing this action, Jane's account is rhetorically organized to undermine another version of reminiscence. The version that Jane seeks to undermine is not stated explicitly in the extract, but is made available indirectly through the reported speech and thoughts of others—*"you'll hear people say (.) ooh he's telling me that story about when he was in the war or (.) when he had- was shot or (.) something"; "if somebody starts talking about the past instead of thinking oh gawd here we go again."* From these reported reactions, we are able to infer that reminiscence is construed here as repetitive talk, which is by implication self-indulgent and of no interest to others. The use of reported speech/thought here has the effect of ascribing this particular view of reminiscence to people other than the speaker (Jane) or her interlocutors (whether student nurses or the interviewer), and thus serves as a rhetorical device for recruiting others to consider this implicit version as problematic or prejudiced (cf. Goffman, 1981; see also Wooffitt [1992] and Widdecombe & Wooffitt [1989] for further examples of the rhetorical uses of reported speech in the marking of alternative positions as problematic). In addition, to the extent that this device serves as a means of indirectly formulating this version, it can also be seen as marking it as "unorthodox" or "dispreferred" in a similar way to that of Mary's in Extract 1.

Formulating the association between reminiscence and later life in terms of social exchange works to counter the version of reminiscence as self-indulgent talk, and marks this version as prejudiced by constructing reminiscence as *meant* for others. This argument builds over the course of Jane's account. First, in introducing the notion of reciprocation, she describes reminiscence as the only resource available to older people in such a process *("that's* all *these people the elderly people have to give in return"; "all they've got to give is their memories"; "that's all they've got to give to say thank you").* This formulation works simultaneously to construct reminiscence as a token of social exchange *and* offer mitigation for its apparent lack of "exchange value." Thus it is the fact that reminiscence is offered as reciprocation that serves as a potential basis for a moral exhortation to *"listen,"* rather than any intrinsic value it might have. One might say "it's the thought that counts" here.

This version of "reminiscence-as-reciprocation" is then used to account for the supposed propensity of older people to reminisce *("that's why you find old people are always going on about the past (.) because that's all they've got to give to say thank you").* This move is interesting in that this supposed propensity is another aspect of the association between reminiscence and old age, besides "function," that has been a focus of empirical research (e.g., Lieberman & Falk, 1971; Revere & Tobin, 1980; Romaniuk & Romaniuk, 1981). Here we see it being used rhetorically. Jane presents it as a "well-known fact" (as something you simply *"find"* going on in the world) and using her version of reminiscence to account for this "fact" increases the plausibility of that version—it "fits the facts," so to speak.

Following this, and building on the theme of social exchange, Jane presents a second version of reminiscence, which might be glossed as "reminiscence-as-wisdom." In this version, reminiscence is construed as having high exchange value, as encyclopedic knowledge, as *"wisdom for the future."* Moreover, it is construed as being of particular value to the nurses she is "talking to"—*"someone of the younger generation I'm 32 but I feel very honoured that I can learn so much about the past."* This version, then, provides a much stronger basis for a recommendation that student nurses listen to their elderly patients. Reminiscence is now of "value" in its own right, and of particular value for their age group. Thus, through the course of the extract, we see Jane formulating versions of reminiscence that accomplish the business of making (or, in this case, reporting the making of) such a moral exhortation.

It is worth noting here that Jane's exhortation to *"listen to the elderly"* is also to be found in the seminal papers on reminiscence referred to earlier. In the work of Butler (1963), Lewis (1971), and McMahon and Rhudick (1964) various formulations of the function of reminiscence in old age are used to argue that reminiscence should be respected, and not treated as "garrulous" or "insignificant." We have argued elsewhere (Buchanan & Middleton, in press) that a major consequence of the naturalization of reminiscence that occurs in these and other papers is to reposition older people in their relations with others to challenge a discourse that legitimates their marginalization through ascribing no value to what they have to say about their lives, and to privilege a discourse that accords value to what they have to say, and hence accords them a right to speak and to be heard. Thus the naturalization of reminiscence as a "function" or "mechanism" in the process of aging, as well as providing one important basis for the development of an arena of reminiscence practice and research, can also be seen as accomplishing this shift. We have argued further that the now commonplace representation of reminiscence as socially valuable oral history can be seen as a further move in this process of repositioning. Just as authors of texts on reminiscence can be seen as deploying this and other versions of reminiscence to argue for change in the way older people are positioned in relation to others, so we can see Jane using similar versions to argue for a change in social relations between student nurses and their elderly patients.

It is important to note, though, that these versions are formulated as arguments. When required to give some account of the value of reminiscence, Jane does not simply say that reminiscence is reciprocation, or that it is the expression of wisdom. Rather, her account has a dialogical form in the sense we have discussed earlier. She formulates versions of the value of reminiscence in contrast to a version that casts it as valueless. Indeed, the dialogicality is underscored here by the fact that the opposing view is voiced through the speech/thoughts of others. In advancing her own argument, Jane must discredit other opposing positions, which are themselves tenable—that reminiscence may also be experienced as boring or repetitive, and irrelevant to the concerns of the care workers who may be its temporarily captive audience.

Concluding Comments

The preceding analysis shows some of the diversity with which care workers formulate the significance of reminiscence in later life, and how such formulations are used in accounting for practice. We have seen speakers using different versions of "reminiscence-and-aging," not only to argue for or against the use of reminiscence work with the older people in their care, but also to argue for or against more general care practices, as Jane does in Extract 3. We have seen too that these versions do not combine together to produce a coherent, internally consistent account of "reminiscence and aging." Instead, we find contradiction and opposition. The accounts we have examined take the form of a dialogue or argument about the nature of reminiscence and its value in later life. Versions of "reminiscence-and-aging" take shape in relation to other, contrary versions, and the accounts themselves embody movement between these versions: reminiscence as past-oriented or present-oriented, reminiscence as self-oriented or other-oriented, reminiscence as socially valuable or of no value to others. Moreover, our analysis has shown that these contradictions are not only present between different speaker's accounts, but are also an important feature of the internal organization of those accounts.

It is the dialogicality of these accounts that is of most interest to us here. The fact that this dialogicality occurs both within and across speakers shows that this talk cannot be accounted for simply in individual terms, as the expression of speakers' beliefs, or the deployment of different versions to suit their own purposes. Neither is it sufficient to say that speakers are drawing from a static "set" of representations of "reminiscence and aging"—rather, these accounts are constructed through movement between contrary positions. What we have here in this talk, then, is evidence of a phenomenon that is at once dynamic and collective.

The dialogicality present in our data has also been noted in other kinds of talk. Billig et al. (1988) illustrate, with examples from a variety of settings, the ways in which talk is characterized by the presence of opposing themes, and can be seen to be handling dilemmas of an ideological and practical nature. They argue that "common sense" is itself made up of contrary themes—that in attempting to account for experiences or actions in commonly sensible ways, people find themselves having to deal with contradictory "truths," and can be seen to seek a balance or compromise between these contradictions in their talk:

> The presence of contrary themes in discussions is revealed by the use of qualifications. The unqualified expression of one theme seems to call forth a counter-qualification in the name of the opposing theme. There is a tension in the discourse, which can make even monologue take the form of argumentation and argument occur, even when all participants share similar contrary themes. (Billig et al., 1988, p. 144)

This is precisely what we have identified in our own data, and suggest it to be a general property of talk. However, to the extent that the talk we have examined pertains to an identifiable arena of practice, it can be seen as revealing the operation of a "common sense" of reminiscence work. The contrary themes we have identified can be seen as the raw materials from which our interviewees construct commonly sensible accounts of their work, the materials with which they literally *make sense* of their own care practices.

It is important to note, then, this sense-making cannot be a once-and-for-all matter. Rather, on each occasion of accounting for practice, the resulting account will not be determined in advance, but will take shape according to the arguments raised and how they are formulated. Such accounting is situated in social action and is sensitive to the interactional business in hand. On this basis, then, we can argue that the "sense" of reminiscence work is being continually reformulated as practitioners talk about their work. Moreover, the sense making practices we have identified can be seen as socially forged, in that individual speaker's accounts are built up using argumentive resources that bear the mark of previous conversational sense-making and discussion. This then leads us to locate the "understanding" of the nature and value of reminiscence work (for both practitioners and analysts) as discursively accomplished. We have no need to look beyond the discourse to a set of representations that informs the talk we have examined here. Rather, this talk can itself be seen as an embodiment of a dynamic "community of discursive understanding," within which practitioners continually formulate and reformulate the nature of their work.

This is not to say that "anything goes" when practitioners talk about their work. On the contrary, any identifiable arena of practice will by definition favor particular ways of representing and talking about that practice. We would argue further that such "ways of talking" play a crucial role in the constitution and maintenance of the regularities and boundaries of practice. In our data, the formative role of this talk is apparent in what we have termed the "preference status" of different versions, and in the way that certain versions are routinely argued for over others. The versions that are both preferred and argued for are those that accord positive value to the reminiscences of older people, as being relevant to the present, as offered to others, as socially valuable knowledge. They are preferred to, or privileged over, versions that construct reminiscence in negative terms, as living in the past, as repetitive or self-indulgent, as irrelevant to others or to the concerns of the present. We can see in these accounts then the maintenance of an "orthodoxy" of reminiscence work at the conversational level. In the detail of the construction of their talk, speakers show resistance to versions that marginalize reminiscence, and through this resist the consequent marginalization of older people as not worth listening to, as having no right to speak and be heard. We have argued elsewhere that the discursive repositioning of older people in their relations with others can be seen as a central concern of reminiscence practice (Buchanan & Middleton, in press). We would argue that the particular and local instances of resistance and privileging identified in our analysis are one means through which this concern is both continually reformulated and pursued.

In describing the versions of "reminiscence and aging" we have documented as "common sense," we should point out that there is also another, more prosaic way in which they might deserve this description. This concerns the notable absence in our data of any reference to academic theories of reminiscence and its significance in later life. We might say, then, that speakers are talking "common sense" in that they do not appeal to scientific evidence to warrant their accounts. This is so even though some of the versions formulated by our interviewees are recognizable as versions of academic theories—for example, reminiscence as the transmission of socially valuable knowledge to younger generations, and this as the social "role" of older people (McMahon & Rhudick, 1964), or reminiscence as a means of affirming identity (Lewis, 1971). This aspect of our data has interesting parallels with current debates regarding the empirical evaluation of the benefits claimed for reminiscence work. As we suggested at the beginning of this chapter, although practitioners have consistently attested to the benefits of such work, empirical investigation has so far failed to substantiate these claims. This failure has tended to result in the dismissal of practitioner claims, rather than the rethinking of research strategies. This debate gives the impression, then, of scientific and "common sense" accounts of reminiscence and aging passing one another by, an impression reinforced by the absence of explicit mention of scientific accounts in our own data.

Gubrium and Wallace (1990) have discussed some of these issues in relation to theories of aging. They present data showing how care workers, older people, and their relatives invoke diverse "theories" of aging in discussing the appropriateness of a particular care regime. They draw attention to the parallels between this "ordinary theorizing" and the theorizing of age done by social scientists, and argue that the separation and the degree of differential status of these two modes of theorizing are unwarranted. They observe that ordinary theorizing shares many characteristics of its scientific counterpart, whereas scientific theorizing, like ordinary theorizing, bears the mark of lived experience and ideology. They suggest a rapprochement between the two, recommending that "scientific theory takes serious consideration of ordinary theorising" and "science no longer has a corrective function with respect to ordinary theorising, but becomes . . . a professional source of insights for understanding experience" (Gubrium & Wallace, 1990, p. 148).

Our analysis can be seen as one attempt to bring such "ordinary theorizing" into serious consideration, and in doing so, can be seen as extending Gubrium and Wallace's discussion. Not only does the analysis reveal parallels between ordinary and scientific theories of reminiscence and aging, and how the former are used to account for action, it also reveals the rhetorical organization of "ordinary theorizing," and its operation as discursively grounded common sense. To treat these versions merely as "lay versions," to be corrected or formalized, would be to miss their crucial role in understanding and accounting for practice, and in the shaping of practice itself.

In these discussions, then, we have offered an alternative to research approaches that study reminiscence as a "mechanism" or "function" associated with a particular stage of lifespan development, and seek to decide empirically between different versions of the significance of reminiscence in later life. This alternative is concerned with the ways in which such versions, formulated in talk, are used by practitioners of reminiscence work to account for and make sense of their practice. Our analysis suggests that these versions form part of a dynamic "community of discursive understanding," which serves as a resource for practitioners in the ongoing business of making sense of and accounting for their work, and which is integral to the constitution of practice. Such an analysis shifts the research focus from the possible benefits of the generic activity "reminiscence" in "old age" to the role of discourse about reminiscence in the constitution of reminiscence work as an arena of practice, and in challenging the marginalization of older people.

Notes

1. Names have been changed where anonymity was requested.
2. The transcription conventions used in the data extracts are as follows:

Overlapping speech	[
Pause of less than 1 second	(.)
Pause of 1 second or more	(no. of seconds in brackets)
Emphasis	*underlining*

Abrupt cut-off	I mean-
Extension of vowel sound	we:ll
Untranscribed vocalization	(laughs)
Context notes	[Mary's group]

3. This use of the terms *preferred* and *dispreferred* is based particularly on Pomerantz (1984) (although see also general discussion in Atkinson & Heritage, 1984; Levinson, 1983; Sacks, 1987). Pomerantz discusses and illustrates the ways in which the design of a conversational response to an assessment offered by another speaker reflects the response's "preference status"; that is, whether or not it is oriented to by participants as being invited by, or relevant to, the initial assessment. In Pomerantz's analysis, one mark of the "preference status" of an action is the degree to which it is explicitly formulated. For example, where agreement is the preferred next action, disagreement will be weakly or indirectly stated. Although the conversational phenomena presented here differ from Pomerantz's data, in that the "assessment" of reminiscence as an unproblematically "good thing" has not been voiced in the immediately preceding conversation, we would argue that there is sufficient similarity between the phenomena described to make the notion of "preference status" both useful and appropriate.

4. Had Mary started her turn a second later, we would have to take its form as a response to the interviewer's *"too much"* ("all the time" clearly being "too much"). However, she starts her turn just as this is said, and thus her choice of this particular formulation can be said to be independent of the interviewer's overlapped talk. It is interesting, though, that the interviewer should come out with an extreme case formulation at the same time as Mary. *"Too much"* reminiscence is, by definition, an undesirable amount, and thus this formulation has the effect of advancing Mary's own argument against doing reminiscence work. Also, this formulation is immediately preceded by the phrase *"not a good idea"* which is strikingly similar to the indirect formulations used by Mary. This suggests that the interviewer, in borrowing Mary's conversational forms, is sensitive to her agenda, and is himself orienting to the potentially "unorthodox" nature of her argument.

References

Age Exchange. (1988). *Lifetimes: Age Exchange reminiscence resources* [Photo pack]. Age Exchange Reminiscence Centre, 11, Blackheath Village, London, SE93 9LA.

Atkinson, J. M., & Heritage, J. (Eds). (1984). *Structures of social action: Studies in conversation analysis.* Cambridge: Cambridge University Press.

Baines, S., Saxby, P., & Ehlert, K. (1987). Reality orientation and reminiscence therapy. *British Journal of Psychiatry, 151,* 222-231.

Bender, M. P., Cooper, A. E., & Howe, A. (1983). *The utility of reminiscence groups in old people's homes.* Unpublished paper available from the London Borough of Newham.

Billig, M. (1985). Prejudice, categorization and particularisation: From a perceptual to a rhetorical approach. *European Journal of Social Psychology, 15,* 79-103.

Billig, M., Condor, S., Edwards, D., Gane, M., Middleton, D., & Radley, A. (1988). *Ideological dilemmas: A social psychology of everyday thinking.* London: Sage.

Bornat, J. (1989, Autumn). Oral history as a social movement: Reminiscence and older people. *Oral History,* pp. 16-24.

Buchanan, K., & Middleton, D.J. (1990). *Reminiscence: Discourse analysis in socio-historical studies of collective remembering.* Paper presented at the Second International Congress on Activity Theory, Lahti, Finland.

Buchanan, K., & Middleton, D. J. (in press). *Reminiscence reviewed: A discourse analytic perspective.* In J. Bornat (Ed.), *Reminiscence reviewed.* Milton Keynes, UK: Open University Press.

Butler, R. N. (1963). The life review: An interpretation of reminiscence in the aged. *Psychiatry, 26,* 65-76.

Coleman, P. G. (1974). Measuring reminiscence characteristics from conversation as adaptive features of old age. *International Journal of Ageing and Human Development, 5,* 281-294.

Coleman, P. G. (1986). *Ageing and reminiscence processes.* Chichester, UK: John Wiley.

Fallot, R. D. (1980). The impact on mood of verbal reminiscing in later adulthood. *International Journal of Ageing and Human Development, 10*(4), 385-400.

Edwards, D. E., & Potter, J. (1992). *Discursive psychology.* London: Sage.

Featherstone, M., & Hepworth, M. (1989). Ageing and old age: Reflections on the postmodern life course. In B. Bytheway, T. Keil, P. Allat, & A. Bryman (Eds.), *Becoming and being old: Sociological approaches to later life* (pp. 133-157). London: Sage.

Freeman, M. (1984). History, narrative and lifespan developmental knowledge. *Human Development, 27,* 1-19.

Gibson, F. G. (1989). *Using reminiscence.* London: Help the Aged.

Goffman, E. (1981). *Forms of talk.* Oxford: Basil Blackwell.

Gubrium, J. F., & Wallace, J. B. (1990). Who theorises age? *Ageing and Society, 10,* 131-149.

Heritage, J. (1984). *Garfinkel and ethnomethodology.* Cambridge: Polity Press.

Kiernat J. M. (1979). The use of life review activity with confused nursing home residents. *American Journal of Occupational Therapy, 33,* 306-331.

Help the Aged. (1981). *Recall* [Audio-visual package]. London: Help the Aged Education Department.

Hobbs, A. (1983). *A study to determine some effect of the Help the Aged's Recall audiovisual programme.* Unpublished dissertation, The British Psychological Society, Leicester.

Lesser, J., Lazarus, L. W., Frankel, J., & Havasy, S. (1981). Reminiscence group therapy with psychotic geriatric inpatients. *The Gerontologist, 21,* 291-296.

Levinson, S. C. (1983). *Pragmatics.* Cambridge: Cambridge University Press.

Lewis, C. (1971). Reminiscing and self-concept in old age. *Journal of Gerontology, 26,* 240-243.

Lieberman, M. A., & Tobin, S. S. (1983). *The experience of old age: Stress, coping and survival.* New York: Basic Books.

Lieberman, M. A., & Falk, J. M. (1971). The remembered past as a source of data for research on the life cycle. *Human Development, 14,* 132-141.

McMahon, A. W., & Rhudick, P. J. (1964). Reminiscing: Adaptational significance in the aged. *Archives of General Psychiatry, 10,* 292-298.

Middleton, D. J. (in press). Talking work: Argument, common knowledge and improvisation in team work. In Y. Engestrom & D. J. Middleton (Eds.), *Cognition and communication at work.* Cambridge: Cambridge University Press. (Reprinted from *Department of Human Science Research Report,* 1991, Vol. 1, pp. 1-35).

Middleton, D. J., Buchanan, K., & Suurmond, J. (1991, June). *Communities of memory: Issues of "re-membering" and belonging in reminiscence work with the elderly.* Paper presented at "Thriving Into the Nineties," the Annual Conference of the British Psychological Society's Psychologist's Special Interest Group in the Elderly (PSIGE), Grey College, Durham University.

Mortimer, E. (1982). *Working with elderly people.* London: Heinemann Educational.

Norris, A. D. (1986). *Reminiscence with elderly people.* Bicester: Winslow Press.

Norris, A. D. (1989, Autumn). Clinic or client? A psychologist's case for reminiscence. *Oral History,* pp. 26-29.

Norris, A. D., & Abu El Eileh, M. T. (1982). Reminiscence groups. *Nursing Times, 78,* 1368-1369.

Perrotta, P., & Meacham, J. A. (1981). Can a reminiscing intervention alter depression and self esteem? *International Journal of Aging and Human Development, 14*(1), 23-30.

Pomerantz, A. (1984). Agreeing and disagreeing with assessments: Some features of preferred/dispreferred turn shapes. In J. M. Atkinson & J. Heritage (Eds.), *Structures of social action: Studies in conversation analysis* (pp. 57-101). Cambridge: Cambridge University Press.

Pomerantz, A. (1986). Extreme case formulations: A way of legitimizing claims. In G. Button, P. Drew, & J. Heritage (Eds.), *Human studies, 9* [Special Issue on Interaction and Language Use], 219-229.

Potter, J., & Wetherell, M. (1987). *Discourse and social psychology.* London: Sage.

Revere, V., & Tobin, S. S. (1980). Myth and reality: The older person's relationship to his past. *International Journal of Aging and Human Development, 12*(1), 15-26.

Romaniuk, M., & Romaniuk, J. G. (1981). Looking back: An experimental analysis of reminiscence functions and triggers. *Experimental Aging Research, 7*(4), 477-489.

Ryden, M. B. (1981). Nursing intervention in support of reminiscence. *Journal of Gerontological Nursing, 7,* 461-463.

Sacks, H. (1987). On the preferences for agreement and contiguity in sequences in conversation. In G. Button & J. R. E. Lee (Eds.), *Talk and social organization* (pp. 54-69). Philadelphia: Multilingual Matters.

Widdecombe, S., & Wooffitt, R. C. (1989, September). *"Well what do you expect looking like that": A study of the construction of a complaint.* Paper presented at the British Psychology Society Social Psychology Section Annual Conference, Bristol.

Winslow Press. (1989). [Products catalog]. Winslow Press, Telford Road, Bicester, Oxon OX6 OTS, UK.

Wooffitt, R. C. (1992). *Telling tales of the unexpected: The organisation of factual discourse.* Hemel Hempstead, UK: Harvester Press.

CHAPTER FOUR

Positioning and Autobiography: Telling Your Life

LUK VAN LANGENHOVE
ROM HARRÉ

Within psychology, two major developments are taking place. One is the growing concern with temporality that is partly expressed in an increasing emphasis on the study of the human life course. This can take the form of an investigation of the pattern of life typical of a certain social group. But increasingly the idea of idiographic studies of the life course of individuals has become popular. Life stories can be told about individual people by others (biography) or by themselves (autobiography). The other major development is a growing awareness that a great many psychological phenomena are not only described in such discourses as accounts and autobiographies, but actually exist as features of those discourses. The most important examples for this chapter are the phenomenon of remembering (Middleton & Edwards, 1989) and the self (Muhlhauser & Harré, 1991).

In this chapter, and in line with this book's priorities, we will explore how biographical studies and discourse analysis can be related to each other. The central insight we will explore is the idea that personal identity and selfhood are manifested in discursive practices, among which are the writing and telling of lives. It seems that people have two kinds of identity. There is the kind of identity traditionally studied by psychologists—social and cultural identity—what it is to be and to be seen to be a certain kind

81

of person. Only philosophers have been concerned with the other kind of identity—personal identity—or what it is to be one and the same individual through a life course (Williams, 1973). Generally people take their individuality for granted, little aware that this deepest aspect of selfhood may be a phenomenon generated in discourse. On the other hand, people are usually quite aware of their social identity as produced by what they say and do—but rarely do they realize the multiplicity of social identities they deploy in their successful management of everyday life (Goffman, 1957). Somehow psychological theory of the self must encompass both stability and uniqueness and variability and multiplicity.

The growth of a sense of personal identity is related in complex ways to the development of a person across his or her lifespan. It is within the beginnings of the lifespan that a human being acquires their personhood (cf. Shotter, 1973, this volume) and it is within his or her life that that personhood is expressed in various ways, characteristic of the local culture. Within the lifespan, while personal identity must at some level be stable, social identity generally changes. One of the most central problems in the psychology of personhood is how continuous personal identity relates to discontinuous social diversity. If one tries to discuss this problem using only the generalized concept of "self," confusion is almost certain to arise—as for instance one finds in the writings of some feminist authors. There seems to be a tension between the multiplicity of selves as expressed in discursive practices and the fact that across those discursive practices a relatively stable selfhood exists as well. In nonpathological cases we want to say it is always the same person who has an identity, but in another sense is always mutable.

We want to argue that the singularity of selfhood, that which philosophers call "personal identity," is equally a product of discursive practices as the multiplicity of selfhood, that which some have called "social identity." Moreover, in order to make it possible for a person to understand him- or herself as a historically continuous unity, he or she will have to engage in very different—possibly contradictory—forms of biographical talk. One and the same person is now this and now that. One can be both keeper of the Queen's pictures and a KGB agent? How is that psychologically possible? Our analysis will show that because both personal and social identities are attributes of discourse there is no onto-logical paradox in the evident existence of contradictions and multiplicities in the discourse. Because there is nothing to which the discourse of selfhood refers except itself, the paradoxical air of internal contradiction vanishes. However, were one's self like one's hat, a real entity existing independently of discourses, a contradictory story told about it could be a cause for concern.

In this chapter, we will try to develop the thesis of discontinuity by drawing upon two recent developments in sociolinguistics. First, we will introduce the concept of positioning and show how, in the ways people position themselves in talk and writing, per-sonal identity can be expressed through the presentation of a biography. Next, we will use some of the differences between "orality" and "literality" to differentiate biographical talk from a literary (auto)biography. Third, we will briefly show how much of the present ambiguity of the concept of self and the related concepts of personhood, biography, and identity emerges out of the mistaken idea that the literary biography can be a source-model for understanding biographical talk. Finally we will dis-cuss the implications of the foregoing for lifespan research.

Positioning Theory

In positioning theory (cf. Davies & Harré, 1990; Harré & Van Langenhove, 1991; Hollway, 1984), the concept of positioning is introduced as a metaphor to enable an investigator to grasp how persons are "located" within conversations as observably and subjectively coherent participants in jointly produced storylines. The act of positioning refers to the assignment of "parts" or "roles" to speakers in the discursive construction of personal stories that make a person's actions intelligible and relatively determinate as social acts. For example, in a conversation between a teacher and a pupil, rights to make certain kinds of remarks will be differentially distributed between the conversants. This is what is meant by identifying "teacher" (P1) and "pupil" (P2) as *positions.* The same utterance will have different social meaning when uttered by the person in position P1 from that which it has when

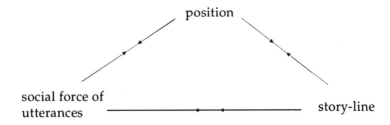

Figure 4.1. The Mutually Determining Triad

uttered by the person in position P2. The utterances that go to make up a conversation unfold along a storyline, say in the form of a tutorial. Thus we have a mutually determining triad, as shown in Figure 4.1.

Several analytical distinctions can be used to identify different forms of positioning. Positions may emerge "naturally" out of the conversational and social context. But sometimes an initial seizure of the dominant role in a conversation will force the other speaker into speaking positions they would not have occupied voluntarily, so to say. Initial positionings can be challenged and the speakers sometimes thereby repositioned. One can position oneself as a commentator upon the positions, social acts, and storylines generated in one conversation by creating a higher order conversation in which the conversation commented upon is merely a topic. One mode of positioning of particular interest to us is the intentional self-positioning in which a person expresses his or her personal identity.

The discursive practices of positioning make possible three ways of expressing and experiencing one's personal identity or unique selfhood (cf. Harré, 1983): by stressing one's agency in claiming responsibility for some action; by indexing one's statements with the point of view one has on its relevant world; or by presenting a description/evaluation of some past event or episode as a contribution to one's biography. How personal identity can be expressed through indexing one's view of the world and one's responsibilities for action by using pronouns is discussed in Muhlhauser and Harré (1991). For example, in so seemingly simple a statement as "I can feel a draft," the content of the utterance (the experience suffered by the speaker) is indexed with his or her spatial and temporal location, and, most importantly, as a claim about a state of affairs it is indexed with its speaker's moral standing. That is, the speaker, by using the pronoun rather than an impersonal form, takes responsibility for the reliability of the claim. The relations between the discursive practices of positioning and the telling of an autobiography can be expressed as follows. First of all, an important distinction has to be made between statements that are part of an autobiography; that is, describe a life event from the point of view of the actor, and statements that are themselves life events. In general, the uttering of a statement descriptive of a life event is also a life event, though statements whose utterings are life events are not by any means all themselves descriptive of life events. Consider the following exchange:

> **A:** I thought you had gone to London.
> **B:** No, I decided to spend the afternoon in the library.

A's remark reports an event in his or her autobiography, and at the same time deletes an item from A's biography of B. B confirms the deletion. But in preparing the relevant item in his or her autobiography, namely a decision, B at the same time provides A with a substitute item for his or her biography of B. By implication, nothing being said to the contrary, B's remark also adds a further item to his or her autobiography, namely an afternoon in the library. The discursive act of positioning thus involves a reconstructive element: The biographies of the one being positioned and the "positions" may be subject to rhetorical redescriptions. The question is how this "rewriting" has to be understood with regard to the personal identity and selfhood. This requires us to pay attention to what exactly "autobiographical" talk is and how such talk relates to the written genre of autobiographies.

Orality and Literacy

A sense of self is always embedded in a particular culture. It can therefore be expected that historical and cultural differences will affect the prevailing sense of self (cf. Logan, 1987). An important aspect of any particular culture is the extent to which it is a literacy or orality dominated culture. In most cultures today language is used in two ways: it is spoken and it is written. This distinction seems so obvious that it is often forgotten that writing is actually a rather recent invention. It developed around the year 3,500 B.C. Before that, all human cultures were exclusively oral cultures. The transition toward literate cultures has been a long and slow process, the technology of writing being not always applauded by everybody. Even Plato in the *Phaedrus* has Socrates say that writing is inhuman, as it pretends to establish outside the mind what in reality can only be in the mind. Moreover, Plato's Socrates urges that writing destroys memory and that the written word cannot defend itself as the natural spoken word can.

All ways of using language, including writing, have structuring effects on thought because they impose structure on expression. One would expect the psychodynamics of orality to be quite different from that of the written word. In recent years, certain basic differences have been discovered between the ways of managing knowledge and its verbalization in primary oral cultures from those in cultures deeply affected by the use of writing (cf. Ong, 1982). We think that this research is of major importance in understanding how, in our literate cultures, personal identity is expressed by biographical stories. Undoubtedly such oral stories are likely to be highly influenced by literary genres, but they are still oral stories with all the properties belonging to them. Biographical talk has to be understood as stories that resemble the Greek oral narrative, the epic, more than they resemble the literary genre of autobiography in the tradition of Augustine and Rousseau. Unfortunately, within the social sciences (including lifespan development, psychobiography) it is the latter that is usually taken as a model in understanding biographical talk. In our view this choice of exemplar is a mistake. In order to show that the written autobiography is not an appropriate source model for understanding how people express their personal identity in biographical talk, we will draw attention to some major differences between orality and literacy and their relation to (auto)biographical stories (cf. Ong, 1982). Four topics will be dealt with: (a) thought and expression in oral cultures; (b) the nature of oral autobiographical stories; and (c) the effect of writing on thought and expression.

Thought and Expression in Oral Cultures

In a culture with no knowledge whatsoever of writing, words have no visual presence. Nothing can ever be "looked up": Words are only sounds that may or may not be recalled. This means that in oral cultures material that has to be recalled needs to be organized in a way that facilitates recall. It has to be so organized that with help of mnemonics and phonetic formulas it can be remembered. For example, the phonetic forms of Anglo-Saxon personal names facilitated remembering family relationships. The most common way to store, organize, and communicate what is known in oral cultures is through stories of human actions. Such oral stories have an important property that distinguishes them from written stories: They are changeable. Actually they need to be changeable in order to function the way they do. Not only are they subject to change because the storyteller cannot make reference back to a written standard, they are also changeable because they are told (or sung) in particular contexts. Stories are the result of an interaction between the narrator, the audience, and the narrator's memory. A storyteller has to speak in accordance with the demands of his or her audience. Mbiti (1966) observed about storytelling in Kenya that "the plot of the story and the sequence of its main part remain the same, but the narrator has to supply meat to the skeleton" (p. 26).

When words are restricted to sounds this not only determines modes of expression but also thought processes. In an oral culture it is essential to think memorable thoughts, otherwise such thoughts can never be effectively recovered. Ong (1982) has listed several characteristics of orally based thought and expression that make for memorability. Among others he noted the additive rather than subordinative style, the aggregative rather than the analytic style, and the redundant or "copious" form of the stories told. All these features of oral narration should be discernible in the told autobiography.

The Nature of Oral Autobiographical Stories

Autobiographical telling is a form of narration. The grammar of autobiographical discourse should, therefore, be similar to that of other forms of narration. A general scheme of pronoun grammar for expressing the narrative voice has been proposed by Urban (1989). It depends upon the common distinction between *anaphora* and *indexicality*. "He" is an anaphor in that it forms a link in a series of expressions co-referential with an original name or definite description, and is rarely used indexically. By contrast "I" is a pure indexical in that its reference is fixed contextually to the speaker of the moment, indexing his or her utterances with the speaker's spatio-temporal location and moral standing. "I" is not functionally equivalent to a proper name. There are two modes of pronominal self-reference in autobiographical telling with subtly different force. Compare "He said that I should repair the fence" with "He said 'You repair the fence.' "

Urban has suggested two principles governing the grammar of the narrative voice. In such sentence frames as "Sharon said 'I shall try to do better next time,' " "I" is co-referential with "Sharon" and so an anaphor. Its indexical force is suspended. But in "Sharon said to me 'You cannot work here any more,' " (a1) "You" is coindexical with "me," the (dative) object of the main clause, and refers back to an introductory but understood "I report that . . . ." Both index the content of the whole statement with the relevant attributes of the speaker. An explicit indexical framing is not uncommon in autobiographical telling: "I want you to know that Sharon said to me 'You cannot work here anymore' " (a2). Or in *oratio obliqua* "I tell you that Sharon said that I could not work there any more" (b). Is there any difference in force between the (a) forms and the (b) form?

Let us call the embedded indexical in both cases a pseudoanaphor, in that the embedded pronoun is co-referential with an indexical expression rather than with a proper name, and so distinct from the simple anaphoric first person in which I report what Sharon said about herself. Urban (1989) points out several important features of these usages in autobiographical narrations. In the (a) forms, the speaker invites the hearer to hear the utterance as if he or she were "momentarily taking on the role of the third person referent" in a kind of play-acting (Urban, 1989, p. 35). It is a kind of metaphor in which only the first person (the [a] uses) provides the "metaphorical pivot" (Urban, 1989, p. 35). But in the disquotative or (b) form the speaker indexes him- or herself as "the concrete representation of a character in discourse" (Urban, 1989, p. 37). We might put the difference thus: In the use of the (a) form I play myself but in the (b) form I am myself. According to Urban (1989, p. 49) "the fundamental distinction is between an 'I' pointing to an everyday self (the [b] form) and an 'I' pointing to an imaginary or assumed self." In the latter case, the individual speakers to whom the "I" points are in fact anaphoric substitutes for characters in a narrative text.

We could express the distinction in forms of autobiographical telling as a difference between merely reporting what went on in a life, the (b) form, and narrating the story of a life, the (a) form. In the former the local conventions of storytelling, plot structure, and so on, are irrelevant. In the latter they may have a dominant role in the organization of and emphases placed on the material. We can now return to the theme of positioning. It is clear that these seemingly unimportant grammatical variations conceal functionally quite distinct positions. Positioning oneself as the subject of mere reporting is quite a different matter from positioning oneself as a character in a lively drama. In the distinction between the (b) form and the (a) form of autobiographical telling we have identified one of the major devices through which speakers adopt positions in telling their lives.

In sketching the logical grammar of first person pronouns we emphasized the double indexicality of their use. They index content with its spatio-temporal location of the embodied speakers and the social force of an utterance with the moral standing of the speakers. Autobiographical acts of telling of the (b) form do not invoke spatio-temporal indexicality. Only in the (a) form does autobiographical telling articulate the speaker's moral commitment to the acts of narration and to the acts narrated. The (a) form is a personal story in a way that the (b) form of autobiography can never be.

Restructuring of Thought and Expression Through Writing

In a literate world, words are not only events (when spoken), they also are things (signs written or inscribed on flat surfaces). The transition from orality to literacy has been a slow process but in today's Western cultures literality dominates orality. Nevertheless, even in our cultures we can find some practices that are in the mold of the old oral tradition. One of them is the oral defense of a doctoral dissertation. Another is the jury system in which jurors have to "hear" a case, without taking any notes (Van Langenhove, 1989). But script, and especially its print form, have had an enormous impact on thought and expression. Postman (1985) speaks in this respect of the "typographic mind." First of all, we no longer have to rely solely on our own or others' memory. When literate people say they know something about, for example, psychology or the battle of Borodino, then this knowledge will refer to something that is eventually available to them in writing. What people experience and needs to be recalled is often transformed into written texts.

Second, the possibility of producing texts has altered the form of knowledgeable things. In writing, "backwards scanning" makes it possible to eliminate inconsistencies. There is no equivalent for this in an oral performance: A spoken word can never be erased, yet oral expressions can be retrospectively revised and redefined very easily. Knowing that texts have been scanned backwards gives them a sense of closure: a sense that what is found in any text has been finalized. Written or printed texts are supposed to represent the words of an author in a definite or "final" form. As recorded, the verbal past takes on an immutable and concrete form. Yet any written record can be challenged, not only with respect to its correctness as a transcription but also with respect to the readings to which it is subject in this or that context.

When a story is written, the reader can only try to grasp the meaning of the texts by interpreting them. He cannot, as in an oral story, intervene to change the text. In telling a story one is never really a soliloquist protected from interruptions. In writing a story one necessarily is. The writer's audience is almost always imagined, tacit. Only rarely is it present at the time of writing. In short, although oral tellings and written records are both subject to negotiation with respect to their authenticity, challenges are directed to radically different kinds of entities.

The Concept of Self in Biographical Perspective

Within social psychology the self has been often regarded as an "information processing structure" (cf. Markus & Wurf, 1987) that uses memories of past events in order to establish a sense of personal identity. This theory, proposed first in the 17th century by Locke, has been very much criticized by philosophers on grounds of internal incoherence. Two different approaches exist within a framework of mainly "social cognition" research. In one, people are seen as skillful at denying personal changes and maintaining biographical consistency. In the other, people are seen as constantly "reinventing" their past in order to fit with current circumstances. In both cases one's personal history is conceived as something "within" the person that has to be "recalled" and that is subject to "cognitive biases." Of course, all this presupposes the continuity of personal identity as a numerical singularity.

Ross and Conway (1986) list three major problems in how people remember their own past: There is selective recall, there is reinterpretation and reexplanation of the past, and finally there is the filling of gaps in the memory by inferring what probably happened. In such a view, the self (once again hypostatized as some inner entity or core of being!) is regarded as a "personal historian." The use of this metaphor leads researchers to extrapolations from "biases and errors of trained historians when they reconstruct and interpret the events of previous eras" (Ross & Conway, 1986, p. 122) to "the average person's remembering of his or her personal history" (p. 122). Greenwald (1980) even pictured the self as a "totalitarian" historian who—as occurs with recorded history in Orwell's novel *1984*—constantly "refabricates" the story of his or her personal past. Greenwald distinguished a further three types of "cognitive biases" that make people revise their history, "thereby engaging in practices not ordinarily admired by historians" (Greenwald, 1980, p. 604): egocentricity (the self is perceived as more central to events than it is), benefitance (the self is perceived as selectively responsible for desired but not for undesired outcomes), and conservatism (the self is resistant to change).

Behind such views is a double conception of the self. On the one hand it is conceived as a "thing" within people that can be "disclosed," "distorted," "perceived," "fabricated," "be subject to inconsistencies," and so on. On the other hand it is the conscious being who perceives and experiences this "thing." Moreover, what people present as their selves or think about as their self is always seen as subject to comparison with the "real" self, which is to a great extent to be equated with the "real" biography or personal history of the person. Within such research, the self is reified as something autonomous within the person that uses personal memories to fabricate itself. But that view conflates the self as perceiver with the self as perceived. It would not be unreasonable to suggest that part of the problem with this approach is the mistaken idea that there exists one real, inner self to which all these things have happened. But there is another possibility, relating to the idea that there exists just one definite and "real" autobiography that can be distorted. It could be that the literate conception of autobiography as a history is, in the first place, wrongly taken as a model for the story of the self.

In recent years, mainstream approaches in psychology have been much criticized. One of the new emerging specialties is "narratology" (cf. Sarbin, 1986) in which the structures and uses of the stories that people tell are the focus of research, rather than people's behavior conceived as the lawful effects of causes. As an intentional action, often deployed in the working out of some project, storytelling, though a sequence of human actions, is not a "behavior" in the sense that this term has taken on in psychology. Within narratology, the self has been studied in a different way from that pictured above. In Gergen and Gergen (1988, this volume) the idea of "narratives of the self" is introduced. By this is meant stories that "serve as a critical means by which we make ourselves intelligible within the social world." Such narratives of the self are seen by Gergen and Gergen not as "fundamentally possessions of the individual, rather they are products of social interchange." In introducing the earlier Gergen and Gergen chapter, Berkowitz (1988) explicitly equated their conception of narratives of the self with the idea that the self is a narrative. This delphic idea seems implicit in Gergen and Gergen (1988) because they assert that the self comes into being in a life story. But if the self is to be taken as a narrative, then the question arises what kind of a narrative it is, a literary or an oral one? And of course, also, who is telling it?

For Gergen and Gergen the answer is, clearly, a literary narrative. This, of course, has its place in the understanding of discursive presentations of life courses—but, we believe, it cannot succeed as a comprehensive theory. This follows from their ideas about the form of self-narratives. Referring to literary criticism, semiotics, and historiography, they have synthesized what they consider to be the components "important to the construction of intelligible narrative in contemporary western cultures" (1988, p. 20). These components are (a) the establishment of a valued end point, (b) the selection of events relevant to the goal state, (c) the temporal ordering of events, (d) the establishment of causal linkages, and (e) the framing of the story by demarcation signs. Consequently, the illustrations of self-narratives they mention are all well-defined episodes such as stories about one's first love affair, the morning's class, or lunch with a companion.

In introducing the idea of written stories, their conception of the self is still a reified one. This follows from their discussion of the "validity" of the self-narrative. Although they rightly assert that such validity is determined by cultural conventions they also state that validity is not matched by the "absolute match between word and thing." But in that way they still emphasize that there is a "real thing" with which socially constructed stories can be matched.

The confusion of thought in this idea of the self as narrative not only derives from privileging the literary model for their conception of an autobiography but confuses "self" as the kind of person I think I am disclosed in the events of my life, and "self" as the unitary person to whom those events occur. Somehow they assume an ego while denying it. The discursive construction of storylines is just one element in the discursive triad; the positioned speaker and the social force of his or her narration are also necessary elements for any narrative to be relatively determinate.

Although it is certainly true that people can and will tell stories about themselves that are modeled upon literary biographical stories, or upon other forms of literature, these are not the only situations in which biographical talk is used. In fact, though seldom telling complete biographical stories, people are constantly engaged in all kinds of self-positioning in which self-narratives occur that are not modeled by any literary plots (Davies & Harré, 1990). Therefore, the self should not be equated with a story having a plot. Rather selves emerge from complex bodies of knowledge that are organized like oral stories, and particularly as stories in the (a) form in which the indexical commitments of the speakers differ throughout the discourse. The self has no plot, only persons (that is selves as expressed in social life) can have plots. The relationship between a self and a person can be understood in terms of positioning and rhetorical redescription. The self refers to the form of inner unity that all discourses of personal experiences must exemplify. While engaged in conversations, people position themselves and others. That tacit self-positioning "reflects the self," that is, creates the necessary order through the grammatical properties of the unfolding language games (Muhlhauser & Harré, 1991).

Constraints for Lifespan Research

Orality and literacy, far from being mutually contradictory poles, can interact and support each other. In our culture both oral and written communication forms exist, and though it is certain that the written word has to a great extent shaped the spoken word, there still seem to be "autonomous" oral worlds. From what has been said above, it should by now be clear that we consider the self to be a feature of a basically oral culture. When people refer to their own or others' histories, they have to rely on recollection. Only seldom is written material available. Consequently, the narrative self has to be treated as a collection of stories suspended from the identity of a person. But, as we have argued, that identity is *also* discursively produced. Whatever is needed to be recalled from a person's life will be organized in stories. But given the usual oral context of such stories, they resemble more the epic than the autobiography, as we have argued above. As indexed with the unifying features of a person's discourse they present a self as not only embodied but responsible. They present character.

Harré (1983) has argued that the self should be regarded as a theoretical entity: the sense of personal identity—how someone experiences his or her unique selfhood—is really the use that person makes of his or her "self" theory. Every person "has a well-ordered if incomplete understanding of the social and individual constituents of the sense of identity" (Harré, 1983, p. 42), that is, is in command of a theory the central concept of which is "the self." According to this point of view, however, that theoretical concept organizes knowledge and action, but has no independent referent other than the person him- or herself. The distinction we have introduced between orality and literacy can be used to refine this notion of the self as a theoretical entity. From the point of view of the philosophy of science, a theory can be regarded as a set of propositions. Theories are represented in texts (scientific publications) and have as such a finalized form. But theories are also used by people or to some extent known by people. In that sense, theories also have a "social representation" (cf. Moscovici, 1983). If we think of the self as the leading concept of a theory a person has about him- or herself, it is in this latter sense: A person has several and changing representations of him- herself, centered on the theoretical concept of a personal unity. The Moscovician idea of a "representation" of knowledge across persons can be used as a metaphor for understanding how a single person has different social or presented selves across all positioning—situations in which she or he occurs as the one and only person. Writing an autobiography, answering questionnaires like the "who-am-I?" can be regarded as the construction of finalized written theories. But, just as it is impossible to write a definite and complete theory on any scientific subject, it is equally impossible to write a similar theory about oneself.

If we take the distribution of knowledge in an oral culture (e.g., child-rearing knowledge among working-class families) as a model for how self is organized, this has important implications for research. We think that the study of lifespan development can no longer be equated with the study of (auto-) biographies. Rather it should be the study of how and for what reason people use autobiographical stories at different ages. In the study of a socially distributed knowledge system a key question is who has a right to use which items of knowledge under what circumstances. Up to now little research has been done on the longitudinal study of biographical presentations of single persons. Moreover, the bulk of lifespan research and "psychobiographical" studies have focused on either describing the major "stages" in the life of persons (see, e.g., Levinson, 1978) or on developing content-analytical tools for analyzing the content of autobiographies (cf. Bromley, 1977; De Waele & Harré, 1979). However valuable these approaches, we think they have to be completed by a study of how people develop rhetorical redescriptions of their own life. The crucial question is which actions of a person are judged by that person to be relevant as part of an autobiographical study? And this takes us back to the points made in the earlier sections of this chapter concerning the discursive triad—position: social force: storyline.

A useful starting point for such a study can be found in the work of Vallacher and Wegner (1985, 1989) on action identification. According to that theory, people have a tendency to reify actions. Actions are assumed to be real (i.e., the act "throwing a brick through a window") even though they are actually mental constructions. Any action can be identified in different ways: "throwing a brick" can equally be identified as "creating a nuisance" or as "breaking glass." Such identifications are not synonyms, they are different psychological and social identifications of what is only in its material form the same. People "act" a whole day, a whole life course long. Most of those actions are never consciously identified although others are, for instance when a person is asked to account for his or her conduct. Whenever the identification of one's own actions is called for, this includes the use of the word *I*. To the question "What are you doing?", a person can answer "I am . . . ." Other questions can be asked. For instance the question "Who are you?" In such cases people will make use of their own action references as well.

All this boils down to the notion that in the many different stories that people tell about themselves, reference to a limited number of past (and possibly future) actions is made in telling their own life. This has nothing to do with "memory": The question is not what people "forget" about their own life, but why they make use in a given situation of this and that action as part of their personal stories. Generally speaking, this will be determined by two things. First, by the stories that they already have told. Once a story is told and retold, it begins to live a life of its own, just as with the stories told in an oral culture. The "self" can be seen as a partly changing audience created by the stories and to which the stories about the self are told. Second, it should be clear that conversations with other people will give rise to new stories because different people will ask different questions. In line with positioning theory, those questions can be regarded as forcing the addressee in certain positions.

Lifespan research can thus simply not take for granted the so widely spread idea in our Western culture that we all live one "biography." Neither can it proceed by studying "individual lives." The problem, then, is that a conversational approach to the study of selves and biographies has to be developed. At present, the work of Hermans (1987, 1989) seems to be closest to such an approach. However, it should be clear that developing a suitable methodology is not enough. Along with that, the people who are "studied" should become aware of their tendency to reify their own lives to a single biography. The above advocated idea of the self as a theory with properties of oral stories thus involves more than a scientific stance: At the end of the day the question is when and why will people think of themselves in such a way? It might well be that for those who are living in a postmodern era, such a view of oneself is more practical than the idea that one is a "round" character.

References

Berkowitz, L. (1988). Introduction. In L. Berkowitz (Ed.), *Advances in experimental social psychology* (pp. 1-14). New York: Academic Press.

Bromley, D. (1977). *Personality description in ordinary language.* London: John Wiley.

Davies, B., & Harré, R. (1990). Positioning: The discursive production of selves. *Journal for the Theory of Social Behaviour, 20*(1), 43-63.

De Waele, J. P., & Harré, R. (1979). Autobiography as a psychological method. In G. P. Ginsburg (Ed.), *Emerging strategies in social psychological research* (pp. 177-224). Chichester: John Wiley.

Gergen, K., & Gergen, M. (1988). Narrative and self as relationship. In L. Berkowitz (Ed.), *Advances in experimental social psychology* (pp. 17-56). New York: Academic Press.

Goffman, E. (1957). *The presentation of self in everyday life.* Garden City, NY: Doubleday.

Greenwald, A. G. (1980). The totalitarian ego: Fabrication and revision of personal history. *American Psychologist, 35,* 603-618.

Harré, R. (1983). Identity projects. In G. Breakwell (Ed.), *Threatened identities* (pp. 31-51). London: John Wiley.

Harré, R., & Van Langenhove, L. (1991). Varieties of positioning. *Journal for the Theory of Social Behaviour, 21,* 393-407.

Hermans, H. J. M. (1987). Self as organized system of valuations: Toward a dialogue with the person. *Journal of Counseling Psychology, 34,* 10-19.

Hermans, H. J. M. (1989). The meaning of life as an organized process. *Psychotherapy, 26,* 11-22.

Hollway, W. (1984). Gender difference and the production of subjectivity. In J. Henriques, W. Hollway, C. Urwin, L. Venn, & V. Walkerdine (Eds.), *Changing the subject: Psychology, social regulation and subjectivity* (pp. 227-263). London: Methuen.

Levinson, D. J. (1978). *The seasons of a man's life.* New York: Knopf.

Logan, R. D. (1987). Historical change in prevailing sense of self. In K. Yardley & T. Honess (Eds.), *Self and identity: Psychosocial perspectives.* Chichester: John Wiley.

Markus, H., & Wurf, E. (1987). The dynamic self-concept: A social psychological perspective. *Annual Review of Psychology, 38,* 299-337.

Mbiti, J. S. (1966). *Akamba stories.* Oxford: Clarendon Press.

Middleton, D., & Edwards, D. (1989). *Collective remembering.* London and Los Angeles: Sage.

Moscovici, S. (1983). The phenomenon of social representations. In R. M. Farr & S. Moscovici (Eds.), *Social representations* (pp. 3-69). Cambridge: Cambridge University Press.

Muhlhauser, P., & Harré, R. (1991). *Pronouns and people.* Oxford: Basil Blackwell.

Ong, W. J. (1982). Orality and literacy. *The technologizing of the word.* London: Routledge & Kegan Paul.

Postman, N. (1985). *Amusing ourselves to death: Public discourse in the age of show business.* Harmondsworth, UK: Penguin.

Ross, M., & Conway, M. (1986). Remembering one's own past: The construction of personal histories. In R. M. Sorrentino & E. T. Higgins (Eds.), *Handbook of motivation and cognition* (pp. 122-144). Chichester: John Wiley.

Sarbin, T. R. (1986). *Narrative psychology: The storied nature of human conduct.* New York: Praeger.

Shotter, J. (1973). Acquired powers: The transformation of natural into personal powers. *Journal for the Theory of Social Behaviour, 3*(2), 141-156.

Urban, G. (1989). The "I" of discourse. In B. Lee & G. Urban (Eds.), *Semiotics: Self and society* (pp. 27-52). New York: Mouton de Gruyter.

Vallacher, R. R., & Wegner, D. M. (1985). *A theory of action identification.* Hillsdale, NJ: Lawrence Erlbaum.

Vallacher, R. R., & Wegner, D. M. (1989). Levels of personal agency: Individual variation in action identification. *Journal of Personality and Social Psychology, 57*(4), 660-671.

Van Langenhove, L. (1989). *Juryrechtseraak en Psychologie* [Juror Sentencing and Psychology]. Antwerpen: Kluwer-Gouda-Quint.

Williams, B. A. O. (1973). *Problems of the self.* Cambridge: Cambridge University Press.

SECTION II

Achieving Control, Transition, and Continuity

The first two chapters in this section share an empirical interest in the social control and acculturation of children. But they approach these issues in very different ways: Aronsson and Evaldsson through discourse analyses of social control being enacted during "sharing time" conversations at two child day-care centers; Prusank by examining parents' accounts of discipline interactions.

Aronsson and Evaldsson take a contrastive perspective, examining data from two different child-care settings in Sweden. They develop careful sociolinguistic accounts of how apparently similar sharing time events enact very different norms and socializing experiences. One, for example, orients primarily to instruction giving and information control, but the other promotes co-narration and cooperation. These different interaction orders entail different models of what it is to be "a child" in the two settings.

Prusank argues that existing, influential approaches to social control have failed to capture the phenomenological experience of these events, from either parents' (controlling) or children's (being controlled) perspectives. Rather than seeing the gap between reports of discipline interactions and actual instances of control as a methodological limitation, Prusank argues that the act of accounting for past instances of control gives valuable access to the motives and rationales for these practices—and this is partly where our understanding of social control needs to be located.

A variety of strategies is documented, for example parents appealing to children's advance knowledge of their misdemeanors as being misdemeanors, which warrants the orientation to discipline as rational, perhaps even obligatory. A model of perceived cultural assumptions about "competent parenting" emerges. As Prusank points out, *developmental* norms for social control can also be accessed through such accounts, and she offers useful comments on how future studies might pursue the issues and priorities she has raised in the chapter.

Staton's chapter develops these concerns in presenting an overview of transitions throughout the (U.S.) student career. The study adopts a "rites of passage" perspective and reviews how students construe their places and goals in the educational enterprise developmentally. Staton finds that students, in their own formulations, orient to elementary schooling as "compliant children," to middle school and high school as "developing and maturing adolescents," and to university as "young adults." These self-construals are also very largely endorsed by teachers and administrators themselves. Although these findings are not surprising, they do make it clear that U.S. students (at least in their overt, public responses) do model themselves in terms actively promoted by the educational institutions themselves. Students seem to construe themselves as following a very predictable maturational path through the school system, progressively building individualism and responsibility.

Finally in this section, McKay assembles instances of grandparents' reflections on their own past lives and their grandchildren's present and future. Their concern for continuity is a dominant theme—the transmission of cultural values, moral lessons, or family knowledge from themselves to their grandchildren. Referring back to Buchanan and Middleton's observations about the presumed functionality of reminiscence, McKay's data do show that grandparents do *in their own discourse* quite explicitly *espouse* the value of linking past to present and future. Indeed, they appear to view it as a moral responsibility upon themselves to promote this continuity of experience. At another level, of course, it may be that this view imposes great constraints upon elderly people, who have many other social roles open to them beyond being mentors for the young.

CHAPTER FIVE

Pedagogic Discourse and Interaction Orders: Sharing Time and Control

KARIN ARONSSON

ANN-CARITA EVALDSSON

In Sweden and many modern societies, official ideology puts great emphasis on children's active participation and democratic rights in everyday institutional settings (schools, day-care centers, etc.). In Sweden, this ideology was implemented in the official child-care policy documents of the 1970s in terms of what was called "dialogue pedagogy," that is, a pedagogic ideology that aspired to focus on learning through reciprocal exchanges, dialoguing in contrast to adult-child instruction (Bernstein, 1990; Kallos, 1978). Such symmetry may be difficult to achieve in real-life settings however, as adult-child encounters are inherently asymmetrical. Children often lack the necessary background knowledge for handling events in fully qualified ways, at least as seen by the institutional standards of schools, pediatric units, and so on. Moreover, children are dependent in the very real sense of being minors, subjugated to the decisions of their parents, teachers, and other seniors. Because of its inherent asymmetry, the adult-child dialogue generally entails conversational dilemmas that concern adult support

AUTHORS' NOTE: We would like to thank Basil Bernstein and Nikolas Coupland for constructive comments on a first draft of this chapter.

103

and direct or indirect control. It is our belief that these dilemmas may be handled in different ways, related to implicit and occasionally explicit child-care ideologies.

In this chapter, we will investigate to what extent interaction orders at sharing time events may reveal anything about more general ways of dealing with intergenerational boundaries. To what extent do different child-care settings form different types of worlds with different implicit rules that regulate the micro mechanisms of everyday interaction? The underlying premise is that discourse practices do not merely reflect pedagogic ideologies and generation bound relationships. Talk also creates and recreates social identities linked to different interaction orders (Coupland, Coupland, & Giles, 1991; Goffman, 1981, 1983a, 1983b; Heath, 1983; Schieffelin & Ochs, 1986).

From the perspective of a dramaturgical analysis of social life, implicit and explicit role ascriptions on a micro level also reflect larger societal preferences and expectations concerning generational and institutional alignments. In line with Brown and Gilman's (1989) recent reasoning, we would argue that social distance between two generations can be described both in terms of vertical distance, that is, power differences between two parties, and horizontal distance, that is, interactive distance or affective distance between two parties. Affect is an aspect of social alignments that has been somewhat neglected in discourse theory. Yet, affect seems to matter in determining stylistic variation in social interaction; in determining choice of personal pronouns, as well as other variables that have a bearing on displaying affinity on the one hand and formal distance on the other.

Role attributions are intimately linked to negotiations about social distance. To what extent are children cast as members of a different age category—pupils—or as members of an equal status category—peers? Do different institutional settings employ different means for underplaying or underlining age differences? In what ways can discourse be used as an instrument in forging intergenerational alignments or in underlining age-category boundaries? These questions tie in with Goffman's (1983b) ideas about the interaction order and participant role structures. In a pediatric setting, Aronsson (1991) has demonstrated how doctor-parent-child encounters at times concern implicit negotiations about the child's (patient's) membership status. Both parents and doctors may at times cast the child as a side-participant in encounters that concern his or her health and well-being, for example by treating child contributions as off-record contributions or by discrediting what the child says. Aronsson has claimed that, in multi-party talk, negotiations about social distance can be seen to concern a participant's personhood, whether he or she should be seen as a participant entitled to full membership or as a side-participant.

Personhood is intimately tied to cultural notions about child rearing and authority. In a comparative ethnographic analysis of caretaker-child interaction in three different societies, Ochs and Schieffelin (1984) have discussed how white Anglo-American middle-class parents interact with their children in ways that require quite a lot of (child-centered) adaptation on the parent's part; for instance, substantial perspective-taking in their listening, and baby talk or other simplified registers in their talking to the child. In contrast, working-class Anglo-American parents and parents in many traditional societies, such as Kaluli, New Guinea, and Western Samoa, expect their children to do the adapting, to listen attentively, and to talk in ways that will be adapted to their listeners. Children who talk unintelligibly do not quite count, as it were.

Goffman's notion of interaction order points to how identities are shaped and reshaped through discourse. Yet, as discussed by for example Strong (1988), Goffman often remains at the level of microanalysis without explicit links to the macro structures of society. In his analysis of visible/invisible pedagogies and social practices, Bernstein (1990) has discussed how societal changes on a macro level can be related to pedagogic practices. Such implicit rule systems can be analyzed in terms of sequencing rules (for pedagogic progression), criterial rules (for what counts), and hierarchical rules (for social interaction). Hierarchical rules regulate domination-subordination in different pedagogic contexts and they are particularly important in that they determine questions concerning legitimacy and authority.

In the microcosmos of the Swedish child-care scene, we have chosen sharing time events for a microanalysis of interaction orders. Sharing time is a recurring activity in child-care settings, where children and staff are gathered to talk about the daily agenda and about matters of common concern (information or instructional matters). Our analyses will be on a local level, but they will hopefully have implications for broader issues related to intergenerational adaptations (cf. Michaels, 1981, 1986). Sharing time events are open to negotiation in that they may concern adult-initiated instruction and/or child-initiated discussions or any mixture thereof. There is no strict curriculum that regulates what may go on during sharing time activities. In Bernstein's (1974, 1981, 1990) terminology, sharing time in Swedish child-care settings is a relatively weakly framed pedagogic activity, which is not sharply set apart from other forms of talk such as, for instance, disciplining talk, everyday conversations, and teaching. This, in turn, means that sharing time events in different settings may reveal local differences in pedagogic practices. In the present context, such differences may be interpreted as different professional styles for handling conversational dilemmas between support and control. These styles may in turn reflect underlying pedagogic ideologies that cast children as pupils or as peers.

Sharing Time Settings

Two after-school centers, the Panda and the Bumblebee (fictional names; although it is conventional to give animal names to child-care establishments) have been studied in two neighborhood areas of a mid-size Swedish industrial city. The children at the Panda are primarily recruited from parents with working-class backgrounds, and there are more people who receive social security benefits in this area. The children at the Bumblebee are primarily recruited from an area with a predominance of middle-class and lower middle-class parents (e.g., people in administrative positions, child-care staff, etc.). According to interviews conducted by Evaldsson (to be reported more fully elsewhere), the Bumblebee parents tend to be somewhat like Bernstein's (1974) prototypical middle-class parent or like Heath's (1983) Maintown parents in that they ascribe to school-oriented, mainstream, middle-class patterns for discursive practices. Moreover, Bumblebee parents tend to give voice to child-care ideologies that are oriented to adult adaptation to children rather than child adaptation to adults (Ochs & Schieffelin, 1984).

After-school centers provide day care for school-age children after school. The Swedish term *fritidshem* literally means "free-time home." Children go to the after-school center after school, arriving between 1:20 p.m. and 2:00 p.m. Many of the children also go to the after-school center before school (depending on parents' working hours and the school curriculum). At both centers, there are 2-3 members of staff, that is carers or so-called *fritidspedagoger* (literally "free-time pedagogues") who are women in their late twenties (or thirties). The women in the present study are all fully qualified with a professional training for this type of work. There are 15 children at each center, aged 6-10.

One of the authors, Ann-Carita Evaldsson, has followed the daily life of the two centers for 18 months as part of an ethnographic study of children's discourse in everyday activities. The main focus in her study is on peer talk in children's playing, teasing, and dispute practices. In addition to fieldwork notes and other types of diary data, she has accumulated more than 200 hours of taped interactions from the two after-school centers. The present sharing time events are transcribed from this larger set of tapes. Three events were chosen from each center, one sharing time event during the first days of school in the fall, one event at midterm, and one event in early spring term.

In Swedish child-care contexts, daily interaction often starts with a meeting between staff and children called *samlingen* (literally: get together). Sharing time generally takes place when all children have arrived at the center early in the afternoon. It is an indoor activity, lasting between 20 and 40 minutes. Sharing time events may be used for administrative information, discussion, instruction, and/or story reading. There is no detailed curriculum that regulates sharing time activities. At the Panda, sharing time generally takes 20 minutes, whereas it varies much more at the Bumblebee. As a rule, a member of staff is seated in front of the children, who are all grouped on a sofa, facing the staff.

Sharing time talk was transcribed in extenso (laughter and pauses included) according to a simplified version of the transcription schemes developed by Jefferson and other ethnomethodologists

Table 5.1   Transcription Conventions

:	prolonged syllable
-	self-editing marker
(.)	audible pause
(pause)	marked pause
CAPITALS	relatively high amplitude (e.g., "but YOU shouldn't . . ."
x	inaudible word
( )	encloses explanation or description of how talk is delivered
underlined text	demarcates overlapping utterances

(cf. Schenkein, 1978) (see Table 5.1). All names are fictionalized in order to protect staff's and children's identities.

Sharing Time Boundaries and Staff as Teachers or Peers

At the Panda, sharing time takes place in a separate room, whereas the event takes place in an open area at the Bumblebee. In other ways, as well, sharing time tends to be a more clearly marked activity at the Panda. There tends to be a ritualized opening: "hello children, hello everybody"; and sharing time always contains certain activities, such as talk about the calendar as well as story reading. At the Bumblebee, staff and children tend to walk in and out of the open area where sharing time takes place and there is no ritualized opening that clearly demarcates when sharing time starts, except for an attention getting device such as "Listen everybody." At the Bumblebee, sharing time boundaries are thus less clearly marked in both time and space.

In the following discussion, each section will contain extracts from recorded interactions from both child-care centers, first from the Panda, and then from the Bumblebee.

Everyday discourse practices shape different ways of setting adults and children apart. The staff at the Panda tend to employ what we will here call an instruction-oriented type of discourse. Talk conforms to pedagogic patterns; for asking quite specific questions, for pinpointing exact times and dates, and for categorizing facts. This can often be seen from the very outset of sharing time events at the Panda, as in the following extract from a sharing time event on a Monday.

Extract 1. Hello Children, Hello Everybody (Panda III:1-10)

1 CARER-A:	Well we'll just have to see how it goes when we get there. Yes hello children, hello everybody
2 Several children:	Good morning
3 CARER-A:	JAKOB! Stop poking at your face and put your hands under the table. I hope you're all feeling good and that you had a nice weekend (lowers her voice)
4 Several children:	Mmm
5 CARER-A:	And that you did something nice together with your parents
6 Mats:	Yesterday we went away, tomorrow we're going too (silently to himself)
7 Tommy:	You know we had a party the day before yesterday. Yes, Friday-fun. No:
8 CARER-A:	Yes but yesterday it was Sunday sweetie, then we <u>didn't-</u>
9 Tommy:	<u>No:, Mats</u> had his party then
10 CARER-A:	That's right, Mats had his party. Then it's best we find out what today's date is because it's Mats' <u>birthday</u>

In its present context, the opening word "well" (turn 1) serves as a topic boundary marker that terminates prior everyday talk and that serves as a linguistic marker of sharing time, that is, serious or pedagogic talk. It is typical for the Panda that sharing time is clearly marked both in terms of time and space, as well as on this pragmatic linguistic level. The carer then continues, opening up by addressing the children as an age-marked collective ("hello children, hello everybody"). This is a ritualized opening phrase that announces most sharing time events at the Panda. In addressing the children as a collective, she also underlines her own position as someone who stands apart from this age-category ("of children"), indexing her own position as an adult. In calling

Jakob to order, she speaks in the voice of adult authority. Also, her two bald on-record directives ("stop poking your face!", "put your hands under the table!") are congruent with the staff member's self-presentation as a responsible adult, standing apart from the group of children. Her directives tie in neatly with the Brown and Levinson (1987) model's predictions of greater directness in the talk of more powerful participants than in the talk of less powerful ones (other things being equal). Thereby she can be said to mark her vertical distance from the collective of children.

The ensuing dialogue about "a nice weekend" indicates an examination type stance in that the staff displays a greater interest in the exact time references of the target party than in what went on during the party (which would perhaps have been the topic of interest from a more progressive child-oriented type of position). Ultimately, this conversational episode is employed as a natural prologue to the ritualized daily discourse about the calendar. The calendar is discussed at every sharing time event at the Panda. In line with Jackson's (1968) observations from U.S. primary schools, early institutional life often revolves around issues that have to do with order (timekeeping and children's movements in space). The calendar is discussed daily at the Panda, but only once a week at the Bumblebee, which seems to reflect underlying differences in institutional concern about sequential order and boundary maintenance.

Sharing time discussions at the Bumblebee often revolve around joint reminiscences or around issues that concern communal arrangements for everyday events (decision making, plans, evaluations). If the staff at the Bumblebee wish to bring up questions about order this tends to be prefaced by excuses or other mitigating devices, as in Extract 2.

Extract 2. A Niggle (Bumblebee III:1-6)

1	CARER-U:	First I've got a niggle to make
2	Anders:	Wha:t?
3	CARER-U:	That those who haven't got any slippers should get some (pause)
4	Anders:	I have told my mum actually

5 CARER-U:	Then you'll just have to go home and niggle. What about you (to Josefin)?
6 Josefin:	What about me, I haven't got any. They're too small

.

.

50 CARER-U:	Well, hello everybody (.) at the same time (said in a low voice)

As can be seen, the carer's admonition is prefaced by a mitigating move. In playing down her own admonition as "a niggle," the staff member can be seen to distance herself from her own position as a niggling adult, if you like. Hence, instead of underlining her own position as someone apart (as in the Panda opening), she can be seen to bracket her adult talk. The request is presented as a type of side-episode (that should not ruin the adult-child alignment).

Eventually, the carer addresses the whole group of children (turn 50, "Well, hello everybody"). In general, sharing time at Bumblebee does not commence with a ritualized opening. Typically, the staff say hello to the children on an individual basis, nodding, smiling or saying hello as the children get seated. Eventually everybody is seated and sharing time can commence. At other times, the staff and children may chat about something and a member of staff may announce the sharing time opening by announcing something in a higher amplitude, calling the children to attention "Listen, listen, all of you." In due time, the staff might introduce different points on the agenda. In the present case, though, the carer indeed says "well, hello everybody," after having discussed her little complaint about slippers. She, herself, comments on this quasi-formal opening, though. In a low voice, she mutters "all at the same time," and a little later (not excerpted here) she explains to the children that, after her Christmas holidays, she hasn't met everybody yet. This explanation can be seen as a type of justification of her somewhat formal opening (by Bumblebee standards). It should perhaps be pointed out that she says "hello to everybody" but not "hello children." That is, she does not specifically address the children as an age-marked collective.

Discourse as Examination or Conversation

If interaction is geared toward instruction and the dissemination of facts, it makes sense to use an examination type question-answer format. At the Panda, the staff may also talk about administrative issues in ways that relate to examination-type questioning (Extract 3).

Extract 3. What Have We Got on Mondays? (Panda I:58-66)

58	CARER-A:	. . . And on monday, we will go on as usual. What have we got on Monday? (pause) Have you forgotten?
59	Jonas:	P.E.
60	Tommy:	Go into the woods.
61	CARER-A:	What do you call the meeting when we assemble on Mondays?
62	children:	Er
63	Malin:	Assembly
64	CARER-A:	Well, precisely, we've got an assembly on Mondays. And then we'll plan for the whole week and decide what we'll do. Do you remember that? And then we'll read a book and on top of that we'll choose a song this term. We will sing a bit more than before. And then we'll choose a song.
65	Sara:	Well, what shall we sing?
66	CARER-A:	And then we'll sing a song, and we will sing it for that whole week. And then we'll have responsibility groups as usual. What should one take care of for a week at a time? (pause) Carita! (Carita has raised her hand)

The carer has a particular type of meeting in mind throughout this episode. As in textbook quizzes, the appropriate response exists in writing, or more specifically in the written agenda of the Panda. The staff rely on the authority of the text in inviting the children's responses. As in prototypical examination-type questioning, there is but one correct response. This particular sharing time event takes place one of the first days of the new term. During spring term, the children have been told about the coming activities of the fall term. Yet, many of them have obviously forgotten what will take place on specific week days. After a few incorrect responses, the adults provide the children with a clue ("when we assemble"). The children seem to be much more concerned about concrete specifics and about the here-and-now than the staff. No one takes up on the general agenda. Sara asks about the concrete activity of singing, though. She also tries to narrow down this activity by asking the staff what song they shall sing (turn 65). The adults thus talk about general principles, whereas the children more often tend to focus on concrete activities of the here-and-now.

Texts or Experience as Legitimate Information

At the Panda, questioning is sometimes situated within a game context. The staff employ a commercially available set of cards, a game called "Hazard," a set of printed cards with a response manual. Individual children are allowed to leave the room after providing a correct response to one of the printed questions (Extract 4). This also means that sharing time closes in a ritualized but playful fashion.

Extract 4. Can You Fly Faster Than Sound? (Panda II:241-251)

241 CARER-A: "Was Hiawatha an Indian chief?" (reads)
242 Sara: (pause) Ye:s
243 CARER-A: Yes, that's right
244 Tommy: Yeah, I knew that
245 Several
   children: Yeah
246 CARER-A: "Can you fly faster than sound" (reads), Mats?
247 Mats: No, yes you can (.) Planes can of course
248 CARER-A: "Can you fly faster than sound?" (reads)
249 Mats: No, you can't
250 CARER-A: No, you can't
251 Carita: That was easy

Hiawatha is probably best known as an American Indian child hero (e.g., Walt Disney's cartoon figure). Yet, the response manual of "Hazard" states that he was an Indian chief, which thus defines this response as the correct one. Thus, correctness is intimately tied to the printed word. The predefined printed responses also guide the ensuing dialogue about "flying faster than sound." In his first response, Mats refers to supersonic planes that may indeed go faster than sound. The carer denies that one can fly faster than sound. In so doing, she implicitly redefines the question into a catch question. Yet, Carita, one of the children, aligns with the staff stating that the question was an easy one. This may indicate that Carita has interpreted the question in terms of *one* correct response, being unaware of the referential ambiguity of "you" ("one" or *man* in Swedish). Or she may merely wish to display her alignment with the interrogator.

At the Bumblebee, adult-child questions more prototypically concern everyday events and quite often events where the children are in the know. Such questions might, for instance, concern the child's recreational activities, as in the following excerpt (Extract 5).

Extract 5. At the Baths (Bumblebee III:108-117)

108	CARER-B:	You had a nice time. I heard, Pernilla told me that it went well at the baths then
109	Kari:	Yeah
110	CARER-B:	I heard that Kristian jumped from high up
111	Klas:	From the fifth level he jumped
112	CARER-B:	What about you
113	Klas:	I jumped from the third level
114	Anders:	Did Krisse jump from the fifth?
115	CARER-U:	Did you, did you dare jump from the third level Klas?
116	CARER-B:	Oh yes he did
117	CARER-U:	It's only Freddy, who else apart from you jumped
118	CARER-B:	And Anders

In the carer's questioning, she refers to the fact that Kristian jumped from high up. It can be inferred that she herself was not present at this event, which is a "B" event in Labov and Fanshel's (1979) terminology, that is an event that the first person does not know about from her own personal experience. She is interested in the children's accomplishments. Yet, she does not fully share the boy's own set of standards. At least, she also tries to boost Klas, who (merely) jumped from the third level (and not from the fifth level). She is aware that he ordinarily does not dare to jump from the third level. Anders, though, does not assume this supportive stance. He does not take any interest in the relative accomplishments of Klas, but only in the success of Kristian. The latter has also provided a standard of excellence within this group of boys.

Later on, during the same sharing time event, one of the pedagogues starts to joke about her boyfriend's daring exploits at the local indoor pool. Evidently, she had dared him to jump from the fifth level, and he had indeed jumped but in so doing, he eventually became quite discolored and scared (Extract 6).

Extract 6. But Did He Dive Then? (Bumblebee III:208-224)

208 **CARER-B:** Anyway, we were there swimming and we'd been on the slide, that's fun. I can't remember what I said, I joked with Conny anyway and that

209 **CARER-U:** Ha ha ha (laughs)

210 **CARER-B:** Ha ha ha (laughs) "you don't dare climb up and dive from the fifth level" It's five meters high up there

211 **Anders:** Yeah, no: ten

212 **CARER-B:** No:, but of course we had been to a party the night before. Then maybe you don't feel too great ha ha (giggles)

213 **CARER-U:** Headaches and so on if you've been up late

214 **Several children:** Mmm mm

215 **CARER-B:** Hee hee (giggles) But anyway, he climbed up (.) God how I laughed. He's not the one to do that sort of thing

216 **CARER-U:** No:

217 **CARER-B:** Just because he had to show me that he dared

218 **Freddy:** Did he dive?

219 **CARER-B:** You said that your heart pounded. You should've seen his heart, he went quite blue in the face

220 **CARER-U + A-C:** Ha ha ha (laugh)

221 **Freddy:** But did he dive then?

222 **CARER-B:**   Yeah he dove
223 **Freddy:**   From the tenth?
224 **CARER-B:**   No, from the fifth. But he hadn't done it for quite a few
                    years . . .

The children listen attentively to this piece of self-disclosure on the pedagogue's part. The other adults laugh at Conny's foolhardiness, but the children do not take part in the laughing. Instead, they seem to focus on Conny's actual accomplishments (cf. Freddy in turn 221 "But did he dive then?"). Apparently, the children do not grasp the mocking stance of the narrative. Yet, they evidently enjoy the mutual storytelling. They have previously told the staff about their exploits at the baths, and, in return, Carer-B now tells the children and the other adults about her boyfriend's (foolish) diving. Storytelling is thus construed as a mutual event where people tell first stories and second stories on a *reciprocal* basis, that transcends generational boundaries. Ultimately, such co-narration may be quite instrumental in establishing what Goffman (1983a) has called joint biographies.

Social Control

Turn-Taking and Topic Control

As we have noted, examination type questioning is common at the Panda, but not at the Bumblebee. Yet, the adults control sharing time talk in many ways at both centers. It is the adults who decide when sharing time starts and terminates, and who decide when and if the children should be invited to talk. Moreover, adults tend to monopolize the discourse space in sharing time events. In reviews of school discourse, teachers tend to use about two thirds of the discourse space (Einarsson & Hultman, 1984). In a Swedish study of six sharing time events in one Swedish preschool unit, the teachers used 70% of the discourse space, as opposed to 30% for all children (Hedenqvist, 1987). It matters little whether there are few or many children who participate in these events; in one case three children share 31% of the discourse space, and in a different case 10 children share 17% of the discourse space (Hedenqvist, 1987). The time distribution is quite similar at the two after-school centers in the present study. On an average, the staff use 72% of the discourse space at the Panda, and 78% at the Bumblebee (when studying the distribution of words for adults, on the one hand, and children, on the other).

In both centers, quite a lot of sharing time talk revolves around the agenda; about planned activities and how to go about them, as well as about the making of plans.

Extract 7. You Know What We're Going to Do Then? (Panda II:94-114)

94	CARER-A:	And you know what we're going to do then, eh. After the meal?
95	Jakob:	No:
96	Several children:	No:
97	CARER-A:	Oh, I hope everyone's got shorts with them
98	Several children:	No:
99	Marianne:	Yeah
100	Several children:	Yeah
101	Sara:	Not me either, I forgot
102	CARER-A:	Sscch! (silencing sound)
103	Jakob:	Black shorts
104	CARER-A:	Well, go in and get changed and put your clothes on your shelves
105	Sara:	I think so
106	CARER-A:	And then go into the er, whadjamacallit (.) No: I don't think we'll do that. When you've got changed, you can line up beside the games hall. Then Ulla and I will demonstrate a bit (.) got it
107	Several children:	Mmm mm (quietly)
108	Karin:	What are we going to do then?
109	CARER-A:	Well, we're going to do something fun and (.)
110	Jakob:	I don't know if my shorts are dry, er we went swimming today and they might be (inaudible)
111	Marianne:	Shall we check

112 Jakob:	I don't know if they're dry
113 Malin:	(to Marianne) <u>Haven't you washed your shorts</u>
114 CARER-A:	We:ll now you know

The children initially do not catch on to what the carer has in mind (turns 95, 96). She then provides a clue, in mentioning that they should all bring their shorts. Somewhat later Karin asks her about what they are in fact supposed to do (turn 108). Yet, the carer only responds that "we're going to do something fun"; turn 109). In so doing, she again turns the planning into something of a question-answer guessing game format, cuing the children about the planned activities, yet without revealing her secret agenda. In her final turn "well now you know," she has still not informed Karin about the afternoon activities. As is quite typical for Panda planning, she does not invite the children's opinions about the afternoon's activities but merely their guesses about what should take place. In fact, the question-answer format is quite similar to school examinations or to fact-finding contests such as the card game "Hazard" (cf. Extract 3 above). In a related quite typical episode, the staff at the Panda talk to the children about "snuggle-up day" (Extract 8).

Extract 8. Snuggle-Up Day (Panda I:98-121)

98 CARER-A:	And then well . . . NO Per and Tommy now I'm disappointed with you Per (pause) you go and sit over THERE now (Per moves to another place on the couch) And you put your hand up if you want something, YOU know that (pause) Don't you (pause) Well that's that. Right, on Tuesday (.) (whispers and holds her arms about herself) we've decided to have snuggle-up day on Tuesdays.
99 Several children:	Yeah
100 CARER-A:	What's snuggle-up day then? (pause) Why do you say yeah when you don't know what it is yet?
101 Tommy:	I know
102 Jonas:	I know
103 CARER-A:	You put your hands up. (Tommy puts his hand up) Yes Tommy

104	Tommy:	Party time or whadjamacallit Friday fun time.
105	CARER-A:	No, not on Tuesdays, we have that on Fridays. You know that.
106	Several children:	Yeah
107	CARER-A:	What do you think snuggle-up day might be?
108	Jonas:	I know, we all lie down and go to sleep.
109	CARER-A:	No (laughs) we're not going to do that when school has started, we just do that now. Although now there are so many kids here so we have story time just after lunch (.) (Lisa puts her hand up) Lisa
110	Lisa:	I'm going to ((XX)).
111	Several children:	(giggle)
112	Sara:	She's got her hand up (points at Carita)
113	CARER-A:	Carita
114	Carita:	We snuggle up all cozy.
115	CARER-A:	Mmm, we didn't really know what to call this day anyhow. But then we thought that on Tuesdays we should take it really easy and be nice to each other =
116	Jonas:	= You should always do that, shouldn't you?
117	CARER-A:	Yes, you should always do that but every Tuesday, we're going to be extra nice to each other (.) And we can play some games and then we can do some collage and we can sit and knit.
118	Jonas:	What sort of collage are we going to do?
119	CARER-A:	You can sit on my lap a while if you want. All cozy and nice and calm =
120	Jonas:	= Is it Tuesday today?
121	CARER-A:	Mmm except we won't start with this until school starts properly. Do you get what I mean?

This time, the guessing game format of the question-answer sequence is quite prominent. The carer has a particular type of activity in mind, and she manages to raise the children's expectations. In a stepwise fashion, she tries to direct the children into the staff's plans about "snuggle-up day." In so doing, she also makes some metacomments about the nature of such examination type sequences, that is that one should not respond if one does not know (turn 100). Also, talking will only be allowed provided that the children raise their hands, bidding for their turns (turn 103). It should perhaps also be pointed out how the children themselves tend to keep track of hand-raising at the Panda, which can here be seen in Sara's turn (112). Speaking rights are less regimented at the Bumblebee, which is also reflected in less child participation at the Bumblebee in this type of official bidding for turns.

Relatively seen, boundaries between different activities are often strong at the Panda. In this respect, the implicit curriculum is somewhat like that of a traditional school with clear-cut divisions between subjects, and not that of an open school with weaker boundaries between activities (Bernstein, 1975). At the Panda, the snuggle-up day is something that may not be mistaken for "Friday fun time." As pointed out (turn 105), Friday fun time should take place on Fridays, not on Tuesdays. The staff laugh at cute answers such as Jonas's idea that everybody should go to sleep. When the staff ultimately reveal that snuggle-up day is when one should be nice to each other, Jonas appears to be somewhat disappointed. Probably, he becomes even more disillusioned as he finds out that there are no specific plans for the snuggle-up day. The staff member makes up plans for Tuesdays in the abstract future, that is for snuggle-up days in general, and she does not respond to Jonas's concrete question about collage making. Furthermore, she does not deal with any immediate activity in that snuggling up is reserved for the abstract future (when school has started, turn 121), not for next Tuesday, or the here and now. The agenda is transformed into an abstraction, if you like, that again accentuates an examination-type stance in the Panda discussions about the agenda (cf. also Extract 3 above or 10 below).

At the Bumblebee, the staff generally tends to discuss events of the immediate future rather than events of an abstract general future. In such a planning sequence at the Bumblebee, the carer discusses the activities of the proximate afternoon with the children.

Extract 9. Playing Games (Bumblebee III:326-340)

326 CARER-U: (hesitates) Sandra! On Tuesday we thought we'd have P.E. and stuff

327	Several children:	YEEEEAH
328	CARER-U:	And WE THOUGHT, listen, that we'd go up and play games instead of normal P.E.
329	Several children:	Yeeeeah
330	CARER-U:	Then you'll have to decide what games we should play. Have you got any?
331	Anders, Klas:	SHIPWRECKED
332	Jan:	Shipwreck(.)ed
333	EVA:	But that's not a game
334	CARER-U:	(hesitates) That's not. That's a P.E. game. You know, normal games
335	CARER-U:	We thought we'd play games
336	Jan:	Tag
337	CARER-B:	Yes, something like that
338	Freddy:	Tag
339	CARER-U:	Tag (writes). Any more suggestions?

As can be seen, the Bumblebee staff try to involve the children in planning the day's activities or coming activities. Yet, the planning is not completely free. In this particular case, it can be seen how "play games" has to be defined in a way that excludes P.E. games and other types of games that are not "normal games." Once this premise has been established (turn 334), the children and the staff get involved in a lengthy and lively discussion about different possible games and their relative drawbacks and advantages (only partly extracted here).

Invitation of Child Initiatives

The closing of sharing time is often preadvertised by an invitation of child questions or child initiatives. On the whole, sharing time talk is regulated by the adults. The staff generally decide what is an appropriate topic for sharing time, and the staff decide about topic shifts or when a topic can be terminated. The children at the Bumblebee tend to make conversational initiatives on their own (or at least, their talk more often results in adult-child dialogues). At the Panda, the children at times may try to initiate different topics but their initiatives are often ignored, as time is more highly regulated. Talk is instruction oriented, which in turn implies that certain types of talk do not fit within the general format of the event as such. At both centers, though, the staff seem to signal that they may relinquish some of the adult control toward the closing phase of sharing time (Extracts 10 and 11).

Extract 10. Any Questions? (Panda III:129-134 . . . 146-161)

129	CARER-A:	(clears throat; addressing the whole group of children) Hrrrmmm Well then, got any questions about the week (.) (to Per) Will you be here all week or what?
130	Per:	Yeah
131	CARER-A:	You'll be here all week then?
132	Per:	Last week
133	Tommy:	Miss, miss, I've got a question
134	CARER-A:	(to Per) What did you say ? . . .
147	CARER-A:	Right then let's see, what were we going to do tomorrow (pause)
148	Robin:	Yeah but I had something else to ask
149	CARER-A:	Now I'm asking what we're doing tomorrow
150	Tommy:	(puts his hand up) I know, I know
151	CARER-A:	Tommy
152	Tommy:	We're going to make things and hang on (xx)-
153	CARER-A:	We're going to make things and hang them on the branch. And what were we going to do on Wednesday then, Carita

In the initial turn above, the carer in charge of sharing time apparently invites questions from the children. Yet, she seems to prevent the children from asking such questions in that she pauses but briefly before venturing upon some questioning of her own ("you'll be here all week then?", same turn). Two boys, Tommy (turn 133) and Robin (turn 148) indicate that they have questions. However, they are not allowed to formulate their questions. The staff have already presented the agenda of the coming week (not extracted here), and the children are required to answer questions about the agenda. Apparently, the initial question about "any questions?" was not an open invitation to discussions, but rather an opening to a rehearsal, an examination about the agenda as it were.

At the Bumblebee, the staff also tend to invite child initiatives toward the closing period of sharing time. The situation is more loosely structured than at the Panda, though (Extract 11).

Extract 11. Has Anyone Got Anything Else to Say?
(Bumblebee III:484-506)

484	CARER-U:	Has anyone got anything else they want to say or ask?
485	Josefin:	Like what?
486	CARER-U:	(in a low voice) Well anything you think you want to say or ask (pause)
487	Anders:	What (pause)
488	CARER-U:	(in a low voice) I wondered if anyone had anything to say
489	Anders:	Well, that it's been a rotten day because school has started, we could've had longer holidays
490	Sandra:	We've had <u>a great time hee hee (giggles)</u>
491	CARER-U:	<u>We've got</u> a day off in two or three weeks. On the 27th of January you've got the day off school . . .
497	Anders:	Aaaw, can't we go to the baths in X-köping then?
498	Sandra:	No:
499	Jan:	But this time I don't think (xx) like you had last time with the bus hee hee hee (giggles)
500	CARER-U:	Who? (.) Do you remember ? hee hee hee (giggles)
501	Several children:	Yeah, yeah, ha ha ha (laugh)
502	Jan:	Yeah we hee hee hee (laughs) just ran around trying to get the bus and you ha ha ha (laughs) <u>(inaudible)</u>
503	A-C:	<u>When was that</u>
504	CARER-U:	<u>Yeah ha ha ha</u> (laughs) we almost didn't get away from X-köping and couldn't find the bus stop
505	A-C:	Yes
506	CARER-U:	And we were running about. Eva and me really upset at each other and 15 kids. To and fro, do you remember

When one carer says that the children may talk about "anything you think you want to say or ask" (turn 486), she actually seems to mean precisely that, and the children initiate discussions about several different topics "longer holidays," a bus excursion in the past, as well as one of the teachers' recent misfortune (a brain hemorrhage; not extracted here), as well as some joint reminiscences about an eventful day off in the past.

As can be seen above, the staff follow up Anders's complaint about starting school in that they initiate the topic of "a day off." Jan and the staff then start a joint narrative about an outing in the past. The staff and the children all laugh about their disorderly behavior at the time. Moreover, one carer (U) reveals how she and Eva (another staff member) were eventually really "upset at each other." The narrative is reconstrued jointly by Jan and the staff. All join in laughing at their own confusion at the time. The staff and the children thus laugh together at the shortcomings of the adults. This type of shared laughter can be seen as an outward manifestation of the relatively weak boundaries between the two generations at the Bumblebee. Generational alignments are construed and cemented through such joint laughter and joint narratives (see also the episodes about the baths, Excerpts 5 and 6 above).

Power, Solidarity, and Participant Status

Speech act theory has it that speech reflects social parameters. Our present data rather show how talk is constitutive of social life and how social distance is continuously being negotiated (cf. Aronsson, 1991; Aronsson & Cederborg, 1991; Aronsson & Rundström, 1989). Along with Brown and Gilman (1989), we differentiate between horizontal distance (affect) and vertical distance (power). Conarration and joint laughter is characteristic of the relationship-oriented discourse at the Bumblebee. In terms of social distance, this institution seems to be oriented toward affective proximity (decreases in horizontal distance), and toward decreased vertical distance between children and adults.

In their different ways of monitoring sharing time, the staff at the two centers seem to define two different types of intergenerational relationship arrangements, two different interaction orders (see Table 5.2). One interaction order is oriented toward instruction and children's adaption to adults, whereas the other is more oriented toward relationship matters such as the construction and reconstruction of shared biographies.

At the Panda, interaction is more oriented toward instruction and the dissemination of facts. This also involves a more regimented curriculum. This orientation toward an agenda in turn involves stronger boundary markings: between sharing time and other activities (work/play), between the two generations (adults/children), between types of everyday regulations (adult-regulated/child-regulated activities), and so forth. Conversely, boundaries are weaker at the Bumblebee.

One important device seems to be the construction of joint biographies. This includes self-disclosures on the part of the adults (cf. Extracts 6 and 11 above). As has been shown in talk with the elderly, self-disclosures seem to play an important part in intergenerational alignments (Coupland, Coupland, & Giles, 1991; Coupland, Coupland, Giles, & Wiemann, 1988). The staff's telling of private stories probably works on two levels. First, it weakens intergenerational boundaries in providing the children with insights into adult worlds. Second, it invites second stories of a similar kind, that is "private" stories from children's lives. Self-disclosure in intergenerational settings thus celebrates weakened boundaries on the one hand, and regenerates such weakening on the other. The Bumblebee staff also try to adapt to the children's perspectives in their way of responding to child-initiated topics, which ties in with the type of child-centeredness that characterizes white middle-class, mainstream cultures in the analyses of Ochs and Schieffelin (1984). On an underlying level, a greater relative occurrence of adult-child sharing of jokes, stories, and laughter (Extracts 5, 6, and 11) also seems to shape intergenerational alignments and social identities. Aronsson (1991) has described how adult talk may cast child patients as persons or nonpersons in pediatric settings. In the present setting, talk does not transform some children into nonpersons. Yet, talk seems to matter in that certain

Table 5.2 Instruction-Oriented and Community-Oriented Types of Adult-Child Discourse

| | Interaction Order: | |
	Instruction Oriented	Relationship Oriented
Sharing time boundaries	strong	weak
Children addressed as	collective (age-marked)	individuals
Participant status of staff	teacher	peer
Participant status of child	pupil	peer
Information exchange	examination	conversation
Prototypical knowledge base	print	experience
Staff self-disclosure	rare	quite common
Prototypical information	facts	shared biography
Topic control	adult agenda oriented	adult community oriented
Topic initiation	adult	adult, child
Intergenerational boundaries	strong	weak
Social control	direct	indirect

professional styles cast child participants as pupils, whereas other styles cast children as peers.

Yet, the two interaction orders cannot merely be reduced to traditional or progressivist pedagogies. Both interaction orders are situated within the Swedish child-care system, based on the child-care ideology of *Barnstugeutredningen* (SOU, 1972), an ideology that celebrates learning by doing rather than learning through instruction, individual growth rather than learning, teacher facilitation or "dialogues" rather than instruction or direct forms of control, and so forth (cf. Bernstein on stage theories; 1990, pp. 68-69). This, in turn, means that both interaction orders can be related to invisible rather than visible pedagogies in Bernstein's terminology. Yet, the relationship-oriented organization of sharing time is more indirect than the instruction oriented, with weaker boundaries toward other types of activities. Sharing time at the Bumblebee is not clearly defined in relation to other events in terms of time and location, or in terms of agendas. At the Panda, there are more distinct criterial rules in Bernstein's terms (1990), for what counts as pedagogic discourse. Sharing time talk at the Panda generally concerns examination type fact-finding, administrative business or order whereas many topics at the Bumblebee demarcate less clearly from any other everyday conversation. In this way, it can be said that the children at the Bumblebee will be better prepared for other types of invisible pedagogies, whereas the children at the Panda will be more attuned to more direct forms of control.

Yet, ultimately, both interaction orders involve adult control. Control at the Bumblebee is more invisible, as in the open schools in Bernstein's model (1975), whereas control at the Panda is more visible. Social control at the Panda is quite direct, which is reflected in such things as bald on-record directives. This seems to correlate with stronger intergenerational boundaries, on the one hand, and with stronger child-child—that is, intragenerational—alignments, on the other (e.g., in the children's playing, disputes, and teasing practices; Evaldsson, 1993). Hence, both models would have drawbacks and relative advantages in terms of intergenerational versus child-child alignments. As in the analysis of child-adult adaption (Ochs & Schieffelin, 1984) or the analysis of codes (Bernstein, 1981, 1990), discursive practices must be understood in relation to socialization requirements in different subcultures.[1]

The two interaction orders must be seen as ideal types that must be understood within their specific cultural contexts. Quite predictably (both from an ethnographic and a Bernsteinian perspective), the instructive orientation is found in a social area characterized by a greater proportion working-class parents, and the community orientation in an area characterized by a greater percentage middle-class parents. Our focus has been on the staff in that they are the ones who monitor sharing time talk and also the ones who do most of the talking. The staff at the two centers are qualified child-care professionals, recruited from a uniform educational background. Yet, they interact in different ways with the children. As was shown, child participation at the two centers accounts for less than a fourth of sharing time talk; if anything, the Bumblebee children talk less than the Panda children. Yet, the children make different types of contributions in the two sharing time settings. At the Bumblebee, the children tend to make initiatives such as telling stories and they take part in joint storytelling with adults. Moreover, they attend less to the bureaucratic order than the children at the Panda (who tend to comment on each others' hand-raising, etc.). The Panda children also take part in things like storytelling and joking, but such speech events would typically be located between peers, that is, between the children and not between children and adults (cf. Evaldsson, 1993). Through the adults' and the children's separated activities, joking and storytelling are thus defined as peer-type events (not intergenerational events). The two interaction orders are thus the joint products of children's and adults' ways of talking.

Asymmetries between children and adults do not merely concern hierarchical order but also background knowledge. In institutional settings it is generally the persons in power who also are the ones in the know. This is also one of the inherent problems with invisible pedagogies (Bernstein, 1975, 1990), in that children may ultimately become assessed by standards that have never been formulated in the open. At times, intergenerational alignments involve collusive aspects. For instance, the staff and the children sometimes listen to the same stories in quite different ways. As an example, the boys enjoy the story about a boyfriend of a staff member and his diving, framing it as a macho-story (of courageous diving), whereas the female carer seems to frame it more as an anti-hero story, laughing in a friendly way at his boyish daredevil attitude (Extract 6). In laughing at the young man, the staff may, of course, indirectly laugh at their co-participants, the young boys who also tend to display quite a lot of boyish competitiveness. McDermott and Tylbor (1987) have demonstrated how discourse is often more or less collusive. In intergenerational talk, this would be particularly true when one generation defines what counts as privileged interpretations of reality; what counts as more mature or more sensible formulations.

People may handle generational status in different ways. In the relationship-oriented type of setting, intergenerational proximity seems to matter more than in other settings, at least as reflected in joint biography making and mutual self-disclosures. The children are encouraged to provide accounts and explanations for their actions, and there is a preference for discussions (rather than directives). Yet, talk does not erase real-life intergenerational differences. Children may become more or less empowered by different discursive practices. Yet, they often lack adult background knowledge for framing situations in ways that counts in society at large, as in school framings and other professional framings. Moreover, children are not the ones who formulate what counts as professional privileged interpretations of events, and they do not have any real share in the professionals' turn taking control or topic control. Hence, adults decide not only about instructional matters but also about what counts as "playing normal games" or what does not count as normal. Control may be more or less direct, but it resides in the hands of professionals, and not in the hands of children. Ultimately then, peer-like conversations in professional settings tend to take place on adult premises.

Note

1. Bernstein has been read differently. To some extent this is because he has often been read through his critics or through his first and most tentative formulations of the 1960s, rather than in his work from the 1970s and 1980s (for an illuminating analysis of these polemic or merely uninformed readings, see Atkinson, 1985, or Silverman & Torode, 1980).

References

Aronsson, K. (1991). Facework and control in multiparty talk: A pediatric case study. In I. Markova & K. Foppa (Eds.), *Asymmetries in dialogue.* Hemel Hempstead, Hertfordshire, UK: Harvester Press.

Aronsson, K., & Cederborg, A.-C. (1991, August). *Facework and participant status in family therapy talk.* Paper presented at the 4th International Conference on Language and Social Psychology, at Santa Barbara, CA.

Aronsson, K., & Rundström, B. (1989). Cats, dogs, and sweets in the clinical negotiation of reality: On politeness and coherence in pediatric discourse. *Language in Society, 18,* 483-504.

Atkinson, P. (1985). *Language, structure and reproduction: An introduction to the sociology of knowledge of Basil Bernstein.* London: Methuen.

Bernstein, B. (1974). *Class, codes and control: Vol I. Theoretical studies towards a sociology of language* (2nd ed., rev.). London: Routledge & Kegan Paul.

Bernstein, B. (1975). *Class, codes and control: Vol. III. Towards a theory of educational transmission.* London: Routledge & Kegan Paul.

Bernstein, B. (1981). Codes, modalities and the process of cultural reproduction: A model. *Language in Society, 10*, 327-363.

Bernstein, B. (1990). *The structuring of pedagogic discourse: Vol. IV. Class, codes and control.* London: Routledge & Kegan Paul.

Brown, P., & Levinson, S. (1987). *Politeness: Some universals in language usage.* Cambridge: Cambridge University Press.

Brown, R., & Gilman, A. (1989). Politeness theory and Shakespeare's four major tragedies. *Language in Society, 18*, 159-212.

Coupland, N., Coupland, J., & Giles, H. (1991). *Language, society, and the elderly: Discourse, identity, and ageing.* Oxford: Basil Blackwell.

Coupland, N., Coupland, J., Giles, H., & Wiemann, J. (1988). My life in your hands: Processes of self-disclosure in intergenerational talk. In N. Coupland (Ed.), *Styles of discourse* (pp. 201-253). London: Croom Helm.

Einarsson, J., & Hultman, T. (1984). *Godmorgon pojkar och flickor.* Malmö: Liber Fölag.

Evaldsson, A.-C. (1993). *Play, disputes and social order: Everyday life in two Swedish after-school centers.* Unpublished doctoral dissertation, Department of Communication Studies, Linköping University, Sweden.

Goffman, E. (1981). *Forms of talk.* Oxford: Basil Blackwell.

Goffman, E. (1983a). Felicity's condition. *American Journal of Society, 89*, 1-53.

Goffman, E. (1983b). The interaction order. *American Sociological Review, 48*, 1-17.

Heath, S. B. (1983). *Ways with words: Language, life, and work in communities and classrooms.* Cambridge: Cambridge University Press.

Hedenqvist, J.-A. (1987). *Språklig interaktion i förskolan. Analyser och exempel.* Stockholm: Högskolan för Lärarutbildning i Stockholm (Institutionen för Pedagogik. Forskningsgruppen för Läroplansteori och Kulturreproduktion. Rapport nr. 5).

Jackson, P. W. (1968). *Life in classrooms.* New York: Holt.

Kallos, D. (1978). *Den nya pedagogiken: En analys av den så kallade dialogpedagogiken som svenskt samhällsfenomen.* Stockholm: Wahlström & Widstrand.

Labov, W., & Fanshel, D. (1979). *Therapeutic discourse.* New York: Academic Press.

McDermott, R. P., & Tylbor, H. (1987). On the necessity of collusion in conversation. In L. Kedar (Ed.), *Power through discourse* (pp. 153-170). Norwood, NJ: Ablex.

Michaels, S. (1981). "Sharing time." *Language in Society, 10*, 423-442.

Michaels, S. (1986). Narrative presentations: An oral preparation for literacy with firstgraders. In J. Cook-Gumperz (Ed.), *The social construction of literacy* (pp. 94-116). Cambridge: Cambridge University Press.

Ochs, E., & Schieffelin, B. (1984). Language acquisition and socialization: Three developmental stories. In R. Schweder & R. LeVine (Eds.), *Culture theory and essays on mind, self, and emotion* (pp. 276-320). Cambridge: Cambridge University Press.

Schenkein, J. (Ed.). (1978). *Studies in the organization of conversational interaction.* New York: Academic Press.

Schieffelin, B. B., & Ochs, E. (Eds.). (1986). *Language socialization across cultures.* Cambridge: Cambridge University Press.

Silverman, D., & Torode, B. (1980). *The material world: Some theories of language and its limits.* London: Routledge & Kegan Paul.

SOU. (1972). *Förskolan del 1. Betänkande avgivet av 1968 års barnstugeutredning.* Stockholm: Liber/Allmänna Förlaget. SOU1972:26.

Strong, P. M. (1988). Minor courtesies and macro structures. In P. D. Wootton & A. Wootton (Eds.), *Erving Goffman: Exploring the interaction order* (pp. 228-249). Cambridge: Polity Press.

CHAPTER SIX

Contextualizing Social Control: An Ethnomethodological Analysis of Parental Accounts of Discipline Interactions

DIANE T. PRUSANK

The main thesis of this chapter is that the discourse acts in which parents describe discipline interactions are actually accounts of those episodes. From an ethnomethodological perspective, parents' use of accounting procedures can be taken to shed light on the methods and practices parents use to make sense of their own (and their children's) behavior within discipline episodes. An analysis of such accounts further serves to explicate several assumptions parents make about their children and about the appearance of social order. An understanding of the features to which parents attend in the discipline situation illuminates the processes through which the discourse of a discipline interaction is co-constructed. This chapter begins with a brief critique of the mainstream research on discipline and social control. Subsequently, it is argued that a reconceptualization of discipline, from an ethnomethodological perspective, brings to the forefront some of what is glossed in the more conventional forms of research. Within this argument an exploratory analysis of parental accounts of discipline interactions is presented. The chapter concludes with a discussion of the implications for research on the discourse of discipline across the lifespan.

Conventional Perspectives on the Study of Discipline

There are essentially two influential lines of research regarding discipline and social control. One line focuses on the strategies parents use to change, modify, adjust, or influence the behavior of their children. Much of this research is consistent with Baumrind's (1967) conceptualization of parental control: "those parental acts that are intended to shape the child's goal-oriented activity, modify his expression of dependent, aggressive and playful behavior and promote internalization of parent standards" (p. 54). The goal of this line of research is to determine the relationship between such parental strategies for control and the outcomes produced, for example, on the child's level of aggressiveness or dependency (e.g., Steinmetz, 1979). The vast majority of this research is conducted via survey methods, where parents are put in hypothetical situations and asked to check off the strategy they would use to discipline the child (e.g., Abelman, 1985). In some cases parents are allowed to provide an open-ended response to the vignette, but in these cases the responses are coded according to a parental style category scheme that generally encompasses permissive, authoritative, and authoritarian styles (e.g., Carter & Welch, 1981).

The second influential line of research also focuses on parental strategies for control (e.g., Bernstein, 1974). However, the goal of this line of research is geared toward an understanding of the linguistic choices parents make in constructing the discipline strategies they use and how these choices are linked to the ordering of social classes. More specifically, these researchers examine the link between a family's relationship to and position within both the larger culture and the immediate community, the linguistic choices and controlling strategies the parents use, and the resultant transmission of culture to the child. This research is generally conducted through face-to-face interviews with the parents, asking them to respond orally to hypothetical regulative situations. The parents' responses are then coded with regard to whether the language choices are universalistic or particularistic, restricted or elaborated, and whether the regulative strategy itself is positional or person-centered.

Although these two lines of research have rather different goals in mind, they use similar techniques to generate data and consequently share some similar assumptions about the nature of discipline interactions. First, because both lines generate data by placing parents in hypothetical situations, there is the underlying assumption that all parents will see the same situations (i.e., the same child behaviors) as warranting discipline or control. Second, because these generic hypotheticals are contextually void both at the micro and macro levels, there appears to be an underlying assumption that the specific context of the discipline interaction is irrelevant to the parent's choice in strategy and the production of the discourse that ensues. For example, at the micro level (i.e., the lock-step sequencing of the utterances produced within the interaction), any parent will attest to the fact that children rarely comply after the parent's first utterance that demands a behavioral change. Yet these conventional forms of research ignore the possibility of a child's reaction to discipline strategies and thus negate the child's investment and subsequent behavior in coconstructing the discourse of social control. At a macro level (i.e., the position of a given episode in the lives of the participants), such research presents discipline episodes as isolated events that are cognitively, emotionally, and behaviorally disconnected from past and future discourse. A simple example comes from the hypothetical situation where the parent is asked to respond to the following: "Suppose (name of child) lied to you? How would you respond?" (Abelman, 1985, pp. 136-137)—is this the first time the child has lied—or has the child exhibited a pattern of lying behaviors?

It becomes evident then that these conventional lines of research fail to capture or even to mimic the complexity of discipline interactions in the methods they use to generate data. Consequently, it is not surprising that this literature tells us little if anything about the phenomenological experience of discipline from either the parents' or the child's perspective. The remainder of this chapter argues that such information can be at least partially derived from participants' recounting of (and thus "accounting" for) these episodes and further that a better understanding of how participants experience discipline episodes will bring to the surface the complexity of the processes involved in the production of discourse at both the macro and micro levels of the discipline context.

Discipline in an Ethnomethodological Framework

Garfinkel (1967) states that "ethnomethodological studies analyze everyday activities as members' methods for making those same activities visibly-rational-and-reportable-for-all-practical purposes, i.e., 'accountable,' as organizations of commonplace everyday activities" (p. vii). From the ethnomethodological perspective, the activities of daily life (generally perceived as mundane) are cast in the light of accomplishments. In studying how everyday activities are accomplished, ethnomethodologists focus on the fundamental practices and bases of commonsense knowledge that actors utilize to both accomplish the order of social structures and in so doing, display their competencies as members of the given culture. Thus, from the ethnomethodological perspective, all activity is ordered in some explainable manner—that is, explainable from the perspective of the participants.

So what researchers may view as "problematic" interactions or encounters, specifically the discipline interaction in this case, contain their own order in that they are accountable and in fact, accounted for. It is the case, then, that even though the participants themselves (i.e., parents and children) see the discipline activity as ordered, and function in a manner to order the event, the behaviors of the child are viewed by the parent, and at times others in the context, as a breach in social structures for which the parent, as a competent member of the parenting community, is responsible. However, parents are not only accountable as parents (i.e., responsible for the child's behavior) they are accountable as any other member of the community for the practices they use in the activity, that is, how and why they behave in the activity is accountable.

That the activity of discipline is seen as accountable (and perhaps necessary to account for) is demonstrated through the data discussed in this chapter. Parents of children between the ages of 3 and 5 years were contacted for the study through day-care centers, mother's day-out programs, and snowball sampling. The data contained in this chapter were obtained through open-ended questionnaires that asked individual parents to provide a written description of a recent typical discipline interaction in which they were the primary disciplinarian. The 37 subjects produced a total of 49 accounts. Specifically, 23 mothers produced 31 accounts and the 14 fathers produced 18 accounts.[1]

What parents actually provided on the open-ended questionnaires were accounts of the discipline interactions in that their "descriptions" contained unsolicited motives, rationales, justifications, special circumstances, and so forth, for the described behaviors. The analysis of accounts is of particular concern in ethnomethodology because its proponents contend that "what counts as social reality itself is managed, maintained, and acted upon through the medium of ordinary description" (Heritage, 1984, p. 137) and further, that "storytelling organizes the perceptual world by making observable and understandable the patterns of collective life and the individual activities which contribute to those patterns" (Wieder, 1977, p. 4). Thus looking at the discipline interaction from an ethnomethodological perspective allows us to view the information provided by parents' accounts as insights into either what parents believe they were doing/accomplishing in the activity and the proposed motives behind those behaviors— or at least what parents believe to be visibly rational behaviors and motives behind behaviors. In either case (i.e., whether we can access what parents actually believe or what they believe others would find acceptable), the accounts demonstrate what issues parents orient to in regard to the discipline interaction.

Retrospective-Prospective Views

Several interpretative procedures form the basis through which competent members of the culture accomplish everyday activities. One is the use of retrospective-prospective views. A retrospective-prospective view suggests that we base our interpretations of any current interaction on past interactions, while leaving a given interpretation open for adjustment contingent upon future interactions as well. That parents orient to the retrospective-prospective view is evident in their accounts as they point to the fact that certain behaviors have been disciplined in prior interactions, or at least warned against. For example, in explaining a discipline sequence that ensued as a child attempted to leave the house after he had wet his pants, the father writes:

[1] We have been battling the wet pants problem for some time and we were all frustrated.

Or take the case where a father explains disciplining his son for irritating his sisters in a wading pool. In describing the event, the father notes:

[2] He was pinching and scratching them—which has been warned against repeatedly.

In these excerpts we see that as parents provide accounts, that is, make visible the rationality of the episode, they point to the macro context as an essential feature of the organization of the social structure. Thus in Excerpt 1 for example, the father makes sense of (and simultaneously makes sensible) the frustration and behaviors within this episode by virtue of the previous interactions labeled here as "battles." These excerpts also demonstrate the parents' attempts to make themselves visibly competent members of the parenting community. As their accounts point to interpreting current actions via past episodes, parents highlight that they have "warned" their children or "discussed" such issues with them, thus qualifying the child's behavior as sanctionable.

As stated previously, conventional research in discipline has ignored the macro context of issue or behavior repetition. Yet parents' accounts of discipline interactions suggest that this feature is one of importance for them as they order the discipline episode. It becomes evident, then, that discipline episodes are not perceived by participants as isolated or disconnected events. If it is the case that parents interpret the present discipline episode in light of previous occurrences of similar events, then it is reasonable to assume that the discourse that arises is constructed on the basis of the retrospective-prospective view. It is suggested then that the discourse that ensues through the repetition of a problem behavior is fundamentally different from the discourse that arises out of a first-time offense. In the case of the repeated problem, parents may now interpret the behavior as "more" problematic than before, they may perceive that previous discipline strategies were ineffective, and/or they may perceive the child as intentionally violating explicit rules. Furthermore, the child is put in a dubious position if he or she also connects the events (i.e., the child recognizes that this behavior has been disciplined before) in that it becomes incumbent upon the child not only to defend the specific behavior, but also to defend the behavior in the light of "knowing better" or "having been warned" not to perform such a behavior.

This discussion concerning the use of the retrospective-prospective view is somewhat constrained by the methods for data collection in that parents were asked to provide information labeled as "discipline" interactions. Garfinkel's (1967) discussion of agreements and the et cetera clause points to the feature of agreements whereby in current states we reassess the agreement:

> The et cetera clause provides for the certainty that unknown conditions are at every hand in terms of which an agreement, as of any particular moment, can be retrospectively reread to find out in light of present practical circumstances what the agreement "really" consisted of "in the first place" and "all along." (p. 74)

In asking parents for information concerning "discipline" interactions, the instructions contain an implicit directive for information that concerns behaviors defined by parents as breaches of agreements. Consequently, the data set reveals few cases in which the et cetera clause is invoked to reread the agreement in such a fashion that the child's behavior is interpreted as in line with the agreement by virtue of special circumstances.

However, the issue that arises from this discussion is important—that is the issue of "what is disciplined" or "disciplinable." Take the following account for example:

[3] My son kept asking me to buy different toys, but I said no, we were only looking (we had discussed this before entering the store). Finally, he found something he *really* wanted and said he'd be my friend if I bought it. (I said he should be my friend anyway—he's

always my friend.) Then he said he *wouldn't* be my friend if I wouldn't buy it for him. I said that made me sad. I said he should ask for it for his birthday. Then he started crying and screaming for it. I told him we'd have to leave the mall if he couldn't stop. He kept it up and we left the mall.

From this account, we may speculate on the use of the et cetera clause as it functioned within the agreement made prior to entering the mall, which required the child to restrain from asking to be bought items. The account seems to indicate that within the agreement, it is acceptable for the child to *request* the purchase of an item, as the mother attempts to have a rationale discussion with the child via his requests. However, persistent *demands* for an item appears to constitute the actual breach of the agreement as defined by the parent (i.e., it is at this point that the child is sanctioned for the behavior). Or take the following case where a child has gotten out of bed once and been sent back, and then arrives in the living room for the second time:

[4] This time I told him in no uncertain terms to go back to bed and not to get up again or he would be spanked hard. He went back to his bedroom and did not come out again, although from the sounds it was clear he did not necessarily stay in bed.

In this case, although the agreement appears to be "don't get out of bed or you will be spanked," the father, himself, points out the fact that the child did not stay in bed, yet was not spanked for this seeming breach of agreement. It appears then that the sanctionable behavior in this case is leaving the bedroom, not getting out of bed. Thus in the case of both Excerpts 3 and 4, the initial agreements between the parents and children are reread as the sequences progress. Children are not disciplined, in these cases, for performing the behaviors they were warned against, but instead disciplined for some variation on that behavior.

It is suggested here, then, that the et cetera clause might usefully be used as an analytic concept by discipline scholars to ferret out just what parents and children view as disciplinable behavior. In focusing not just on those behaviors that are disciplined, but those behaviors that are not disciplined as they stand in contrast to parent/child agreements (e.g., Excerpt 4) may lend further insight into what discipline interactions are all about. To do so, scholars must focus on the discourse that produces the agreement as well as the discourse that surrounds the circumstances in which the agreement is and is not invoked.

The Corpus of Commonsense Knowledge

The above discussion concerning the retrospective-prospective views and the et cetera clause begins to highlight what appears to be an important feature of the parents' accounts—that is, what parents believe their children know. At the center of ethnomethodological theory is the "corpus of commonsense knowledge." The corpus of commonsense knowledge encompasses "what everyone knows" about the practical actions of everyday life. Garfinkel (1967) refers to such knowledge as the "socially-sanctioned-facts-of-life-in-society-that-any-bonafide-member-of-the-society-knows" (p. 76). Such knowledge is treated by members as shared and taken for granted, and so the display of its use through action constitutes certification as a competent member. Garfinkel's (1967) breaching experiments attest to the strength of response members display when these socially sanctionable facts of life are violated, that is, when members' actions display a lack of, what is assumed to be a shared basis of, commonsense knowledge. It is interesting to note an *analogous* issue that arises in the parents' accounts of discipline interactions. Excerpts 1-3 as well as the following exemplify how parents make reference to what they believe their children know. In Excerpt 5, the mother allowed each child to take one toy with them on their trip to the post office. As she describes the argument that ensues she notes:

[5] It turned out that my three year old son had a stuffed animal which they both know was given to my daughter.

In the following excerpt, the mother describes her failed attempts to get her son to take a bath, she notes then that she began to count aloud and writes:

[6] he knew that if I counted to three before he responded I would spank.

And in an account that describes how a mother made her child clean up the paint she and her friend had spilled on the carpet, the mother refers to what her daughter "knows" very clearly:

[7] she knew paint on the floor was unacceptable.

From these excerpts we see, first, that in making sense of the discipline interactions, parents make assumptions about what knowledge their children hold and, second, that these statements display an assumption that children will/should use this knowledge. Consequently, such statements within parents' accounts function to make visible the rational nature of the parent's own disciplining behavior. To see how this is so, one may simply imagine how irrational the parent may appear if the opposite were true—that is, if the child did not "know better," if he or she had no information that would help them to see that such an action was not acceptable. In essence then, these statements within parents' accounts of discipline interactions suggest that the existence of such a knowledge base within the child is sufficient grounds to make behavior to the contrary a disciplinable action. In essence, parents make reference to "what everyone knows" in the modified version of "what my child knows."

Once again we begin to see how the discipline process may be a much more complex event than is suggested within conventional research. Specifically, conventional research in discipline ignores what it is the parents believe that the child "knows" about particular actions. More importantly, by ignoring this feature of the interaction, we also escape the issue of "what is being disciplined." When parents use "what they believe their children know" as a way to interpret the child's behavior, we must question whether the child is being disciplined for performing the actual known unacceptable behavior (e.g., painting on the floor) or if instead, the child is being disciplined for not behaving in accordance with what he or she knows. As Heritage (1984) states, "constitutive expectancies of the attitude of everyday life are treated by mundane actors as profoundly normative, and morally sanctionable, matters" (p. 101). In painting on the floor, the child not only creates the "mess" of paint on the floor, but the child also behaves in a manner incongruent with his or her knowledge base, that is, he or she displays incompetence.

Finally, by performing an action that one "knows better" than to do, the child creates a scene for which the parent must make some sense. Here is an example of how one parent made sensible the incongruity between what the child reportedly knew and how the child reportedly behaved:

[8] Her attitude was a happy one, enjoying being defiant.

It appears that this parent has made sense of the child's behavior by interpreting it as intentionally violating or ignoring what she knows. Given that parents orient to such features of the child's behavior and knowledge within their sense making of these episodes, we may suggest that the resultant discipline in this type of encounter may then stem from: (1) the disturbance caused by the actual behavior; (2) the child's seeming unwillingness to utilize what he or she knows to be socially sanctionable facts; and/or (3) displaying intentional defiance or disregard for parental authority.

The complexity of discipline interactions becomes more relevant as we look at the layers of issues parents point to in their accounts of these interactions. As we begin to see the many possible rationales for disciplinary action made visible through these accounts, the question of what is being disciplined comes to the forefront. Furthermore, questions arise as to whether the parents themselves are cognizant, as they proceed through such interactions, of exactly which behavior at which point in time they are attempting to change or modify. And the same problem is of course applicable to the child from a different perspective. It would certainly be of interest to gain some insight into how the children in such interactions would make sense of these events— particularly in regard to what they believe they are being disciplined for—if it is even the case that they see the same issues as relevant to making sense of the scene. One way to uncover what it is that children believe they are being disciplined for is to analyze the arguments they construct as they attempt to refute their parents' moves to discipline them within such episodes. That children do, in fact, participate actively in co-constructing these episodes comes to light in the following section.

Reconstituting the Scene

Up to this point, the analysis of parents' accounts has focused on the methods parents use to make sense of their children's behaviors that supposedly initiate or provoke the initiation of the discipline episode. That children's behavior and discourse continue beyond their initial behaviors is an equally important feature of the episode, a feature glossed by more conventional studies of discipline. Such a gloss is most likely grounded in the belief that children have little or no power by virtue of their role relationships with parents. This belief is naive given that each utterance in the sequence (regardless of the supposed "power" held by its producer) functions to reconstitute the scene, that is, "actions reflexively and accountably redetermine the features of the scene in which they occur" (Heritage, 1984, p. 107).

Heritage's (1984, pp. 106-108) discussion and explication of initial greetings serve as an example of the importance of each actor's action within any given sequence. This example begins with two parties, who are mutually disengaged as they pass through a hallway. At the moment that one of the actor's offers a greeting to the other, the scene is immediately reconstituted, whereby an offer is made for mutual engagement. The second actor then is placed in a situation of choice. If the second actor reciprocates the greeting, the scene is transformed from a proposal for mutual engagement to an acknowledgment and ratification of the proposal. Thus the scene is now altered in a particular direction toward mutual engagement. If the actor does not reciprocate the greeting, the scene is also reconstituted by this action, and as Heritage (1984) points out, "although a circumstance of mutual disengagement may well ensue from such action, it will not be the 'same' circumstance of mutual disengagement as existed prior to the first greeting" (p. 107). It is the case then that any action within the sequence reflexively acts upon that scene, in that "the unfolding scene . . . cannot 'mark time' or 'stall' for a while; it will unavoidably be transformed" (p. 107).

Parents' accounts of discipline interactions do highlight how children reconstitute the scene as is demonstrated in the following excerpt where the mother finds that her daughter has drawn on the wall:

[9] I immediately blew up as she had done this with crayon once before. She got defensive and said that her little sister had done it. I told her that it wasn't possible because her sister couldn't write yet, and the drawings had the alphabet on them. She knew she was caught in her lie, and I explained how lying was very bad. I also told her that this time she was to clean every bit of it . . .

This excerpt is typical of many accounts where parents suggest that once confronted by the parent, children make choices in the sequence that are not in their best interests with regard to punishment. In lying about the drawing, the child reconstitutes the scene in such a manner that the trouble is compounded. As demonstrated by the mother's account, *two* disciplinable behaviors are now reportably visible in the scene. The data for this study indicate that tantrum-like behaviors have a similar effect, as suggested in the next excerpt. Here the account begins with the father explaining that he was attempting to get his children to clean up their toys. When they refuse, he promises them a story if they comply. The two children begin to fight:

[10] They got louder and louder so I yelled at them to get their attention. My oldest daughter ran in her room crying and screaming. After getting on to her for screaming and running in her room I told her if she didn't straighten up that I wouldn't read her a book.

Again we see in Excerpt 10 that the child's contributions to the interaction are visibly reportable and thus reflexively reconstitute the scene. The child here is "gotten onto" for the tantrum-like behavior and further threatened with the deprivation of a story for "not straightening up." When confronted with the discourse of discipline, whether through a threat, an explanation for the need for a change of behavior, a demand for different action, the child is placed in a situation of choice. And whether the child chooses to comply, to ignore, to refuse, to throw a tantrum, to lie, or to defend, *that action* will redefine the scene and thus place the parent in a new situation of choice, and so on. Thus it is as important to understand and analyze the child's contribution to the construction of the discourse in process, as it is to understand and analyze the parents' contributions.

Several important points arise from this issue. First and foremost is that discipline interactions, like all other forms of discourse, are inherently coordinated events. Each party has choices to make in regard to what actions he or she will take, and each party must make sense of the unfolding scene in process, to do so. That parents orient to the "here-and-now" of these interactions is best exemplified by the note one mother wrote on her husband's description sheet:

[11] My husband said he was not filling out this because he thinks this is not right because you can't predict how a child will act when disciplined at certain times. There is no way to tell what will happen when they are disciplined at a particular time.

Second, in focusing on how parents make sense of these types of interactions as unfolding scenes, the importance of the micro level of context is highlighted and the notion that parents have one particular style of disciplining begins to lose ground. As parents attempt to order the events of discipline interactions, their parenting strategies are reported as varied and contingent upon the contributions of the child both within the micro-level sequencing of a particular episode as well as within the macro-level context of previous similar events. It is not uncommon to find within these accounts parents reporting that their initial strategies for dealing with a discipline behavior would be classified by conventional discipline scholars as "love-oriented positive" techniques, like reasoning with the child, only to find that the final strategy the parent reported would be classified in the same category scheme as "love-oriented negative" or "power assertive" techniques, such as ignoring the child or hitting the child.

Finally, although the parents in Excerpts 9 and 10 through their reports make visible the differences in how they dealt with specific behaviors in the interaction (e.g., telling how lying was bad and making the child clean the drawing off the wall), in some cases it is not clear which behavior within the sequence is being disciplined.

> [12]   The other afternoon my son was chasing his 10 month old sister in the living room trying to take off her diaper—he had his friend and sister over and I believe he was showing off. He proceeded to get the job done. I grabbed him and spanked his bottom and put him in his room. I did this because I have repeatedly told him not to do that. He just laughed and of course so did his friends making him continue with his actions—putting him in his room made him mad he screamed— . . . he knows its not a funny matter with me. We have an understanding!

In this account, the mother makes visible a variety of the child's behaviors that may be deemed as disciplinable, the least of which is his chasing his sister around. In addition, he attempts to and accomplishes showing off, laughing with his friends about his defiance and violating an understanding with his mother.[2] Again we are faced with the question of exactly what is being disciplined in these cases, and furthermore, whether either the parent or child even contemplates such issues.

Competent Parenting

As has been noted throughout this chapter the issue of what is disciplined and disciplinable has not been resolved by analyzing parents' accounts of discipline interactions—rather this exploratory analysis simply served to point to this *as an issue*. What we can glean from accounts is that in making visible and reportable (i.e., making sense of) the discipline interactions in which they participate, parents invoke the breaking of rules, agreements, and understandings as rationales for disciplining their children as well as orienting to how "what their children know" often stands in contrast to what their children do, and how children's behaviors reconstitute and further complicate the scene in calling for further or different disciplinary actions. In essence they provide the methods by which parents may account, and thus provide evidence, for their competence as members of the parenting community.

From the analysis contained in this chapter, then, the list of disciplinable behaviors provided by parents would include: (1)

when a child repeats a behavior that has been disciplined before; (2) when a child breaks an agreement made with a parent; (3) when a child does the opposite of what he or she knows better than to do; (4) when a child disturbs the discipline sequence in some manner, and the list could go on. The important point is that this is a list of accounting methods, rather than a list of rules to follow when disciplining. Though parents themselves may contend that the above is a list of "rules" that guide competent parenting behaviors, the above explication of these accounts pointed to the fact that they confused rather than made clear exactly what the child was being disciplined for, that is, which disciplining rule was being invoked. This confusion arose first because, more often than not, parents pointed to several of these "rules for disciplining" within any given account. Second, the analysis indicates that these "rules" are not always invoked immediately in the sequence; some breaches are left unattended until parents are further provoked. This should not be surprising. It has been argued elsewhere that "rule-governed" or "rule-compelled" behavior is simply not possible because it is *impossible* to know, *and* to know in conjunction with another, all of the contingencies under which rules may or may not apply in any given situation (e.g., Garfinkel, 1967; Heritage, 1984; Weider, 1974).

The action of invoking a rule, then, serves as a frame by which members interpret the behaviors that surround them—whether those behaviors are interpreted as being in accord with the rule or as a deviation from the rule. It is argued, then, that parents' use of invoking the breaking of rules, agreements, and so forth, is used within the accounts to provide the reader (or hearer) of such accounts with a framework to interpret the child's behavior as warranting discipline. And once this interpretive template is placed on the child's behavior, the parent's behavior in response to the child further constitutes the episode as a discipline interaction; and finally, the framework functions to stand as support for the parents' competence in an "episode of this type." Thus the utility of the production of any of the items on the aforementioned list within an account and/or within an interaction lies in the reflexive nature of the action itself.

It is interesting to note that although parents' accounting practices highlight the "rules" for what is disciplinable, less frequently found are "rules" for the types of actions to take with the child, that is, what "discipline techniques" to use. When parents did attend to this feature of the account, the information they provided reflected the popular media's influence on parenting. For example, after providing a specific account of an interaction, one father attached a separate sheet on which he wrote a step-by-step plan for discipline. The procedure laid out by this father might be labeled the "enlightened parent's model" for disciplining where what the parent goes through, with the child, is akin to the rational model of decision making:

[13] 1. explain the problem
      2. identify the causes
      3. offer your help
      4. ask for their help
      5. agree on specific solution
      6. set follow-up date
      7. make sure you follow up!

When other parents did comment on specific techniques, these comments appeared as caveats about using physical punishment with children, as noted in the excerpts below:

[14] I talked to him while changing his clothes and then swatted his (about twice softly) bottom and told him to go sit on the couch.

[15] Then I grabbed the toy away . . . and swatted him once (softly) on the butt. He cried a phoney cry but I could tell he knew he was wrong.

[16] I don't like to spank, but I do resort to it at times.

In Excerpt 14, the caveat put in parentheses by the parent, and placed in her written text just above "his bottom" seems to indicate that in reading her own account, the mother felt the need to qualify the action of striking the child—as if it did not read how she had intended for it to appear. In Excerpt 15, the father attests to the weakness of his swatting behavior, not only by noting in parentheses that it was done softly, but by also accounting for the child's crying as "phoney." And in Excerpt 16, the mother indicates her own unwillingness to physically punish the child. These excerpts along with other similar accounts contained in the data appear to be written in the context of the current state of our culture, which not only places a stigma on parents who use physical punishment, but is also very much in tune with the problems and implications of child abuse. These caveats then serve to demonstrate that despite the use of physical punishment, these parents' actions are, nonetheless and for all practical purposes, in line with culture specific perspectives on "competent parenting." Again the production of these caveats, as with the production of the "reasons" for disciplining, provide methods by which parents make their own behaviors visibly sensible and rational.

Studying the Discourse of Discipline Across the Lifespan

Although this chapter does not provide definitive statements about how discourse functions in the discipline context across the lifespan, it does provide a series of issues for research. First, in studying discipline interactions, researchers must begin to focus on how parents use the above explicated "rules" for what is disciplinable within these interactions. That parents point to these features is evident in their accounts, but how they are utilized in the sequence of the interaction is not known. Even more to the heart of the matter may be an analysis of when these "rules" are and are not produced in discourse, as well as how they are produced. Accordingly, a focus on how each action in utterance in the sequence reconstitutes the scene is imperative. Both parents and children are put in the "situation of choice" with each interlocking utterance and the choices they make have serious consequences for each participant simultaneously. Such analyses of discourse will tell us a great deal about what both parents and children see as a disciplinable behavior, especially if we focus on interactions that are successfully reconstituted as "nondiscipline" interactions, as well as those that are reconstituted at each utterance as a discipline interaction. Such an analysis will also tell us much about how parents and children use discourse in action, as ways of making sense of the episode.

That the discourse that surrounds and creates discipline inter-actions will change over the lifespan should be self-evident. As suggested earlier, the discourse that evolves in a situation where the child has committed a repeat offense must be fundamentally different from the discourse in the first offense situation, if for no other reason than that the parent may now choose to point to the child's previous behavior as part of the current scene. But beyond these incidences that may occur within months of each other, cer-tainly as years pass, the discourse may change. It is easy enough to point to the fact that as children age they are more cognitively prepared to reconstitute the scene in many new ways, and thus the discourse they produce will present more of a challenge for the parent. And equally obvious is the point that these "children as adults" will increase in their capacity to perform more serious offenses than asking for toys in the mall.

In addition, I would argue that the feature "what my child knows" becomes even more central as children age, and this so for several reasons. First, as children age, parents become less and less responsible for their child's behavior. In fact, when parents invoke the "what my child knows" rule, we may be seeing the beginnings of how parents distance themselves from "parental responsibil-ity" and simultaneously make their child accountable. It should not be surprising to find parents increasingly abdicating respon-sibility for the child's behavior, and consequently for disciplining it, as children move through adolescence. Parents are also relieved of this responsibility to some degree at this point because their children are now disciplinable by a variety of people including teachers, school administrators, and the police. And thus the responsibility for *discipline* is encompassed by a wider net that may be better cast as *social control*.

It is here that "what my child knows" becomes even more imperative. Performing a behavior that the child should know better than to do is punished much differently when performed by an adult. Take the simple example of a 4-year-old child putting a candy bar in her pocket. If the cashier notices, it will likely be laughed off by both the parent and the cashier, and perhaps later the child will be punished by having a privilege taken away or perhaps a spanking. An adolescent would be treated differently, the cashier would not laugh-off the event, nor are the child's parents likely simply to spank the adolescent as punishment. And later we realize that bona fide shoplifting by a full-fledged adult is, of course, punishable by law, not by a spanking. Or take the case of the boy who kept trying to pull his sister's diaper down. One might well imagine the punishment that may ensue for an adult with the same fetish—this same act is now treatable as a form of molestation, an illegal act. What changes as children become adults is not only "what they know" but *how* they are to know these things—they are to know them differently as they age. And simultaneously, acts that stand in contrast to what we assume children know are accountably punishable through the invocation and interpretation of rules, whereas many acts that stand in contrast to what adults know are accountably punishable through the invocation and interpretation of laws. Thus the ultimate contrast in the discourse that evolves in discipline interactions over the lifespan may be the contrast between the parent disciplining the child for stuffing the candy bar in her pocket and the full-fledged adult in court for shoplifting. Though the initial disciplinable action is virtually the same, the behaviors are interpreted differently by virtue of the template placed over them to account for, or make sense of, the action. Although these cases represent the extremes of the continuum, they also indicate that much happens in between.

And finally, it must be noted that as the lifespan of parents and children reaches the point where the parents are elderly and children are actually adult children, the participants find themselves in a reversal of roles regarding who is disciplining whom. That is, adult children find themselves in the position of "disciplining" their parents. Though it is unlikely that such discourse is peppered with the same types of threats used on children regarding taking away privileges such as television time or spanking, we might speculate that the discourse does encompass issues regarding what the elderly parent knows (e.g., that particular medications must be taken at certain intervals). And ironically enough, elderly parents may attempt to reconstitute the scene by invoking their age as evidence that they know better/more than the adult/child. Such interactions may be further complicated by the health of the elderly parent, a condition that may serve as the basis for invoking the et cetera clause on a given day (i.e., agreements made with elderly parents may be reread on the days when the elderly parent is not feeling well, or being forgetful). In any case, an analysis of the discourse produced by elderly parents and their adult children should reveal the special circumstances that render these interactions different than those produced at earlier stages in the lifespan.

Conclusion

"With all the interest quite naturally focused on what the actors substantively report, empirical researchers have only intermittently had occasion to reflect on what the actors might be accomplishing in and through their acts of reporting" (Heritage, 1984, p. 138). The work presented in this chapter suggests that such an analysis provides a starting point for a better understanding of what it is that researchers are viewing when they witness discipline interactions. The methods parents used to make sense of their own and their children's behaviors are features of the practice of accounting. The practice of accounting (i.e., making action visibly understandable), however, is not a practice that occurs only when one is asked to do so—the practice of accounting is a visible feature of all actions in progress and thus of all discourse as it is co-constructed. Consequently, researchers in the area of discipline should find greater insights into such interactions by focusing on how parents and children co-construct accounts of the interactions they are in, as these interactions are unfolding.

Notes

1. The data discussed in this chapter were collected in conjunction with a larger study on discipline. Consequently, within the data collection process, some subjects were asked to provide two accounts of discipline interactions while others were asked to provide only one, thus the discrepancy between the total number of subjects and the total number of accounts produced. It should also be noted that because the data were obtained in written form, the punctuation contained in the excerpts comes directly from the parents' writing with the exception of ellipses used by the author to abbreviate an account.

2. Excerpt 12 is particularly interesting in that within the account the mother points specifically to the public nature of the interaction (i.e., that there are witnesses) and further that the child has managed to engage the witnesses in behaviors that support the child's defiance. It may be argued that face-saving issues come to the forefront in these contexts. A rather complex problem arises in these public situations in that the parent must display competence in gaining the child's compliance, yet the publicness of such events may restrict the use of "socially inappropriate" strategies such as hitting or screaming at the child.

References

Abelman, R. (1985). Styles of disciplinary practices as a mediator of children's learning from prosocial television portrayals. *Child Study Journal, 15,* 131-145.

Baumrind, D. (1967). Child care practices anteceding three patterns of preschool behavior. *Genetic Psychology Monographs, 75,* 43-88.

Bernstein, B. (1974). *Class, codes and control* (2nd ed.). New York: Schocken Books.

Carter, D., & Welch, D. (1981). Parenting styles and children's behavior. *Family Relations, 30,* 191-195.

Garfinkel, H. (1967). *Studies in ethnomethodology.* Englewood Cliffs, NJ: Prentice-Hall.

Heritage, J. (1984). *Garfinkel and ethnomethodology.* Cambridge: Polity Press.

Steinmetz, S. K. (1979). Disciplinary techniques and their relationship to aggressiveness, dependency, and conscience. In W. Burr, R. Hill, & R. I. Nyes (Eds.), *Contemporary theories about the family* (Vol. 1). New York: Free Press.

Weider, D. L. (1974). *Language and social reality.* The Hague, The Netherlands: Mouton.

Weider, D. L. (1977). Ethnomethodology and ethnosociology. *Mid-American Review of Sociology, 2,* 1-18.

CHAPTER SEVEN

Transitions Through the Student Career

ANN Q. STATON

An important dimension of lifespan development occurs within the realm of schooling in American society. Being a student is a requirement, indeed a legal mandate, for most young people in the United States between the ages of 7 and 16 (Calvert, 1975). This 9-year period is generally agreed upon as encompassing the years of "childhood" and "adolescence," two major developmental phases in the lifespan. In reality, the majority of young Americans begin formal schooling at age 5; many others attend school well beyond the age of 16, moving from "high school adolescents" to "young adults" enrolled in a college or university. Still others continue on to a graduate or professional school. Finally, a growing number of adults over the age of 25 enter or re-enter higher education each year, either at the community college, college, or university level.

Being a student is the full-time career of all young Americans for some 9 to 12 years. It is the "job" of young people to attend school. Out-of-school activities (e.g., socializing with friends, pursuing hobbies) may actually be more desired and more important to the students than classroom learning, but it is the role of student that is considered the full-time occupation of young people. At the outset, the student career ("studentship") is a forced one; that is, young children are not given a choice about entry. Although parents may allow their children some voice in determining the school to attend, it is the state that dictates attendance. In later years, the decision to attend school may be a voluntary one by students, but for the early years it is not.

"Studentship," although a full-time occupation during at least the years of 7 to 16, is but a temporary career. It is well within the norm for a person to begin school at age 5 and emerge at age 30 with an advanced degree in hand. It is not unusual for a person to have a career as a "student" for as long as 25 years. Despite the potential longevity of the career and the fact that it occurs over the lifespan, however, it is never a permanent one. That is, nobody remains a student forever. The career of being a student is not an end in itself, but is a means to achieve another goal(s). It is a pathway, a road map, to another, more permanent career.

As one begins to examine the student career—as enacted by children, by adolescents, by adults—it becomes readily apparent that "studentship" is not a static career, but an ever-changing one. The role of student changes as young people progress through the school system, and these differences are due, in no small measure, to age-related development in students themselves. As children mature in age and progress through the student career, the role changes. To be a student as a child is different than being a student as an adolescent or as an adult.

In providing an understanding of the student career and the student role across the lifespan, this chapter focuses on communication:

> the process by which people attempt to negotiate shared meanings, thereby validating their perceptions. It is a process of interpretation which begins when people assign meaning to the behavior of others and seek to make sense of their environments. At a fundamental level, communication is the process by which people create shared understandings with others in society through symbolic activity. (Staton, 1990, p. 11)

It is through communication that children construct their initial student role, learn about it, and make sense of it. As they interact with an array of others (e.g., classmates, teachers, administrators, parents), the student role is formulated, developed, negotiated, and altered.

The theoretical framework that guides the examination of communication during the student career is that of "status passages." This concept was derived from the seminal work of Arnold van Gennep

(1960) in his *Rites of Passage*. Movement through the student career is not considered a series of life crises, however, but a series of status passages. Building upon the concept of passages, Glaser and Strauss (1971) discuss age-linked statuses. When extended to the arena of schooling, the status passages can be depicted as follows: As young people grow older and mature from childhood to adolescence to adulthood, they progress from elementary to middle to high school to a college or university. As they move through the various levels of schooling, they "pass through" a series of different student statuses. The transitions and passages to a new status are the focus of this chapter.

An understanding of the changing student career is provided through a communication perspective. Four transition points during the career, with distinct student roles, are examined:

1. becoming an elementary school student (compliant child),
2. becoming a middle school student (developing adolescent),
3. becoming a high school student (maturing adolescent), and
4. becoming a university student (independent young adult).

These roles were derived from analyses of communication data collected by the author and two co-researchers.[1] Data included: (a) interviews with students regarding their perspectives about their new student status, (b) written responses by students to open-ended questions about what it means to them to be in the new student role, (c) observations of students and teachers in school environments (e.g., classrooms, lunchrooms, playgrounds), and (d) interviews with teachers regarding their perspectives about the changing role of their students. Data were collected in schools in the Pacific Northwest region of the United States over a period of several years, always during the Autumn term as students were embarking on a new student status.[2]

Becoming an Elementary School Student: Compliant Child

Although there is not complete uniformity, most elementary schools in America begin with kindergarten and end with the fifth or sixth grade (Spodek, 1986). Kindergarten can be considered the start of the student career for youngsters, with passage into subsequent grade levels constituting changes in status. Data drawn from a case study of one class of kindergartners (at a private, parochial school) indicated the conceptualization of elementary school students as *compliant children*. At the elementary school level, the role of student is clearly one of learner; young children have to learn to be students and also to learn content (Mehan, 1980). The notion of compliant learner centers around the belief of the classroom teacher that because of their young age, elementary school children need to be compliant in order to learn. Responses from interviews with kindergartners indicated elementary students as compliant learners in both academic and social domains. Kindergartners were asked, "What does it mean to be a kindergartner?"

Academic Domain. The academic dimension of being a kindergartner includes such activities as learning, studying, working, doing homework, writing numbers, counting, and writing in workbooks. As one girl commented: "[Kindergartners] do homework and stuff. Learning little letters. And they start learning how to read. And they probably make designs and cut out things."

The kindergartners had a clear sense of the teacher as the authority figure who was in charge of their academic learning. Regarding academics, students responded with comments such as "[The teacher says] raise your hand if you don't know what to do." "She helps us read." "She helps me draw." "She teaches me." "When we ask her questions, she listens." "She helps me do things when I'm stuck." "She reads us books." "Go ask her [if we don't understand]." "Listen to the teacher." When asked what they would do if they did not understand their work, only rarely did students comment that they would ask another student for help or would just continue to try to get it on their own. It was consistently the teacher who was the focal point of their attention and classwork.

Social domain. The social dimension includes such activities as "playing outside," "going outside for recess," "talking to my friend about going to [her] house," "talking to my friends about if they want to play a game or if they want to swing," "going on field trips and having fun," and "sing[ing] songs and watch[ing] movies sometimes." Similar to their views about the teacher as academic authority, the children also considered the teacher as the one who gave them social privileges: "[The teacher] lets us have snacks. Lets us play on the playground." "She tells us to go outside."

To Be a Good Kindergartner Is to Be Compliant. When asked what it takes to be a good kindergartner and to provide advice to a hypothetical newcomer, the children responded with comments indicating compliance: "Be a good listener." "Be quiet when you take a nap." "[I would] tell her the rules." "Don't be bad—only be good." "Do a lot of work." "Be nice." "Know the rules." "To know how to try and work hard, to follow the rules, do what Mrs. _ says. Be very, very, very good." "Know that you have to be good." "Don't break rules." "Know the house rules." "Be good and do what the teacher says." "Listen to rules, follow instructions, do what teacher says." "To be good." "Be good." "The rules." "To be nice so she wouldn't have to go to the principal." "To be a good girl." Taken in conjunction, these responses are suggestive of children who had internalized, at least on a surface level, the importance of obedience for success in the classroom.

Teacher as Authority Figure Who Demands Compliance. When the kindergartners were asked who was the boss in the classroom, all 20 responded that the teacher was. When asked why they do what the teacher tells them to do, responses were of two types:

1. fear of punishment: "I don't want to get in trouble." "You might get a hit on your bottom." "I might have to sit in the corner or something." "Get in big trouble—[she] might call your name." "Maybe we go sit in time out." "Sit in the closet." "Because I don't want to get a spanking." "I might be sent home." "I [would] have to go to the principal or miss my recess." "So I don't get my name on the board." "She'll put us by the wall."
2. acknowledgment of teacher as the authority: "Cause she's the teacher." "Because she's our teacher and she's supposed to tell people what to do." "Cause she's the grown-up." "So you don't do it wrong." "Cause she wants us to." "Cause we're not the teacher." "Because we need to be good."

Only 1 of 20 children indicated compliance because of a positive reinforcer: "Cause we get a listening award."

Compliance Learned Through Classroom Discourse. Children learned the expectations for conformist behavior and constructed their own roles as compliant learners as they interacted with others in the classroom. Classroom observations indicated that the teacher encouraged and fostered compliance in four ways: establishing herself as the authority, issuing imperatives, giving rewards, and sanctioning students. First, the teacher maintained herself as the authority figure by: (a) referring to herself in the third person (e.g., "Ms. Lane wants you to get out your crayons and close your box."), and (b) reminding the class that she was the person in charge (e.g., "Who's the boss around here?"). A second strategy for encouraging pupil compliance was that of giving directives to students, related to: content, procedures, social norms, and restriction of their verbal and nonverbal activity. Third, the teacher rewarded students for their compliant behavior, thus seeking to reinforce and extend it. She rewarded the kindergartners by: (a) giving compliments (e.g., "Nice job."), (b) encouraging self-rewards (e.g., "Pat yourself on the back."), (c) distributing concrete rewards (e.g., "Those who remembered may come up and get a sticker."), and (d) offering privileges (e.g., "Edward, you may be the first to get a drink of water."). Finally, the teacher sanctioned students for instances of non-compliant behavior by: (a) reprimanding verbally (e.g., "Cut out the chatter."), (b) calling students back (e.g., "Angie, get out of the line and go back to your seat. . . . "), (c) withdrawing privileges (e.g., "You will not get to see the movie with the rest of the class if you continue to talk."), and (d) threatening public humiliation (e.g., "If you cannot get your work done without disturbing your neighbor, I will have to put your name [on the chalkboard].).

Children also learned compliance through interactions with one another. Two major categories were evident from classroom observations: child reprimands and child imitations. The category of child reprimands included instances in which one child overtly reprimanded the behavior of another, either verbally ("John, put your box away,") or nonverbally (pushing, shoving, giving dirty looks). The category of child imitation included instances in which one child imitated directly the behavior of another in order to help her or him complete a work-related task.

Kindergarten as Passage Into Elementary School Student Status. Considered as a passage into elementary school student status, entry of these children into kindergarten can be characterized as: a *regular, scheduled* occurrence, *central* to the children and *desirable* to them; a *collective* passage with full *awareness* of its occurrence and explicit *communication* about it; and occurring with a certain degree of *formality*, a particular set of rituals, and *clarity in the signs of the passage.* Becoming a kindergartner is an inevitable prospect for most children, and when interviewed about their desire to attend kindergarten, 19 of the 20 children in this case study indicated genuine enthusiasm. Children make the passage to kindergarten as a group, not in isolation. Observations in the classroom and on the school grounds indicated considerable explicit talk about being new kindergartners (e.g., classroom discourse about needing to establish rules because the students were new), as well as structural and procedural devices to mark the transition to kindergarten (e.g., being dismissed early during the first week of school, lining up and being formally escorted into the school building by the teacher each morning, being segregated from the older students at recess). For this group of children, kindergarten was a clearly marked passage to elementary school and the role of compliant student was the one articulated and emphasized by the school.

Becoming a Middle School Student: Developing Adolescent

Middle schools in American society were instituted to serve as gateways for the passage from elementary school to high school (Noblit, 1987). The middle school years are generally designated as those encompassing sixth, seventh, and eighth grades. In some school systems, the classification is that of junior high school and incorporates only seventh and eighth grades. Data drawn from interviews with approximately 100 sixth graders suggested the characterization of middle schoolers as *developing adolescents.* In the discourse of both students and teachers, the distinction between being a child and being an adolescent was directly addressed and discussed. The conceptualization of developing adolescent emerged from the perspectives of teachers (and the students themselves) that these sixth graders were merely embarking on adolescence, but had not yet reached it fully. Responses from interviews with sixth graders suggested middle schoolers as developing adolescents in academic and status domains. They were asked, "What does it mean to be a middle school student?"

Academic Domain. The academic dimension of the role of middle school student centered around the increased difficulty of school work and homework: "Means you're gonna have to do a lot more work than elementary school." "It feels great to be learning new things." "Feels like I'm getting smarter every day. You learn more." "With all the tests it's hectic; have a big LA [Language Arts] test today." "Going to different classes. Having projects in science." "Have more responsibility . . . more homework. I have to be organized." "You have to work harder, study more, have to be a good listener, a good student. . . . You learn more, better skills, you listen. It's a little bit hard." "You have six classes . . . and in elementary school we had one grade and one class." "There's a lot less time to do things. You have to rush wherever you go. You have to really pay attention cause the teachers don't repeat." The sixth graders emphasized the importance of the more difficult school work and their own responsibility for accomplishing it.

Status Domain. The status dimension of the role of middle school student centered around the age-related change in their conceptions of themselves. They were aware of a new status as adolescents, distinct and superior to that of elementary school children, yet inferior to that of the older middle-schoolers.

A number of their responses to what it means to be a middle school student emphasized development, change, and maturity: "Means that I've moved up from elementary." "It kinda means like I'm growing up, kind of like a birthday. It reminds me that you're growing up. It's mixed." "Means I've grown up more, can take more responsibility. Makes me feel that people can trust me more." "Better than elementary, not ruled by the teachers." "Big. In elementary school they pushed me around." "Pretty special—I been waiting all my life for middle school. It feels like I'm really high in my education. I've come a long way." "You're grown up, not a kid anymore. You're a kid still but you're grown up." "Done with elementary school and gonna be in high school in a couple years. [Feels] nice, fun." "Kind of more independent." "It means that I'm closer to high school—kind of in between." "Means that I'm kinda grown up; people don't treat you like a baby no more. It's fun." These comments suggest a positive view of being a middle schooler.

Still other responses indicated a sense of being "at the bottom." As sixth graders, these students had surpassed elementary school children, but were the youngest in the middle school: "Gotta be older, but still the youngest person in the school." "Feels scary at the beginning—gonna be big kids who would beat you up." "It's hard because I came from fifth grade being the oldest and here I'm the youngest." "I feel kind of down because . . . I'm the youngest again, have to start all over." "You're a puny little sixth grader— the seventh and eighth graders are older, boss you around." "Going from oldest to youngest feels strange." These responses suggest a view of being a new middle schooler that focuses on a lower rather than a higher status.

Strategies for Making the Passage to the New Status of Middle School Student. As indicated by classroom observations and interviews, sixth graders engaged in various strategies to gain needed information to make sense of middle school and construct their student role. These included: asking direct questions (of teachers, classmates, and siblings in the school), getting to know others (trying to make friends, conversing with those seated nearby, being nice to teachers), being indirect (using indirect questions to check one's progress against that of others without overtly asked the teacher), testing limits (challenging or violating known rules in order to discover their limits), and observing the behavior of others (watching classmates who are accepted and noting what they wear, how they act). Some of these strategies involved face-to-face verbal communication (e.g., asking questions, getting to know others, being direct, and testing limits). The strategy of observation, however, is indirect and requires no discourse.

Sixth Grade as Passage Into Middle School Student Status. Entry into sixth grade marks the passage into middle school, characterized as: *inevitable, regular, scheduled,* generally *desirable, central, accompanied by explicit signs, formal, occurring within a collective,* and accompanied by *awareness of the collective* and *communication with others* during the passage. Administrators in both middle schools accorded the new status of developing adolescents to the sixth grade students. This was acknowledged formally in the discourse during the orientation session for new sixth graders. Contrasts between elementary and middle schoolers were articulated, including positive changes (e.g., more privileges such as a combination lock on one's locker, selecting one's own coursework) and potentially negative ones (e.g., the capability of now committing "adult" crimes such as larceny, assault, and battery in contrast to such "childish" offenses as chewing gum). In addition, the notion of developing adolescents was also stressed by discussion in orientation of the students' changing bodies.

As a way of acknowledging and affirming the collective, teachers continually referred to these students as "new sixth graders." Several special assemblies were held only for the sixth graders. In addition, structural arrangements (e.g., having all of the sixth grade lockers on one hallway, having all of the sixth grade homerooms in close proximity) served to reinforce the sixth grade collective and facilitate communication among the students. And, finally, as a way of fostering the transition to being middle schoolers, not just sixth graders, both schools held combined gym classes for sixth, seventh, and eighth graders.

Becoming a High School Student: Maturing Adolescent

For many American youngsters, the high school experience is the culmination of the student career. In 1989, for example, 40% of high school graduates did not continue on to a college or university (Office of Educational Research and Improvement, 1991). The high school years typically encompass ninth, tenth, eleventh, and twelfth grades, referred to respectively as: the freshman, sophomore, junior, and senior years. Data drawn from written responses of some 750 ninth graders to open-ended questionnaires suggested the characterization of high school freshmen as *maturing adolescents*. In the written discourse of these students, they characterized themselves as more mature, more responsible, and more serious as high school students than they were as middle schoolers. At the same time, however, they expressed a tension between the overall increased responsibility and maturity of being in high school with the situation of still being the youngest in high school, as freshmen. In responding to the question, "What does it mean to be a high school freshman?", two of the predominant categories of comments were that of the academic domain and the status domain.

Academic Domain. The academic dimension of the role of high school freshman focused on an awareness that as mature freshmen there were increased expectations and greater demands for academic performance. Student comments included: "So I can study more works and learn more things." "I worry about the work that the teacher gives." "High school gives too much complex homework and too many new things you don't understand." "It means I must work harder at my old school assignments because it will count on my record." "I feel it's more important to get good grades here because now they really count." "The final part of my free education! I'm trying to do my best scholastic[al]ly. It means I must do my best to achieve my goals!" "You have to be serious about your school work." In the views of these students, this academic experience of high school was more important than work during previous years of schooling.

Status Domain. The status dimension of the role of high school freshman had both positive and negative elements for the students. The positive aspect was related to the maturity involved in being a high school student: "Means that I'm almost grown up and being a freshman is helping me get started." "I'm a year older and have more freedom." "I feel a little maturer and more smarter." "It means that I have more responsibilities now and a few more years until I go on my own." "Means I'm grown up and people expect me to be responsible." "Means I'm not a kid any more." "I'm glad to be getting older and getting more rights and responsibilities." "Means I started a new grade level and more independence." "It means that I am a newcomer to this school and from now until I'm a senior I get a chance to participate in most school activities and I get a chance to say how this school should be run. It makes me think that I am more mature and I'm getting ready for the real world." "I think it's a great feeling looking down on others because you're at the top and they are still climbing." "That I'm getting older and more mature and I have to take on more responsibility." "It means that we are now ready to be treated like responsible people." "The time where you are more serious and looking forward to the big time." "It feels RAD because you're in a high school and it feels good and I'm proud to be a freshman."

There were, however, some negative aspects associated with the role, namely that of being the youngest in the school: "Means that you get thrown in garbage cans and given swirlies." "Starting over at the bottom." "You have older guys pick on you." "It stinks. I'm tired of the other classmen yelling, 'freshmen.' It drives me nuts." "Means being treated bad cuz we're the baby beavers. It also means that older kids can pick on us." "It means being on the low rung again." "It's terrible because people look down on us. If the upperclassmen could just accept us as people it would be easy." "It means the bottom." "Being in high school is a killer but being a freshman sucks." "It means being at the bottom of the pile."

Function of Communication in Making the Passage to the New Status of High School Student. As a way of determining their perspectives about the function of communication in their transition to the role of high school student, freshmen were asked several additional questions about: the importance of communication in helping them adjust to high school, the people who had been most helpful to them, their sense of belonging, and what helped them to feel a part of the school. From their viewpoint, communication served two primary functions: informative and integrative. Through general communication strategies such as asking questions, talking with teachers and other students, as well as listening to others, students learned about school regulations, procedures, and academics (i.e., informative function). Communication that functioned to integrate students international the role of high school student served to meet their emotional needs (i.e., moral support) as well as to facilitate their making friends and gaining a sense of belonging. Five strategies for making friends emerged from analysis of their responses: participating in school activities, being interpersonal, being myself, being introduced by common friends, and impression management.

Ninth Grade as Passage into High School Student Status. The passage to the status of high school student had characteristics similar to the passage to middle schooler: *regular, scheduled, inevitable, formal, accompanied by clear signs, central,* generally *desirable,* experienced as a *collective* with *conscious awareness of the collective,* and *communication* among those in the collective. All of the high schools observed had formal orientation sessions during which time the school administrators referred to the newcomers as "the freshman class," as a way of highlighting the collective. The emphasis of the orientation programs was on academics and not on social aspects. This was an acknowledgment by the administrators that these students were mature adolescents and that the high school experience was "the real thing" in terms of the importance of grades and what was learned. This was in contrast to the consideration of elementary and middle school as being preparatory learning experiences. Also in keeping with the view of mature adolescents, the freshmen were accorded more freedom and greater autonomy than they had experienced previously throughout their schooling (e.g., permitted to smoke on the school grounds, leave the school premises at lunchtime).

Becoming a University Student: Independent Young Adult

The college/university years constitute what is known in American society as "higher education." This form of education is not mandatory and, indeed, is not available free of charge to most students (exceptions, of course, being those students who receive scholarships). Although not compulsory, there are large numbers of students attending colleges and universities. In 1988, for example, there were some 11.3 million undergraduates enrolled in institutes of higher education in the United States (National Center for Education Statistics, 1990).

Data drawn from written responses of approximately 150 freshmen (at a large, state-supported university) to open-ended questionnaires suggested the characterization of university freshmen as *independent young adults*. In response to the question, "What does it mean to you to be a college/university freshman?", a predominant theme was that of independence with a new sense of responsibility, choice, and accountability: "It means you're having your own responsibility. You're out on your own and making choices that affect your later life. Only you are responsible for your actions like going to class, studying, and joining in activities." "It means self-discipline and independence." "To be an adult and independent. To find a way of life by myself." "It means a beginning of adulthood, a new start." "It means that my life is changing and the change is bringing maturity, independence, and knowledge of how to survive on my own." "I'll learn how to live, become totally independent, to survive in such a big, fast world." "It means I am finally an adult and for all practical purposes, the master of my own destiny." "This is the start of my real life, independent of anyone. I make or break this one myself." "Academic challenge combined with complete responsibility and independence." "Self-reliance and responsibility." "I am here to gain knowledge and finalize the process of living independently in the financial sense." "This is the start of my real life, independent of anyone. I make or break this one myself."

For some, the sense of independence was referred to specifically as independence from parental authority: "It means having the chance to become my own person through the choices that I will make. By being independent of my parents at this period in my life, I will have [the] opportunity to make either right or wrong choices, with the knowledge that it was a result of my own decision." "I notice it's time for me to be an adult and take over for myself (instead of my parents taking over)."

Function of Communication in Making the Passage to the New Status of University Student. To determine the views of new university freshmen about the function of communication in their transition to the new student status, they were asked to: "Please describe how important you think communicating with other people has been in helping you adjust to the university." From their perspectives, communication was vitally important in the transition process and was the means by which they received both needed information (informative function) and emotional support (integrative function).

The freshmen were adamant that communication was of critical importance in their transition: "Communication is the only way I will survive here." "Without communication I would not be sitting here—it's vital in any sort of day to day life." "Very important to feel comfortable in new situations." "Communication is the key to survival at the university." "Communication with other people is one of the key tools to help in adjusting to the university." "I would say this [communication] is the most important thing in helping my adjustment." "It [communication] has been the only thing that really matters, it is very important. Without it I could not adjust and would not be here." "Communication with others is very helpful in adjusting to the University, even if it is just a 'hello' or 'how are you doing?' "

More specifically, communication was the means by which they gained the information they needed: "Very important! I have needed important questions answered." "Communication is the key. . . . It is up to you to get the information you need to know, i.e., when intramurals start, where classes are, and what extracurricular activities there are." "I know my way around campus much better and I know what the campus has to offer and what the U-district has to offer by *asking* people and *reading* about things." "Communication is important. Like when we have floor meetings or when one talks to their RAs. They give great advice." "It has been really helpful to have people who tell you right at the start, 'If you have any questions, just ask,' and they mean it sincerely." "Talking to my friend and brother, who are already out of college, also helps. They give me hints on 'how to survive.' " "To ask them about a class, or what I need to do, or what class should I choose."

Communication also served an integrative function, that is, providing the means by which they gained emotional support: "It [communication] helps me feel more at home with what I do and less intimidated by the whole thing." "When people walk by you and smile and say 'hi' it makes you feel like you belong." "I think communication has been very important. For example, talking to other freshmen helps to reassure you that you aren't the only scared, confused person on campus." "You can't make friends very easily without talking to people and friends make my life here much more comfortable." "I think communication is very important because when you talk to other students you get emotional support by knowing that they are in the same basic situation you are in." "We need the communication to know we are not alone." "I think talking to a person with the same situation you are in makes me much more comfortable."

Freshman Year as Passage Into University Student Status. Similar to the passages to elementary, middle, and high school, the passage to the status of university student is characterized by *formal mechanisms, clear signs of passage, centrality, desirability,* and *existence of a collective.* Unlike the previous passages, however, the transition to university student is not necessarily accompanied by awareness of the collective and built-in mechanisms for communication among those in the collective. Although new freshmen at a university do constitute a distinct group and all are aware of the existence of the collective, freshmen are isolated as a group only rarely. This occurs during formal orientation and occasionally in intact classes for freshmen. For the most part, however, freshmen are not set apart structurally from university sophomores, juniors, or seniors. They are not usually segregated according to classes taken, activities engaged in, or living arrangements. Thus, although it certainly occurs, communication among members of "the freshman class" is not fostered by the institution. Instead of an emphasis on being a freshman, a sense of self as a university student and as an independent adult is encouraged.

Entry into a university can be considered an "ecological transition" (Bronfenbrenner, 1977, 1979). Although the kindergartners, sixth graders, and ninth graders discussed previously all entered a new school building as they made the transition to a new student status, the ecological transition for most freshmen university students is much greater than that for others. Upon leaving the familiar high school building and discarding the status of high school senior, the new freshman enters the inevitably larger university campus where she or he takes classes generally in an array of buildings. University students, unlike elementary, middle, or high school students, have almost complete freedom of movement throughout the campus. This is a change from the previous years of schooling in which students generally are monitored closely and restricted from coming and going at will.

Coupled with this type of ecological change is typically a change in place of residence (Johnson & Staton, 1990). Although some new freshmen continue to live at home when they enter a university, many change their residence to campus dormitories, fraternity or sorority houses, or their own apartments. Often, for the very first time, these students live apart from their parents and on their own.

The nature of these ecological transitions is salient vis-à-vis the changing student career and contributes, no doubt, to the freshmen feelings of independence and of being young adults instead of adolescents. As indicated in their discourse about what the new freshmen experience means to them, it is communication with an array of others that enables them to make sense of and negotiate the new environment and student role.

Conclusion

As indicated by the data reported in previous sections, the role of student changes continually over the career of "studentship." Evidence has been presented that elementary schoolers are characterized as compliant children, whereas middle schoolers and high schoolers are viewed as developing and maturing adolescents, and university students are considered independent young adults. Interestingly, the views young people express of themselves in the various student roles are remarkably consistent with the perspectives of teachers and administrators.

When the transitions from one student role to another are examined as status passages, there are some similarities across the student career. For the child and adolescent student roles of elementary, middle, and high schooler, entry into the new status is characterized as *regular, scheduled, central, generally desirable, inevitably, formal, and collective passage* with *awareness* of its occurrence, explicit *communication* about it, and *clarity in the signs of the passage*. The new role was articulated explicitly by teachers, administrators, and students, and was accompanied by structural and procedural devices within the schools to signify entry into the role.

Students were *aware* consciously of their new status, that they were part of a *collective,* and that *communication* with others was a vital aspect of their transition.

For the *adult* student role, the passage is neither routinely *regular nor inevitable.* Continuing in the student role as an adult (or taking it on after a lapse of time) is usually a voluntary decision. Perhaps the independence of the role can be attributed, in part, both to the older age of the students and to the role not being a required one. Similar to the passage to child and adolescent student roles, however, the transition to being a university student seems to be generally *desirable* and *formal.* And although there was a similar conscious *awareness* of the new status, an awareness that they were part of a *collective,* and an acknowledgment of the importance of *communication* in making the transition, there was less explicit communication about the freshman student body as a collective.

It seems clear, then, that the student role is a changing one across the lifespan from child to adolescent to adult. The career of "studentship" is a central one in American society that can be examined usefully as a series of status passages. Analysis of student and teacher discourse about the role is one way of illuminating the understanding of the career.

Notes

1. The author thanks Dee Oseroff-Varnell for assistance in collecting and analyzing data for the section on middle school students. These results are reported more fully in a coauthored chapter, "Becoming a Middle School Student," in A. Q. Staton, *Communication and student socialization* (Ablex, 1990). She also thanks Geri Johnson for assistance in analyzing data for the section on university students. These results are reported more fully in *Communication in the Socialization of New University Freshmen* (Staton & Johnson, 1989). The sections on kindergartners and high school freshmen are reported more fully in A. Q. Staton, *Communication and Student Socialization* (Ablex, 1990).

2. Readers should note that the number of students who participated in the studies varied across the student career. At the elementary school level, results were derived from a single case study of a kindergarten class in a private school. At the middle school level, interviews were conducted with approximately 100 sixth graders in two public schools. At the high school level, approximately 750 freshmen from four schools (three public and one private) responded to open-ended questionnaires. At

the university level, approximately 150 freshmen at a public institution responded to open-ended questionnaires.

References

Bronfenbrenner, U. (1977). Toward an experimental ecology of human development. *American Psychologist, 32,* 513-531.

Bronfenbrenner, U. (1979). *The ecology of human development.* Cambridge: Harvard University Press.

Calvert, B. (1975). *The role of the pupil.* London: Routledge & Kegan Paul.

Glaser, B. G., & Strauss, A. L. (1971). *Status passage.* Chicago: Aldine Atherton.

Johnson, G. M., & Staton, A. Q. (1990, November). *An ecological perspective on the transition of new university freshmen: A preliminary study.* Paper presented at the annual meeting of the Speech Communication Association, Chicago.

Mehan, H. (1980). The competent student. *Anthropology and Education Quarterly, 11,* 131-152.

National Center for Education Statistics. (1991). *Digest of educational statistics 1990.* Washington, DC: U.S. Department of Education, Office of Educational Research and Improvement.

Noblit, G. W. (1987). Ideological purity and variety in effective middle schools. In G. W. Noblit & W. T. Pink (Eds.), *Schooling in social context: Qualitative studies* (pp. 203-217). Norwood, NJ: Ablex.

Office of Educational Research and Improvement. (1991). *Youth indicators 1991: Trends in the well-being of American youth.* Washington, DC: U.S. Department of Education, Office of Educational Research and Improvement.

Spodek, B. (Ed.). (1986). *Today's kindergarten: Exploring the knowledge base, expanding the curriculum.* New York: Teachers College Press, Columbia University.

Staton, A. Q. (1990). *Communication and student socialization.* Norwood, NJ: Ablex.

Staton, A. Q., & Johnson, G. M. (1989, November). *Communication in the socialization of new university freshmen.* Paper presented at the annual meeting of the Speech Communication Association, San Francisco.

van Gennep, A. (1960). *Rites of passage* (M. B. Vizedon & G. L. Caffee, Trans.). Chicago: University of Chicago Press.

CHAPTER EIGHT

Making Connections:
Narrative as the Expression
of Continuity Between Generations
# of Grandparents and Grandchildren

VALERIE CRYER McKAY

What is a grandparent? They have a past of their own and a
future which belongs to everyone.
                                        Exley and Exley, 1990

To consider the telling of a story as a means of coming to understand one's life is to accept the importance of narrative as the
process by which this understanding might be achieved. Clearly,
to accept the notion of lifelong development it is necessary to take
into account not only the individual's present position in his or
her lifespan, but the past upon which both the present and future
are built (Huyck & Hoyer, 1982). Likewise, to examine the narrative phenomenon, one must also understand "the developmental
process of that communicative event" (Nussbaum, 1989, p. 3).
What part does the telling of one's life story play in the developmental process? What part does the relationship, in which the
story is shared, play as the individual approaches the reality of the
impermanence of human existence? What are the consequences if
the story is never told?

It is the purpose of this chapter to explore the possibility that, by sharing information and events with grandchildren (and ultimately developing a meaningful intergenerational relationship), grandparents achieve a sense of continuity in their own lives. Consistent with this view, continuity is realized by engaging in those strategies or activities for the purpose of maintaining and developing personal identity with, and understanding of, the past, present, and future. In addition to reviewing current literature in the areas of narrative, continuity, and the grandparent-grandchild relationship, this chapter illustrates the importance individually attached to achieving continuity—evidenced as grandparents recount stories of the past, contemplate the present, and speculate about their future and the future of their grandchildren.

Narrative and the Grandparent-Grandchild Relationship

Perhaps there is no communicative event as salient to the grandparent-grandchild relationship as narrative—the sharing of life stories, events, advice, or family history. The benefits intrinsic to this type of information exchange, for both grandparents and grandchildren, have been the focus of previous research. For example, Baranowski (1982) found that grandparents provide grandchildren with a source of identity development by sharing stories about the grandparents' past experiences and other accounts of family history. Moreover, grandparents achieve a sense of satisfaction knowing that ideas, beliefs, values, and memories shared with grandchildren are carried on into the future (Mead, 1974).

The individual who shares the story—the storyteller—also plays an integral part in both the characterization and content of the story told. This view is supported by Farrel (1984) who comments that the purpose or intent of narrative may be to delight, instruct, or move the listener—whether or not these objectives are achieved is largely dependent upon the character of the individual imparting the story. Within the context of the family, therefore, the role of grandparent as storyteller becomes particularly important for several reasons: They are often the oldest generation of family lineage (although great-grandparents are becoming an increasingly common family phenomenon); they are the bearers of family information about past generations, parents as children, and grandchildren as very young children; they can communicate information about their participation in historical events that is otherwise unavailable to grandchildren except in textbooks; and finally, they have collected a lifetime of experience and wisdom that can be passed on to future generations in the form of advice or lessons learned.

The grandparent-grandchild relationship is unique in that it can provide both generations with a link to the past, present, and future. Through intergenerational interaction, then, grandparents have the opportunity to achieve continuity, both in terms of understanding their own life experience and influencing the lives of their grandchildren, such that "in the presence of grandparent and grandchild, past and future merge into the present" (Mead, 1972, p. 282).

Why is it important for grandparents to tell their story? What happens if the story is never told? A review of research in the area of oral history, which clearly encompasses narrative activity, suggests that telling one's story in many ways satisfies higher order personal needs such as self-esteem or self-actualization. "Oral history provides a way of making concrete one's experiences and wisdom and of creating from them a heritage to hand down to one's family and communal heirs" (Baum, 1980, p. 49). "Oral history signifies their being included in the continuum of history" and thus offers the opportunity for the individual and his or her cohort group to achieve recognition for their participation in historical events (Baum, 1980, p. 51). Telling one's story offers the opportunity for interpretation and expression of one's experiences in order to further authenticate those events (Handler, 1987). Oral history has a cultural function as the means by which ideas/values are transmitted through conversation between generations (Ong, 1980). Recounting oral history provides the teller with the opportunity to interpret how a life event occurred (Ricoeur, 1977); and finally, narrative functions to bind together discrete events into a more understandable and interpretable whole (Goldberg, 1982).

These studies illustrate the personal and functional importance attached to conveying one's life experiences to others. Narrative, then, is the process by which individuals can verbally connect past experiences with the present and future, and at the same time achieve a degree of self-actualization in knowing that their life has meaning not only for themselves but for future generations.

In summary, the purpose or intent in telling the story, the content of stories shared (e.g., perceptions, past experiences, family history, participation in historical events), and the role of storyteller (e.g., grandparents) merge together as justification for examining the grandparent-grandchild relationship as a highly salient context in which to observe and interpret narrative. In this chapter, continuity is purported to be both the outcome of and motivation for narrative as a pattern of communication within this intergenerational relationship. What is continuity and how might it be evidenced by communication within the grandparent-grandchild relationship?

The Concept of Continuity

Continuity is conceptualized as both internally (psychologically) and externally (psychosocially) experienced. The latter results in feelings of security and comfort with one's environment. The former is more closely associated with psychological identity that is developed through the process of connecting past and present life events, and by which the present is reinforced by change and ongoing interaction with others. Continuity, then, is viewed as a healthy capacity to see inner change as connected to the individual's past and the sense of self-satisfaction achieved is relevant not only to that individual but others with whom he or she is associated (Atchley, 1989, p. 184). Likewise, internal and external continuity should not be viewed as distinct, but *complementary* aspects of individual continuity.

Atchley (1989) suggests that by reflecting upon life events, an individual comes better to understand his or her own existence. Moreover, the individual can utilize this "new" information for guidance in future endeavors or in advising the endeavors of others. In the process of telling their story, then, individuals are better able to contemplate the nature and course of life events that were most important in their lives—or those events that have particular meaning for them. Consistent with the lifespan perspective, then, continuity becomes an integral aspect of individual development; in coming to terms with the past, an individual is better prepared for the future. Moreover, although self-reflection is one way in which contemplation or retrospection can occur, verbal exchange of experiences with others provides the individuals with a sense of contentment knowing that their story is "passed on" and will become a part of the future—mitigating the pervasive fear of mortality. In this way, the grandparent-grandchild relationship functions as an agent for achieving continuity: *Internally* it offers the aging grandparent the opportunity to reconnect with the past by reevaluating and reinterpreting life experiences in retrospect, while *externally* providing an opportunity to contemplate the present and, by bonding with grandchildren, the future.

Consistent with this view, Coupland, Coupland, Giles, Henwood, and Weimann (1988) contend that a natural consequence of aging is the process of reducing uncertainty about one's participation in the course of life events. Their focus is upon painful self-disclosure (PSD) sequences as a functional form of personal discourse. Not surprisingly, Coupland et al. suggest that younger generations play an integral part in this process in terms of providing affective or relational support during disclosive sequences.

> Ageing individuals (and doubtless others, perhaps including the terminally ill) will be drawn to question their own life-positions, and employ social encounters (perhaps above all new encounters) as a forum for this appraisal. There will be prospective assessment, conjecture about what is left to endure or enjoy, and about the energy investment needed to pursue any future worthwhile goals. Retrospectively, the elderly are likely to review significant life-events, good and bad. (Coupland et al., 1988, p. 128)

Clearly, then, interaction with younger generations provides elders with the opportunity to exchange information about, and come to terms with, their lives. These opportunities become the window "through which individuals create coherent pictures of the past and link the past to a purposeful, integrated present" (Atchley, 1989, p. 187). In the empirical section of this chapter, my purpose is to explore aspects of continuity, both in grandparents' descriptions of their roles and relationships with grandchildren and in accounts of stories they have shared. Interviews with more than 100 grandparents were completed during the summer of 1990. These interviews were conducted by trained interviewers, tape-recorded, and transcribed.

Questions exploring grandparents' perceptions of their relationship with a selected grandchild, activities in which they engaged with that grandchild, topics shared/not shared in conversation, similarities and differences in personality, and perceptions of their role as grandparent were addressed. The only criterion for grandparents' selection of a grandchild was that the grandchild be 12 years of age or older as grandchildren were to be contacted for subsequent interviews. The age criterion for grandchildren was implemented based upon developmental research suggesting that children 12 years of age or older are better able to approach more formal operations in thinking (Piaget, 1954), and thus reflect upon relational elements of their interaction with grandparents (Kahana & Kahana, 1970). All of the interviews were scheduled in advance; grandparents were originally contacted through senior citizen activity centers, newsletters distributed in retirement communities, and minimum nursing care facilities.

Creating a Framework for the Analysis of Internal/External Continuity

Although a comprehensive framework for identifying aspects of continuity within grandparents' discourse has not yet been developed, an inductive analysis of text derived from grandparent interviews indicates that attributes consistent with the notion of internal/external continuity are central to grandparents' descriptions of their roles, relationships, and accounts of information exchanged with grandchildren. These attributes include: *reevaluation* (determining the reasons, motivations, intent, and/or consequences of actions taken), *reinterpretation* (determining new meaning for life events and the involvement of others), and *reflection* (reconstructing events, recounting memories) and were clearly illustrated. *Time frame* (past, present, future) emerged as process;

in other words, retrospection of the past resulted in contemplation about the present, and often, speculation for the future—especially in terms of *how* the information would be useful to grandchildren. The following examples illustrate the presence of these constructs interwoven within the text derived from grandparents' interviews.

Extract 1: George and Todd

In the first example, the focus of the disclosure is on George's grandson, Todd; yet, one key statement revealed that the information being conveyed was a reevaluation of George's own educational and occupational experiences as a young man.

> [Todd] hasn't yet focused on what to do for his living. He hasn't decided what branch or field of endeavor to earn a living. So he is working odd jobs. But he's going to have to get more schooling in. He graduated from high school, but he'll have to get more schooling or some trade or some profession which he enjoys. Otherwise life will be rough for him—*because if you don't like doing the type of work you are doing for a living you're not going to enjoy working.* I've talked to him about that. I told him the more education he gets, the more money he'll make, and the more credit he'll have. And it will be easier to make a living—he won't have to work as hard physically if he gets an education. It will be easier for him in the long run. He should choose something he likes to do.

This information had been exchanged with Todd with the hope that he would take full advantage of educational opportunities in order to secure his future career. In this way, George reinterpreted his inability to get an education as the motivating factor for Todd to continue his. George revealed that he had obtained what he perceived to be a less than adequate education; as a result, his work had been in a profession with which he was generally dissatisfied. This had had a profound effect upon George, who felt that one of the most important objectives in his relationship with Todd was to convey the importance of "getting an education," and, if necessary, to help finance Todd's college education in order that he be spared a similar fate.

Extract 2: Ralph and Casey

In a similar circumstance, Ralph expressed concern that his grandson "follow in [his] footsteps" and pursue the career of a doctor. In order to accomplish this, Ralph disclosed that,

> I'd like to have a good heart-to-heart talk with [Casey] about his future. He's at the place now where he's got to make up his mind if he's going to college, what kind of courses he's going to take . . . I'd like to talk to him about that and give him some advice; how he can make his personality be of some use to him in his life.

Ralph went on to say that in his "talk" with Casey, his objective would best be accomplished by recounting a story told to him by his father, and his grandfather before that—a lesson in life.

> There are certain things that have happened in my family that are important . . . well, with my parents. For instance my grandfather lived in Iowa and they passed a law that you could not shoot any deer. Because one of the fathers there had a bunch of deer and they got out, and they bred in the wild, and there were so many deer out there that they were eating all of the crops. Finally, they killed off the deer so much that there were hardly any left. And the state wanted to keep some of the deer around so they passed a law saying you couldn't shoot any so my grandfather went out, and found a deer eating out of his corn crib and shot him and killed him. He called the sheriff and said come and get me, I just killed a deer. Well, grandpa had a right to protect himself and his corn crib to keep his profit from the corn and to feed his animals with the corn. The deer was eating it and he couldn't get him away. He did what he thought was right. He turned himself in but they never prosecuted him for killing the deer. That story has been passed down through our family and it illustrates what kind of person he was, and I am, and I expect Casey to be. And if Casey knows something is right—he should do what is right.

In this example, a very meaningful aspect of family heritage is to be conveyed as a lesson in expectations for future endeavors. The story itself has meaning for Ralph, but more importantly, Ralph intends, by sharing this story, that Casey should understand something of the character of male members of the family.

Ralph perceived that his conveying this story to Casey was, perhaps, a grandfather's responsibility—accomplishing this task would provide Ralph with a sense of satisfaction that he had contributed something he knew about his own father's past to Casey's future.

Extract 3: Mary and Camber

Mary, Camber's grandma, spoke of her regret that she had never shared family information with her own grandmother—"ages ago." In reflecting upon this unfortunate circumstance, Mary stated that this had been a mistake and she did not intend to make the same error with her own granddaughter; thus, she had gone to great pains to secure the past for her granddaughter's future.

> As I look back on my grandmother I wish so much that I had sat and listened, but she died when I was 16 and she was quite old. The last time Camber was over she wanted to see some old photos so I showed her and talked to her about them. I share some things to try to give her some examples of how things work out so that she'll know that once I was young, too, and had some of the problems that she is having, and maybe how I handled those problems.

Mary also expressed her interest in passing on family genealogy; she had gone to a great deal of trouble to prepare a family history journal, along with a collection of personal effects belonging to her own parents.

> I have put together some genealogy books with family histories in them so she [Camber] has my mother's personal history and some personal things from her grandfather. It's important to give you continuity in belonging to this thread that goes on. You didn't just start here, but your genes go way back and with my own grandfather's journal I've come to know him; I just know all about him from what he wrote in his journal—I think that's very important.

Clearly, Mary was attempting to make Camber's past more concrete—not only by providing information about other family members, but by collecting personal artifacts from which Camber would better know and understand her family heritage. In addition, Mary has made careful attempts at establishing a trusting relationship with Camber in order that she be able to offer advice—based upon similar experiences—comfortably and confidently.

Extract 4: Betty and Cheryl

Our next illustration emerged from our interview with Betty, Cheryl's grandmother. Betty explained that it was very important for her to be there in her relationship with Cheryl. The reason for this became evident as we asked Betty about sharing her past experiences and family history with Cheryl.

> I didn't have any family to talk about. My mother and father left each other and I didn't have anyone, I had two sisters and a brother and still I was alone. I never talked about them to anybody. I was raised in a children's home. I was 17 years old before I saw my mother again; and I was married with three children before I saw my father because he went to Indian Territory. I don't know if my father wanted my mother to go with him, or if he just got up and went. I was 4 years old when we were all put into the children's home.

In Betty's case, her own past was somewhat uncertain. In reevaluating the absence of close family ties in her own life, and to spare Cheryl the same sadness she herself felt in not knowing her parents, Betty conveyed that she made efforts to talk about Cheryl's parents, and especially, her dad's childhood. In this way, Betty was able to provide family connections for Cheryl, even though her own were not well defined.

Extract 5: Helen and Sonya

Helen was an African-American grandmother well over 80 years of age. She shared many life experiences with us, emphasizing that the same stories were used as sources of inspiration for her granddaughter, Sonya. Helen shared one of the stories she often tells Sonya:

> Sometimes when I'm pressing her hair we talks about how hard it was for me growing up in Louisiana out in the cotton fields. That why I brought my children to California. I want her to finish her education and become someone. I tell stories so that she can learn

from them . . . I came to California in 1970. I brought four children to California and I couldn't bring all of them at one time. So when I got off that bus in '70 on the third day of January, I had three dollars, no way to lay my head I could call my own—living with my niece. You see a lot of people down the county, I don't because I took the money like I was supposed to. So in February I saved and sent for five more of my children. In June I got five more and we lived in two bedroom apartment. I had six girls in one room and six boys in the other and I slept downstairs in the living room. My babies didn't have a change of clothes—so you see how good the Lord has been (she points around to the house she now owns). The good Lord and the county and me—we did it. And just about all I own I earned.

Evidence from Helen's example supports the contention that grandparents use their own life experiences to influence, guide, and advise grandchildren in their own endeavors. The purpose in telling these stories ranged from inspirational to practical, yet, a close examination of *how* the stories were told suggests that Helen perceived "telling" as part of her family responsibility, her family role. In fulfilling this responsibility, then, Helen completed a connection between her own difficult yet rewarding past and Sonya's future.

Summary and Implications

The purpose of this chapter has been to explore the possibility that, by sharing information about family and life experiences with grandchildren, grandparents achieve a sense of continuity in their own lives. At the beginning of the chapter, three questions were posed: the implications drawn from the data presented suggests answers to them.

First, what part does the telling of one's life story play in the developmental process? People appear to draw on their past as a means of (1) making decisions about the future, (2) establishing a sense of integrity regarding their own past, and (3) using this information as the basis for accepting the role of *guide* in their grandchildren's lives. Intrinsic to this perspective, then, is the recognition that, first, people reevaluate, reinterpret, and reflect upon the past, and, second, recognize the importance in *communicating* newly found insight to younger generations. Substantial research advocates that narrative is one form of communication by which people come to know themselves and the part they have played in their own life story. Narrative is characterized by (1) conscious intent for conveying the story, (2) purpose, and (3) a need to share. Furthermore, the storyteller plays an active and creative part in the story being told; grandparents play an integral part in the creation of family culture by telling their story and the stories of others in the presence of younger generations. In this way, grandparents also come to understand their own lives by passing on their memories, life experiences, and ultimately, advice to younger generations.

Second, what part does the relationship in which the life story is shared play as the individual approaches the reality of the impermanence of human existence? Implicit in the conceptualization of continuity is the recognition of human mortality: We need to know that we will live on in the minds of others, and this is accomplished by creating our own memorable moments as we share stories of the past with significant others. The grandparent-grandchild relationship has unique potential in this regard.

Finally, what are the consequences when the story is never told? The reality exists that some grandparents rarely or never experience the consequences of rewarding interaction with grandchildren. Fortunately, however, even among grandparents who comment that geographical distance is a factor resulting in infrequent visits with grandchildren, the bonds between them appear to transcend any obstacles. Does this mean that continuity is always achieved? Although the answer to this question is beyond the scope of this chapter, the importance in achieving continuity is perhaps best illustrated in the following passage:

> There is a lot that I know. I think it is important to tell. I think it is important for somebody to know. There is going to be a lot of things when I die that are going to be lost forever and nobody is going to know unless I tell them . . . I have to tell them. (Fa's granddad)

References

Atchley, R. C. (1989). A continuity theory of normal aging. *The Gerontologist, 2,* 183-190.

Baranowski, M. D. (1982). Grandparent-adolescent relations: Beyond the nuclear family. *Adolescence, 17,* 375-384.

Baum, W. (1980). Therapeutic value of oral history. *International Journal of Aging and Human Development, 2,* 49-53.

Coupland, N., Coupland, J., Giles, H., Henwood, K., & Weimann, J. (1988). Elderly self-disclosure: Interactional and group issues. *Language and Communication, 8,* 109-133.

Exley, R., & Exley, H. (1990). *Grandmas and grandpas.* Great Britain: Exley Publications Ltd.

Farrell, T. B. (1984). Narrative in natural discourse: On communication and rhetoric. *Journal of Communication, 34,* 109-127.

Goldberg, M. (1982). *Theology and narrative.* Nashville, TN: Parthenon Press.

Handler, R. (1987). Overpowered by realism: Living history and the stimulation of the past. *Journal of American Folklore,* pp. 337-341.

Huyck, M. H., & Hoyer, W. J. (1982). *Adult development and aging.* Belmont, CA: Wadsworth.

Kahana, B., & Kahana, E. (1970). Grandparenthood from the perspective of the developing grandchild. *Developmental Psychology, 3,* 98-105.

Mead, M. (1972). *Blackberry winter.* New York: William Morrow.

Mead, M. (1974). Grandparents as educators. *Teachers College Record, 76,* 240-249.

Nussbaum, J. F. (1989). Introduction. In J. F. Nussbaum (Ed.), *Life-span communication: Normative processes* (pp. 1-4). Hillsdale, NJ: Lawrence Erlbaum.

Ong, W. J. (1980). Literacy and orality in our times. *Journal of Communication, 30,* 197-204.

Piaget, J. (1954). *The construction of reality in the child.* New York: Basic Books.

Ricoeur, P. (1977). The model of the text: Meaningful action considered as text. In F. R. Dallmayr & T. A. McCarthy (Eds.), *Understanding and social inquiry* (pp. 316-334). Notre Dame, IN: University of Notre Dame Press.

SECTION III

Discourse and Intergenerational Relationships

The four chapters in this third section all address social relationships across the lifespan. The first two relate to mother-daughter relationships. The second two are concerned with marriage and couple relationships. Each, however, is a unique blend of theoretical and empirical priorities.

Henwood and Coughlan establish their theoretical base very carefully; it lies at the intersection of feminist, developmental, and social constructivist concerns. From this position, they undertake a richly detailed review of diverse literatures on family relationships, then specifically mother-daughter relationships. They point out how it is often difficult to assess the semantic and relational values of commonly used terms such as *conflict, attention,* and *interest* that often function as interpretive primes in these studies. For this reason, they devote their empirical efforts here to deconstructing how "closeness" and "intergenerational solidarity" are in practice constructed in the discourse of mothers and daughters themselves, "from the perspective of women's lives." A range of metaphorical resources to do with closeness is indeed important for women's construals of their mother-daughter relationships, though these resources are employed to express a wide range of more and less favored relational dimensions.

In Cicirelli's chapter, the main concern is the ethical dilemma potentially associated with decision making when a family member is very elderly and very frail. Cicirelli starts with a retrospective on lifespan theory, sharply pointing to some important distinctions within this field (lifespan psychology versus lifespan developmental psychology; aging psychology as different from these in turn). His own conception is of the individual confronting and engaging with multilevel environmental forces to construct momentary life-relevant events—reminiscent, then, of Giddens's and Shotter's approaches as we considered them in the Introduction. However, Cicirelli goes on to argue that the beginning and end of the lifespan need to be represented differently from mid-life, as periods when the individual is relatively "separable in time and space from the environment" and operating in a relatively "closed system." He therefore wishes to qualify the social constructivist perspective, in claiming that, in late old age, the reduced quality of interaction leads to "a predetermined direction of aging."

Controversial as this sounds, Cicirelli is concerned here with typically post-85-year-old individuals, and he is right to point out that evidence has accumulated that there is a much-reduced communicative environment for many people in very late life. Cicirelli then produces data showing how "paternalistic" initiatives are increasingly associated with decision making for frail elderly family members, and he highlights the moral issues that this raises.

Sillars and Zietlow ask what the typical ways are in which couple relationships change as they age. A fascinating question for the theme of this volume is whether couples in some respects take on a *joint* identity over time. Because they are looking for trend data, Sillars and Zietlow first provide statistical analyses of questionnaire responses. Evidence suggests that what they call an increasing "we-ness" is indeed experienced in longer relationships, which tend to be more passive but more satisfying and tend to show less conflict. Then, in a more textually based thematic study of couples' conversations, they show how, for example, retired couples often focus more on shared activities, beliefs, and interests rather than on the projection of two complementary individual identities.

Wilmot and Hocker's approach to couples discourse is from the perspective of *intervention*. As analysts and practitioners in this area, they discuss how couples often make their relationships meaningful to each other through myths and metaphors of various sorts. And it is through the reshaping of these myths and metaphors that some of the most successful interventions can be achieved by third parties. For example, couples can have divergent images of "who they are" together and separately. Introducing candidate metaphorical definitions for a couple's own consideration, or facilitating metaphor shifts, can open up new possibilities for relational healing and growth.

These last two chapters lead the interpretation of lifespan identity away from the individualistic conception that has tended to dominate past theorizing. Understanding collaborative processes of identity formation and change is an important challenge for future research, consistent with Shotter's earlier insistence that "the primary human reality is face-to-face conversation."

CHAPTER NINE

The Construction of "Closeness" in Mother-Daughter Relationships Across the Lifespan

KAREN HENWOOD

GERALDINE COUGHLAN

Until fairly recently the implications of motherhood and daughter-hood for women's identities and relationships had been paid relatively little attention in human or social science research. Pioneering attempts to reflect on the experience and institution of motherhood and the mother-daughter bond relied heavily on their representation in literature, art, and personal biography to augment information from medicine, history, anthropology, and psychology (see, e.g., Friday, 1977; Rich, 1976). Many probable explanations for this situation come to mind, including the general exclusion or neglect of women and "women's issues" from social science prior to the mobilization of feminist opinion in the 1960s and 1970s.

The identification of an androcentric bias in research has fueled a good deal of criticism of the human or social sciences within feminist circles. One persistent argument has been that women should be "added in" as practicing scientists and research participants, and by extending the range of topics of inquiry to include those that are of particular concern to women. Because a major concern here is with eradicating unwanted sources of distortion or bias from the research process, this idea is wholly consistent with the view that social scientists should imitate the natural sciences by seeking to establish the objective, universal laws of human behavior through controlled experimentation (Harding, 1987). Other criticisms of social science research within feminism, however, have focused on problems that derive specifically from the adoption of a natural science (or "positivist") approach to the study of human thought and conduct. Smith (1974), for example, has criticized the "norm of objectivity," which assumes that the knower and the known can be unambiguously separated in research. Du Bois (1983) has argued that social science cannot be described as objective and value-free because scientists' activities are always constrained by societal values and assumptions. And Parlee (1979) has pointed out that a concern for universal psychological laws tends to abstract thought and behavior from its social and historical context.

Feminist research that is critical of positivist social science is therefore part of a broader movement in the philosophy of science (see, e.g., Feyerabend, 1975), sociology of knowledge (see, e.g., Woolgar, 1988), some parts of psychology (see, e.g., Gergen, 1985), and other social science disciplines (e.g., social anthropology) that has been given the label of social constructionism, and that informs the chapters in this volume. Social constructionism is the thesis that knowledge is an interpretive activity and a product of social, cultural, and historical circumstances, rather than a more or less direct reflection of a world of objectively defined facts. It has given rise to the analogy of social life as a text (Shotter & Gergen, 1989). This analogy enables researchers to concretize the constructionist thesis by conceptualizing the "objects" of study as signs that stand in relationships of meaning with other signs, and whose significance is therefore always renegotiable in relation to context of use.

Feminism, as with some other versions of the social constructionist thesis, resists a slide into total relativism, however, by making the assumption that interpretations of women's experiences must contribute to women's advance and liberation. Kitzinger (1987), for example, rejects "liberal" and "gay affirmative" constructions of lesbianism because these represent a new development in the oppression of women on the one hand, and a depoliticization of lesbianism on the other. Instead she argues for the generation of constructions of women's lives that enable them to bond together to achieve shared political goals.

In this chapter we consider theoretical analyses and empirical studies of mother-daughter relationships and how they have been influenced by the perspectives of feminism, lifespan research, and discourse analysis, thereby considering them in relation to the emerging social constructionist paradigm in social science. Particular attention is paid to the "closeness" of relationships between mothers and daughters and how this may be variously constituted across the lifespan. This is an appropriate focus because the concept of closeness articulates both with preexisting theoretical and methodological interest in the quality of family relationships and its measurement *and* with the concerns of women who have been interviewed about their family relationships. We begin by reviewing research on relationships between women as mothers and daughters that falls within two broad intellectual paradigms, first the sociology of intergenerational family relationships and, second, psychological research into the development of female identity. Finally, we consider some examples of research that are anchored explicitly within the complementary perspectives of feminism and social constructionism.

Research on Intergenerational Family Relationships and Mother-Daughter Closeness

In the field of intergenerational family relationships research, sociologists and social gerontologists are interested in the structure and functioning of, and relationships within, families. Initially such research concentrated on early stages in the life course, for example, on relationships between parents and non-adult children. However, with the aging of modern, industrialized societies interest has increased in the later years of life, such that family relationships research often now focuses on relationships with older family members (Johnson, 1988).

A dominant trend in this research is to conduct empirical investigations into the factors potentially affecting the quality of family ties, including those between mothers and daughters. One possible reason for the popularity of these kinds of investigations is their frequent relevance to issues in applied social problems research, such as the detection of factors predicting elder abuse as opposed to quality care (see, e.g., Noelker & Townsend, 1987; Steinmetz, 1988). The studies tend to follow the prescriptions of a natural science perspective on social scientific inquiry by seeking to discover causal or correlational connections between specific variables in an implicit attempt to determine the universal laws of family relationships and functioning. For example, Suitor and Pillemer (1988) have studied the effects of the presence of an adult daughter in the parental home, finding that this was unrelated to mother-daughter "conflict." Aldous (1987) tested the hypothesis that parental "attention" tends to be focused on those offspring who have children themselves but discovered that attention was greater for those daughters who are in greatest need (e.g., who are divorced with children). Kulis (1987) investigated the effects of offspring occupational mobility and gender on parent-child relationships. In this study, parents were found to show less "interest" in their downwardly mobile sons (but not daughters), and services, such as help with domestic chores, to parents were reported to be especially burdensome for upwardly mobile daughters.

In describing the reported findings of the above studies we have used the global terms (conflict, attention, interest) that are used by the original researchers to refer to aspects of the quality of relationships under study. However, it is necessary to note how, without returning to details of the way the experimental variables are operationalized and measured, it is rather difficult to know what precisely is being measured or each term's specific meaning.

Young and Wilmott's (1957) study of marriage and kinship among working-class families in Bethnal Green, London, is an important early instance of research on intergenerational family relationships and a seminal work on relationships between mothers and daughters. In this study, close and interdependent relationships between mothers and their married daughters were identified as the linchpin of family life, in the sense that contact between family members across the generations tended to be with the maternal family of descent or origin. The quality of closeness between the mothers and their adult daughters in this study was explained by Young and Wilmott as due to their shared roles as wives and mothers, the assistance given by mothers to daughters in finding accommodation, and the alcoholism then widespread among men in Bethnal Green that forced women to rely on one another for support. More recently, Wilkinson (1988) has used Sussman's (1953, 1960) research on kinship ties as a means of studying the connectedness between mothers and daughters in the context of sociocultural change. Sussman is attributed with conducting the original research that appreciated the significance of patterns of mutual help as an indicator of linkages between generations, even in nuclear families. Wilkinson found that there has been no diminution in the filial responsibility of adult daughters over the past 30 years despite a continued structural shift to nuclear family arrangements; the apparent move away from rigidly stereotyped gender roles; and the social, economic, and personal costs to increasing numbers of women who, with demographic changes, find themselves caring for long-term, functionally disabled parents.

However, some researchers have questioned the assumption of the universal and unique closeness of relationships between mothers and daughters that has tended to follow from accepting the seminal importance of Young and Wilmott's study. The use of single dimensions such as "frequency of interaction" or "exchange of aid" to assess the quality of intergenerational family relationships has been identified as a serious impediment to research and an alternative, multidimensional construct of "intergenerational solidarity" has been proposed (Mangen, Bengston, & Landry, 1988; Roberts & Bengston, 1990). A related point is made by O'Connor (1990) when she criticizes the frequent equation of closeness with "tending" (meaning the servicing of needs) in mother-daughter research. She sees this as an illustration of the ideological acceptance of "caring" as a natural extension of a feminine identity.

O'Connor's research was based on intensive interviews with 60 daughters (aged 20-42 years) that ranged over many aspects of these women's lives. In the course of their interviews, respondents were asked what they meant by having someone to whom they felt "very close" and whether they would describe anyone in this way, besides their husband and children. Subsequently, O'Connor explored the content and quality of women's relationships as reported in the interviews using a number of central concepts. These included "intimacy," which O'Connor describes as the disclosure of private information about the self to the other person, "attachment" (the extent to which the other person contributes to a sense of safety and security), and "solidarity" (deep feelings of being special to the other person, loyalty, a history of shared experiences, an ability to accept criticism without offence). Only 16 of the daughters in her study (less than one third) described their relationships with their mother as very close. And where this was the case, the relationships tended to be characterized by high levels of visual contact and felt attachment, but not necessarily by high levels of practical help and ongoing dependency, and only rarely by intimate confiding. Moreover, relationships with sisters were chosen almost as frequently as relationships with mothers as very close, and were reported to have a higher level of intimacy, solidarity, and a pleasurable interactive quality that was not said to be typical of relationships with mothers. O'Connor infers from her study that the perception of mother-daughter relationships as very close is, therefore, a popular belief that reflects current definitions of femininity and an idealization of the mother role, rather than being an intrinsic property of those relationships.

The influence of feminist thought on O'Connor's research is readily apparent in her concern for the liberatory potential of her conclusions for revealing the "distorting" and "inhibiting" factors in the development of mother-daughter relationships. Certain essential elements of social constructionist thought are evident too in her identification of mother-daughter closeness as a feature of wider cultural and ideological systems of belief. O'Connor's research is particularly informative, however, in its methodological aspects since her intensive interviews allowed her to combine a concern for concepts (attachment, solidarity, etc.) that she derived from preexisting research on the quality of mother-daughter relationships with a sensitivity to the particular terms used by the women in her study to account for their own experiences. Within feminist literatures, qualitative interviewing is highly recommended (see, e.g., Measor, 1985; Oakley, 1981) along with other research strategies that give appropriately motivated researchers the flexibility to begin to see through the eyes of participants themselves, rather than necessarily interpreting participants' responses through instruments formulated to test specific theoretical ideas. This is deemed to be important because there is no absolute guarantee that any one theory will be relevant to understanding a new set of data or accounts. The commitment in feminist research to qualitative research as a means of seeing through the eyes of participants themselves is itself derived from the conviction that the researcher and the researched are and should be interdependent in social science investigations. Feminist writings therefore provide a rich source of insight into research as an inherently interpretive, constitutive, social activity.

In addition to feminism, lifespan research has also begun to influence inquiry into the quality of mother-daughter relationships. Lifespan research is critical of the assumption of stability and consistency over the life course that tends to follow from accepting that the goal of social science is to establish the universal laws of behavior that obtain irrespective of social and historical context. Instead it points to the potential for instability and change over the life course, suggesting that to talk in terms of development at all would seem to require some acceptance of the possibility of change over time (see, e.g., Abeles, 1987). Where it has been recognized that lifespan development involves change over time, such changes have often been attributed to the unfolding of maturational processes. Neither stability nor change need necessarily be assumed to refer to aspects of an underlying developmental process, however. Both may be conceptualized alternatively as influences on the way lifespan development is represented and constituted.

Fischer (1981) specifically considers the temporal dimension to mother-daughter closeness in her empirical research into transitions in mother-daughter relationships over the life course. She found that marriage and first pregnancy was associated with an increase in daughters' desire for closeness and intimacy with their mothers, thereby encouraging a "reordering of the mother daughter relationship . . . toward greater dyadic interaction" (Boyd, 1989, p. 296). Research by Baruch and Barnett (1983) contradicts this claim because, despite the generally positive feelings of daughters for their mothers in their study, daughters who had children themselves reported finding relationships with their mothers less rewarding than daughters without children. This apparent contradiction has been accounted for by the reported lack of satisfaction by divorced women in the sample. Where research allows for the possibility of temporal change, women have most frequently reported feeling more satisfied with their relationships with their mothers as they grow older (e.g., Baruch & Barnett, 1983; Berti, 1981).

Mother-Daughter Relationships From the Perspective of Research on Women's Psychological Development

The second tradition of research, which forms the basis of most attempts to account for mother-daughter relationships theoretically, is focused on women's psychological development. Numerous studies have been informed by the perspective of social learning theory, assessing maternal influences on daughters' sex-role attitudes, orientations to work, self-concept, and personality (see, e.g., Macke & Morgan, 1978; Rollins & White, 1982; Wingrove & Slevin, 1982). However, these have a less developed conceptual emphasis than psychoanalytic research into the psychosexual and identification processes associated with parent-child relations and their differential significance in the emotional lives of women and men.

Sigmund Freud spoke of women's psychology having its origins in young girls' recognition of genital difference and their experience of "penis envy." By this account, young girls harbor ambivalent feelings for their mothers and develop heterosexual attachments to their fathers in the hope of gaining a longed-for penis, which they unconsciously equate with having a baby. Freud's concern with the instinctual basis of parent-child attachments and psychosexual development influenced early writings on the psychological foundations of motherliness in women. Here it is argued that all women have a natural instinct to mother (Benedek, 1970), that women develop a deep-rooted "feminine core" (comprised of passivity, masochism, and narcissism) in association with their reproductive function (Deutsch, 1944), and that childbearing and -rearing is a major determinant of psychological maturity in women (Benedek, 1970).

Today, however, the majority of research on women's psychological development and mother-daughter relations is informed by what is called the "social object relations" school of thought where concern for the role of instinctual gratification and events in the Oedipal period is displaced by consideration of the way a child's sense of self develops in relation to others (called social objects) during the pre-Oedipal stage. It is assumed that mother and child exist, initially, in a state of symbiotic union, where each experiences the other as an extension of themselves, and that a major developmental task for the child is, therefore, the achievement of a separate sense of self beginning around the age of 6 months (see, e.g., Mahler, 1957). The primary caregiver (usually the mother) is said to play a vital role in children's development by providing them with an adequate sense of security and degree of autonomy to explore and thereby discover the boundaries between themselves and objects in the external world; the phrase "good enough mother" has been used to encapsulate those maternal qualities that are thought to be adequate to facilitate a child's psychological development (Winnicott, 1965).

In her now classic text *The Reproduction of Mothering*, Chodorow (1978) draws on the approach of social object relations theory, making specific reference to the particularity of mother-daughter relationships in women's psychological development. Her argument is that, in a society structured in terms of gender (and particularly where parenting is organized asymmetrically), boys can come to recognize themselves as different from their primary caregiver (their mother) fairly early in life, but girls tend not to do so because of a "double identification" with their mother as women. A major consequence of this prolonged period of mother-daughter emergence is said to be that girls develop a "feminine" identity, where they define themselves in terms of their connectedness to others, whereas boys grow up with a developed "masculine" sense of separateness from others. Also, women are said often to suffer extremely ambivalent relationships with their mothers, due to unresolved conflicts over the need for autonomy and separation.

Magrab (1979) is similarly concerned with the ambivalence of mother-daughter relationships in her analysis of the "life cycle of the mother daughter relationship" (p. 115). She argues that conflict often remains unresolved between mothers and daughters in adulthood through mothers not allowing their daughters to separate and/or because daughters continue in a state of infantile dependency. Both Chodorow and Magrab echo many of the ideas expressed in the popular feminist writings of Friday (in *My Mother, Myself*, 1977) and Rich (in *Of Woman Born*, 1976) who originally connected the problems of their own and other women's insecurity, dependency, and sexual guilt with their relationships with their mother as children, and an unwillingness to question the mother-daughter bond for fear of loss of maternal love.

Research with empirical foundations in the analysis of women in psychotherapy has filled in many of the details of the origins of ambivalence between mothers and daughters. Both Deutsch and Benedek have alluded to the conflict between mothers and daughters that can be awakened during pregnancy and motherhood, and Chodorow has suggested that this occurs because memories of a daughter's own infancy may be evoked. A fuller analysis, however, is given by Flax (1981) beginning with her observation that many of her female patients reported having felt pressure to mother their own mothers. The explanation given for this is that mothers have more difficulty being emotionally available to their daughters than to their sons during the symbiotic phase, in some large part because their own childhood needs were not met by their mothers, and because the strong identification between mother and daughter as women leads to a diffusion of boundaries and lack of clarity about who is mothering whom. Also, most mothers within patriarchal society are said to experience unconscious psychic conflict about being female and to be ambivalent toward their daughters' femininity. Flax believes that a woman's wish to have babies therefore represents an unconscious desire to be mothered. However, infant daughters cannot of course provide such care and in this way a source of conflict between mothers and daughters is passed down through generations of women. The inadequacy of the symbiotic phase for girls makes it difficult for them to differentiate because they lack a firm emotional base from which to explore being separate from their mothers. Furthermore, there is less requirement for girls to differentiate because they are expected to carry out the same tasks in adulthood as their mothers have done. Little girls feel forced to choose between autonomy and their mothers' love because they cannot have both. As adults women rarely receive the nurturance they need from their male partners because masculine gender formation requires men to suppress the "feminine," nurturing part of themselves. For the same reason, mothers look to their daughters and not to their sons to provide the love they missed out on in infancy.

The account of mother-daughter relationships as unconsciously conflicted due to gender-specific problems in the achievement of psychological separation has achieved acceptance in diverse areas.

It is characteristic of much feminist writing on women's identity formation within societies and systems of meaning that are structured in terms of gender in ways that disadvantage women. It is also part of a particular view of child development that has prevailed since the post-World War II years. An illustration of the second case is a discussion of child development for pregnant mothers where it is suggested that a woman's sense of her own mother must shift in a positive direction, or mother-daughter reconciliation be achieved, before she can make an attachment with her own child (Ballou, 1978). Nevertheless, criticism of the account for leading to a view of women as infantile, immature, and as developmentally retarded (see, e.g., Bart, 1981/1983) has had to be met. Hence, the position of the feminist psychotherapists Eichenbaum and Orbach (1983) is that there should be less concern with separation per se and more interest in finding ways for women to achieve genuine intimacy without feeling threatened by loss of self.

A number of unconnected theoretical reservations have also been lodged. Sayers (1989), for example, has questioned the neglect of Kleinian theory, which made the original challenge to paternalism and began the shift toward mother- as opposed to father-centered relationships, within classical psychoanalysis. And Benjamin, in her treatise *The Bonds of Love* (1989), draws on Stern's (1978) claim that babies never exist in a state of total emergence with their mothers because they are born with an "emergent sense of self" to argue for the reciprocal relationship between separation and relatedness in an "intersubjective" process of "mutual recognition" between mother and child. Finally, interviews with younger and older adult women about their relationships with their mothers have suggested that, rather than struggling to break those ties that token dependence, women are engaged in "refashioning," "reworking," or "transforming" their relationships so that they are better able to accommodate the changing circumstances of women's lives and senses of self (Apter, 1990; Hancock, 1990). These efforts are interpreted not as attempts by daughters to seek out the love, comfort, and security they missed in early childhood, but as a potentially "subversive" (Hancock, 1990) means of empowering mothers and daughters to challenge the attributes of weakness and dependency that are culturally attributed to them as women (see also Bart, 1981/1983).

Mothering as Discourse: A Social Constructionist Approach to Mother-Daughter Relationships

Some aspects of the previously reviewed accounts of mother-daughter relationships and women's identities are consistent with the view that women's experiences over the lifespan are constructed socially. Feminist theory and research is concerned, generally, with the way women's experiences and relationships are determined within a particular set of (patriarchal) social and historical relations, and Chodorow's (1978) thesis is a clear example in describing how "all aspects of psychic structure, character and emotional development are social, constituted through a history of object choices" (p. 50). However, a line of criticism has been taken by researchers who argue that popularized versions of post-Freudian ideas function as part of the social regulatory apparatuses that both prescribe what women should do when rearing children and constitute them as mothers (see, e.g., Urwin, 1985). Urwin uses the post-structuralist concept of "normalization" (the construction of norms to identify deviance and regulate the rest of the population) to point up the way that "theories initially based on clinical cases or forms of pathology have contributed to the role of the normal mother" (p. 171). The idea that a place of safety is necessary for children to be able to develop through creative exploration and play, as described already in this chapter, is identified as defining the role of the mother in terms of assumptions about children's needs and propensities. Moreover, Urwin supports this view with empirical research in which the mothers she interviewed tended to evaluate their own competence by comparing the performance of their children against other children and age-based developmental norms.

In a similar vein, Griffith and Smith (1987) are critical of the preoccupation with mothering as an "intimate relationship within which the wellbeing of a child is dependent on his or her mother" (p. 87). They try to counter this preoccupation by investigating mothering as work, or as a "set of activities orientated to the child and to the institutional relations in which the family is embedded" (p. 87). This allowed them to reveal the presence of a "mothering discourse" as central to the experience of being a mother and leading to the standardization of maternal practices. For Griffith and Smith (1987) the reported experiences, accounts, and actions of the mothers in their empirical study remained largely inexplicable until they were seen to be structured in terms of a set of standards "organised extra-locally in a discourse on parenting and on child development which sets up the parameters for 'normal' child development and the parenting required to develop and maintain that normalcy" (p. 96). As an example, they note one particular mother's insistence on asking the researchers for advice on how best to deal with her child's problem at school. This would seem to indicate the mother's acceptance of her maternal responsibility to find a solution for the child's problem and the interviewers as representatives of "expert knowledge" on child development and the educational process. A defining feature of Griffith and Smith's "mothering discourse" is its idealized or moral dimension that positions mothers as responsible for their children's normal development and as morally culpable if developmental standards are not being achieved. Because it seems to apply irrespective of the practicalities and conditions of women's lives, the moral dimension is deemed to be responsible for the experiences of guilt so often reported by mothers.

Empirical Research Illustrating Aspects of the Construction of Closeness in Mother-Daughter Relationships

The view that women's experiences, identities, and relationships are discursive products or constructions, rather than fixed, natural realities, provides the background to our own empirical investigations. In following this view, we have adopted Weedon's (1987) definition of discourses as practices that inhere within social and historical relations, thereby avoiding the charge sometimes leveled at constructionist research that it admits of no reality beyond the text. Practically, the research uses feminist research methods, a basic principle of which is the seeking-out of women's accounts of their experience, whose validity must be accepted in their own terms (see, e.g., Duelli-Klein, 1983). Evidently, this principle must be equated with the view that all experience is a meaningful construction. Harding (1991) and Hollway (1989) among others have argued successfully that, although there will always be some connection, accounts need not necessarily be a *direct* reflection of experience. The task of the feminist researcher is, therefore, to interpret the relationships between women's accounts and experiences starting from the perspective of women's lives.

We interviewed 61 women approximately half of whom were mothers (aged 47-86) and half daughters (aged 24-47); two thirds of the women comprised mother-daughter pairs. The "mothers" in the sample were women who had at least one daughter, and who may also have had grandchildren; rarely, however, did they have a living mother themselves. The "daughters" all had living mothers, and characteristically had dependent children, although some were unmarried and without children or had semi-independent children. About 70% of the mothers were of retirement age, although a small number still worked part time. More than 50% of mothers had a living spouse with whom they lived, roughly one third were divorced or widowed and lived alone; only one lived with her daughter and family and one was a single parent who had two adolescent daughters still living at home. The daughters either worked full time (1/3), part time (1/3), or were full-time housewives (1/3). Mothers and daughters mainly lived in close geographical proximity (a walkable distance or less than 30 minutes drive) or quite close (an easy round trip in a day). In terms of socioeconomic status, and using the occupational status of the woman if she worked or her partner if she did not, roughly 50% of the women could be categorized as "professional," 35% as "skilled nonmanual," and 5% as "unskilled." The remaining 10% were difficult to code using this three-way schema.

The women were asked about their lives, experiences, and relationships with their mothers or daughters. The interviews were semistructured to ensure the relevance of topics discussed and sufficient flexibility to follow up those issues that appeared to be important to the women themselves. A notable feature of the interviews was the women's preparedness to talk in terms of the closeness or lack of closeness of their relationships with their mothers or daughters. Using Potter and Wetherell's (1987) terminology, closeness appeared as a potent "interpretive repertoire"

in our women's accounts. We, therefore, felt confident to proceed
with a specific focus on this topic since it evidently had relevance
and meaning for the women themselves.[1]

Where the term *closeness* is used explicitly, it often seems to
place a specific evaluative gloss on the relationship in question.
This is illustrated, for example, in Extract 1 where J B (a 30-year-
old woman, married with two very young children) spontaneously describes her relationships with her mother as "quite close,"
having first described how much she relied on her mother, particularly as someone to whom she could off-load her troubles.

Extract 1

```
 1  JB:   I tend to off-load everything onto mum onto
 2         her actually      in fact I rely quite heavily on
                         [    ]
 3  I1:                   yes
 4  JB:   her really
                    [    ]
 5  I1:             yes and is it mainly at the end of the
 6         'phone or do you go to see her or
 7  JB:   mainly at the end of the 'phone I don't
 8         have a car so I can't really get
 9         out very much     now and again I can ask
                         [     ]
10  I1:                    right
11  JB:   John to take to go into work with somebody
12         else and then I have the car       but on yes
                                          [    ]
13  I1:                                       yes
14  JB:   mum and I we are really quite close in a way
```

Labeling a relationship as close or not close would seem in part,
then, to perform the same function as a direct evaluation of a
relationship, as when J B's mother S K spontaneously describes
the two women early in her interview as having a *a good relationship*. An evaluative label need not, however, be applied directly to

the mother-daughter relationship itself. Describing one's other relationships and other people's relationships as close/not close or good/bad can also have the effect of evaluating a mother-daughter relationship in a particular way where such comments set up implicit comparisons and projected evaluations. This happens in our data, for example; when M H (a 43-year-old mother with living parents) comments on her first husband's poor relationships with his own family, leading to the implication that both of them were far "closer" to her parents. Also, an elderly mother who describes her daughter as having been "very close to her father" seems to be using this as an indirect tactic for acknowledging the problems her daughter evidently experiences in their relationship.

There seemed to be a strong preference among the women who were interviewed for describing their relationships with their mothers and/or daughters as very close or intimate. However, what the women precisely meant by describing their relationships in this way, and how this was achieved, was variable and multi-faceted. Some women were able to describe their relationships in terms of global feelings of fondness, love or affection, as illustrated in Extract 2.

Extract 2

```
1 MH:   I'm very fond of my mother        yes
                                         [    ]
2 I1:                                        yeah and in
3        the past would you describe it always as
4        fondness
5 MH:    (3.0) yes I have always been (.) I have
6        always been but I bitterly regret (.) that whilst I was with my
         first husband it was tinged (.) with (.) a dissatisfaction which I
         didn't feel but which he felt and that rubbed off onto me
```

Extract 2 is also of interest because is suggests that reported feelings in relationships are not unidimensional and fixed, but differentiated and capable of evolving in relation to specific circumstances and lifespan developments. One recurrent theme to emerge from the interviews is that mother-daughter relationships in adolescence are remembered as traumatic and difficult, but that women may grow together as they accumulate more common life experiences. However, the accumulation of common life experiences in itself is no guarantee of closeness among mothers and daughters in adult life, because there were no obvious differences in the extent of shared experiences between those women who did and those who did not project warm and intimate relationships. In consequence, there would seem to be some explanatory value in viewing the attribution of relationship difficulties to earlier phases in the lifespan as a powerful accounting device that contributes to the construction of closeness in adult mother-daughter relationships.

A further way of describing the closeness of mother-daughter relationships is in terms of ease of interaction and lack of self-consciousness in the presence of the other person. S W, a newly retired mother with four adult children, for example, distinguishes between her two living daughters in terms of the former being "on her wavelength" and the second being "prickly," where the latter term means likely to take offence or feel slighted by innocent remarks. A tendency to disclose private, personal information is also frequently mentioned, as in Extract 1, together with mothers and daughters having a routine involvement in one another's lives. As C C, a single parent with five daughters proudly remarks, *all my daughters are always round here* (that is, at her home). The daughter to whom C C expresses feeling particularly close is the one with whom she exchanges *small itty critty things* (personal thoughts that are of consequence only to themselves) and who is most likely to vacuum her mother's living room without inquiry or comment. K B, a 38-year-old daughter who is also a mother of four young children, comments on many aspects of this more practical view of mother-daughter closeness in Extract 3, where she contrasts her relationship with her childhood carer and current helper (B D) and her natural mother.

Extract 3

```
 1  KB:   it actually sounds from this conversation
 2        that she (B D) is much closer to me than my
 3        mother and I suppose in a way she is       but that
                                              [    ]
 4  I2:                                         mm
 5  KB:   could be because I see quite a lot more of her
                                              [         ]
 6  I2:                                        yes yes
 7  KB:   and she's more she seems to have a more
 8        sympathetic attitude than my mother does . . .
 9        so I suppose if she did have a problem she
10        would tell me about it whether I could do
11        anything to help       would be another matter
                            [    ]
12  I2:                       yes
```

However, we are reminded here that we are dealing with closeness as variably constituted, and often in contradictory ways, as opposed to the essential properties of relationships. This is the case because K B's mother's understanding of the relationship is that it is close because mother and daughter intuitively know one another's feelings, and therefore have no need to express themselves to each other in words.

Renderings of feelings of closeness appeared to be most intense where members of the mother-daughter dyad alluded to their feelings of we- or one-ness. This is illustrated in Extract 4. R M is an active elderly mother who lives next door to her daughter.

Extract 4

```
 1  R M:   well that's the strange part about it she's so
 2         like me to look at and when she was younger she
 3         was very like me in everything as a child I
 4         could tell what she was thinking . . . I don't know
 5         what it is something (3.0) I can't describe it
 6         there's something there that we're like one
 7         person
```

Her daughter K M, in a separate interview, reciprocates this sentiment by commenting that she, unlike other girls, never really wished to leave home for university, always returned home during her period of study at weekends, found it difficult to leave her mother for her husband on her wedding day (returning to the parental home for breakfast the next morning), and sometimes experienced an intense need simply to be in her mother's presence.

Among women (always daughters in this study) who described their relationships as highly conflicted, a common element was the tendency to draw on powerful metaphors. In Extract 5, for example, D P draws on the metaphor of mothers and daughters as connected by a string, which can be used to bind them together.

Extract 5

1	DP:	she'd always liked to keep I felt that she'd
2		always liked to keep me on the anything I say
3		is just my own opinion (laughs) I'm afraid
		[ ]
4	Il:	yes
5	DP:	to keep me on a string . . . in the end you want
6		to pull away further because you're getting
7		this pull back all the time

Another woman (J D) similarly describes her own late development into adulthood as occurring only when she managed *to cut a bit of the apron strings*. Extract 6 continues the theme of daughters having to cut the ties that bind them to their mothers, but superimposed upon this is the idea that the mother is *clutching* onto her daughter, almost as if she were a bird with prey.

Extract 6

1	CN:	I was actually strong enough to cut the ties
2		and the best thing I ever did was to move I
3		wish I'd done it sooner because once I got out
4		of (named village) I was out of her clutches

Later C N provides support for our interpretation of her remarks in this way when she comments that she experienced moving further away from the maternal home as if she was *flying away like a bird*.

Psychoanalysis of all of these women could, possibly, reveal the origins of their feelings in early parent-child interaction around issues of separation and individuation. However, for our purposes the women's accounts would seem to serve as useful illustrations of the way highly intense or problematic relationships can be rendered personally intelligible and socially meaningful. In the latter regard we would conjecture, for example, that drawing on powerful metaphors is one effective way of communicating personal experiences to others because it makes connections with ideas and images of mothers that are available as part of the cultural stock of knowledge. Raphael-Leff (1991) has described how the simultaneous idealization and devaluation of women as mothers in contemporary Western societies is made manifest in images of mothers as "placental containers." However, we make the more simple point in relation to our data here that drawing upon metaphors of binding and clutching is one way of articulating with those negative cultural stereotypes that portray women as powerful and possessive in relationships.[2]

Conclusion

Adrienne Rich gave notice in 1976 that mother-daughter relationships were a great unwritten story. This story is now being written apace within many disciplines in social science. Although the prevailing theoretical view is that many mothers and daughters have highly conflicted relationships due to unresolved issues arising from the need for daughters to achieve psychological and emotional separation from their mothers in infancy, a contrasting approach is to study the discursive production of mother-daughter relationships over the lifespan. Some examples of research of the latter kind have been considered in this chapter, including that which has identified the role of psychological theory in the construction of women as "normal" mothers and some preliminary research on the construction of mother-daughter closeness. In contrast to positivist science, both psychoanalysis and social constructionism share a common concern with interpreting the meaning of experience. However, it is our view that a close examination of the practical and discursive ways in which women negotiate and construct their own relationships and identities will lead to a welcome increase in the range of understandings available for women to make sense in their everyday lives.

Notes

1. See Hammersley and Atkinson (1983) for further remarks on the role of emergent "member categories" in interpretive research.

2. In Greek mythology, harpies are monsters with women's faces and bodies and a bird's wings and claws. Given the powerful emotions of disgust and hate that C N recounts in her relationship with her mother, this picture of specifically female monsters constitutes one possible source informing her particular choice of metaphor.

References

Abeles, R. P. (1987). Introduction. *Lifespan perspectives and social psychology* (pp. 1-15). Hillsdale, NJ: Lawrence Erlbaum.

Aldous, J. (1987). New views on the family life of the elderly and the near elderly. *Journal of Marriage and the Family 49*, 227-234.

Apter, T. (1990). *Altered loves: Mothers and daughters during adolescence.* Hemel Hempstead, UK: Harvester Wheatsheaf.

Ballou, J. W. (1978). *The psychology of pregnancy.* Toronto: Lexington Books.

Bart, P. (1983). Review of Chodorow's The Reproduction of Mothering. In J. Trebilcot (Ed.), *Feminist views on mothering* (pp. 147-152). Lanham, MD: Rowman & Allanheld. (Originally published 1981)

Baruch, G., & Barnett, R. C. (1983). Adult daughters' relationships with their mothers. *Journal of Marriage and the Family, 45*, 601-606.

Benedek, T. (1970). Motherhood and nurturing. In E. Anthony & T. Benedek (Eds.), *Parenthood: Its psychology and psychopathology* (pp. 153-165). London: Brown & Co.

Benjamin, J. (1989). *The bonds of love: Psychoanalysis, feminism and the problem of domination.* London: Virago.

Berti, B. (1981). Women's relationships to their mothers at two stages of adulthood (Doctoral dissertation, University of Michigan) *Dissertation Abstracts International, 42*, 2514B.

Boyd, C. J. (1989). Mothers and daughters: A discussion of theory and research. *Journal of Marriage and the Family, 51*, 291-301.

Chodorow, N. (1978). *The reproduction of mothering: Psychoanalysis and the sociology of gender.* Berkeley: University of California Press.

Du Bois, B. (1983). Passionate scholarship: Notes on values, knowing and method in feminist social science. In G. Bowles & R. Duelli-Klein (Eds.), *Theories of women's studies* (pp. 105-116). London: Routledge & Kegan Paul.

Duelli-Klein, R. (1983). How to do what we want to: Thoughts about feminist methodology. In G. Bowles & R. Duelli-Klein (Eds.), *Theories of women's studies* (pp. 88-104). London: Routledge & Kegan Paul.

Deutsch, H. (1944). *The psychology of women* (Vol. 1). New York: Grune & Stratton.

Eichenbaum, L., & Orbach, S. (1985). *Understanding women.* Harmondsworth, UK: Penguin.

Feyerabend, P. (1975). *Against method.* London: Verso.

Fischer, L. (1981). Transitions in the mother-daughter relationship. *Journal of Marriage and the Family,* June, 613-622.

Flax, J. (1981). The conflict between nurturance and autonomy in mother-daughter relationships and within feminism. In E. Howell & M. Bayes (Eds.), *Women and mental health* (pp. 51-69). New York: Basic Books.

Friday, N. (1977). *My mother, my self.* New York: Delacorte.

Gergen, K. J. (1985). The social constructionist movement in modern psychology. *American Psychologist, 40*(3), 266-275.

Griffith, A. I., & Smith, D. E. (1987). Constructing cultural knowledge: Mothering as discourse. In J. S. Gaskell & A. T. McLaren (Eds.), *Women and education: A Canadian perspective* (pp. 86-103). Calgary: Detselig.

Hammersley, M., & Atkinson, P. (1983). *Ethnography: Principles in practice.* London: Routledge & Kegan Paul.

Hancock, E. (1990). *The girl within: A radical new approach to female identity.* London: Pandora.

Harding, S. (1987). *Feminism and methodology.* Milton Keynes, UK: Open University Press.

Harding, S. (1991). *Whose science? Whose knowledge? Thinking from women's lives.* Milton Keynes, UK: Open University Press.

Hollway, W. (1989). *Subjectivity and method in social psychology: Gender, meaning and science.* London: Sage.

Johnson, C. L. (1988). Relationships amongst family members and friends in later life. In R. M. Milardo (Ed.), *Families and social networks* (pp. 168-189). Newbury Park, CA: Sage.

Kitzinger, C. (1987). *The social construction of lesbianism.* London: Sage.

Kulis, S. (1987). Socially mobile daughters and sons of the elderly: Mobility effects within the family revisited. *Journal of Marriage and the Family, 49,* 421-433.

Macke, A., & Morgan, W. (1978). Maternal employment, race, and work orientation of high school girls. *Social Forces, 57,* 187-204.

Magrab, P. (1979). Mothers and daughters. In C. B. Kopp (Ed.), *Becoming female: Perspectives on development* (pp. 113-125). New York: Plenum.

Mahler, M. (1957). *The psychological birth of the human infant.* New York: Basic Books.

Mangen, D. J., Bengston, V. L., & Landry, P. H. (Eds.). (1988). *Measurement of intergenerational relations.* Newbury Park, CA: Sage.

Measor, L. (1985). Interviewing: A strategy in qualitative research. In R. G. Burgess (Ed.), *Strategies of educational research* (pp. 55-57). London: Falmer Press.

Noelker, L. S., & Townsend, A. L. (1987). Perceived caregiving effectiveness: The impact of parental impairment, community resources, and caregiver character-istics. In T. H. Brubaker (Ed.), *Aging, health and family: Long-term care* (pp. 58-79). Beverly Hills, CA: Sage.

Oakley, A. (1981). Interviewing women: A contradiction in terms. In H. Roberts (Ed.), *Doing feminist research* (pp. 30-61). London: Routledge & Kegan Paul.

O'Connor, P. (1990). The adult mother/daughter relationships: A uniquely and universally close relationship? *Sociological Review, 38*(2), 293-323.

Parlee, M. B. (1979). Psychology and women. *Signs: Journal of Women in Culture and Society, 5*(1), 121-133.

Potter, J., & Wetherell, M. (1987). *Discourse and social psychology* London: Sage.

Raphael-Leff, J. (1991). The mother as container: Placental process and inner space. *Feminism and Psychology, 1*(3), 393-408.

Rich, A. (1976). *Of woman born: Motherhood as experience and institution.* New York: Norton.

Roberts, E. L., & Bengston, V. L. (1990). Is intergenerational solidarity a uni-dimensional construct? A second test of a formal model. *Journal of Gerontology (Social Sciences), 45,* S12-S20.

Rollins, J., & White, P. (1982). The relationships between mother's attitudes and daughter's sex-role attitudes and self-concept in three types of family environ-ment. *Sex Roles, 8,* 1141-1155.

Sayers, J. (1989). Melanie Klein and mothering—A feminist perspective. *Interna-tional Review of Psychoanalysis, 16,* 363-375.

Shotter, J., & Gergen, K. J. (1989). *Texts of identity.* London: Sage.

Smith, D. (1974). Women's perspective as a radical critique of sociology. *Sociological Inquiry, 44,* 7-13.

Steinmetz, S. K. (1988). *Duty bound: Elder abuse and family care.* Newbury Park, CA: Sage.

Stern, D. (1978). *The interpersonal world of the human infant.* New York: Basic Books.

Suitor, J., & Pillemer, K. (1988). Explaining intergenerational conflict when adult children and elderly parents live together. *Journal of Marriage and Family, 50,* 1037-1047.

Sussman, M. B. (1953). The help pattern in the middle class family. *American Sociological Review, 18,* 22-28.

Sussman, M. B. (1960). Intergenerational family relationships and social role changes in middle age. *Journal of Gerontology, 15,* 71-75.

Urwin, C. (1985). Constructing motherhood: The persuasion of normal develop-ment. In C. Steedman, C. Urwin, & V. Walkerdine (Eds.), *Language, gender and childhood* (pp. 164-201). London: Routledge & Kegan Paul.

Weedon, C. (1987). *Feminist practice and poststructuralist theory.* Oxford: Basil Black-well.

Wilkinson, D. Y. (1988). Mother-daughter bonds in the later years: Transformation in the "help pattern." In S. K. Steinmetz (Ed.), *Family support systems across the lifespan* (pp. 183-195). New York: Plenum.

Wingrove, C. R., & Slevin, K. (1982). Age differences and generational gaps: College women and their mothers' attitude toward female roles in society. *Youth and Society, 13,* 289-301.

Winnicott, D. (1965). *The maturational processes and the facilitating environment.* New York: International University Press.

Woolgar, S. (1988). *Science: The very idea.* London: Tavistock.

Young, P., & Wilmott, M. (1957). *Family and kinship in East London.* New York: Penguin.

CHAPTER TEN

Intergenerational Communication in the Mother-Daughter Dyad Regarding Caregiving Decisions

VICTOR G. CICIRELLI

Although some research exists concerning communication during dyadic decision making among younger adults (e.g., Kenny & Acitelli, 1989; Poole & Billingsley, 1989; Sillars & Kalbfleisch, 1989), and some research exists concerning communication in general with elderly people (e.g., Atkinson & Coupland, 1988; Coupland, Coupland, Giles, & Henwood, 1988), little is known about communication in dyadic decision making among elderly parent-adult child dyads in family caregiving situations. The present chapter is concerned with the latter topic.

Communication in dyadic decision making among elderly parent-adult child dyads is a significant topic in view of the increasing number of dependent frail elderly in American society and the central role of the family in providing care to elderly family members (e.g., Brody, 1978, 1990; Cantor, 1975, 1985; Noelker & Townsend, 1987; Shanas, 1979). On average, about two thirds of the elderly receive help from family members, with daughters caring for elderly mothers constituting the most frequent caregiving unit (Brody, 1978, 1990; Cantor, 1985; Cicirelli, 1981; Coward & Dwyer, 1990; Horowitz & Dobrof, 1982). In family caregiving, one or both members of the dyad must make decisions regarding the types and amounts of care to be provided as well as its mode and timing. Communication in such dyadic caregiving decision-making situations has yet to be investigated.

Communication in Relation to
Lifespan Development and Aging

Before proceeding to intergenerational dyadic caregiving decision making, it is important to provide some rationale as to the nature of human beings and how they change over time as a basis for understanding communication in decision making.

Lifespan Psychology. A psychology of the lifespan provides a broad frame of reference from which to interpret an individual's behavior such as decision making. A lifespan perspective allows one to interpret the significance of decision making at different points in a person's life. The interpretation of decision making may be different at different time periods relative to any past behavior that may exist as well as projected future behavior.

Lifespan Developmental Psychology Perspective. The lifespan developmental psychology perspective goes beyond lifespan psychology per se in that it provides a more elaborate background to understand the discourse of decision making for helping elderly parents.

A lifespan developmental psychology perspective is based on a contextual/dialectic metamodel or worldview. Change is considered possible throughout the lifespan. Change may be continuous, with apparent stability in certain domains merely representing a very slow rate of change. On the other hand, the onset, duration, and termination of change may vary across the lifespan, depending on the domain involved. Whatever the domain, change is always possible and has priority over stability. Such change is both qualitative and quantitative.

Change is multilinear (i.e., linear or nonlinear for different functions or behaviors), multidirectional, (i.e., change can take many directions over the same or different functions), and reversible (plasticity) depending upon the situation. Thus the direction of change is not predetermined nor is there any end point to change. Change is open-ended, and often times unpredictable. Also, all types of change are considered developmental changes; therefore, aging change is synonymous with, or part of developmental change (Baltes, 1979; Lerner, Hultsch, & Dixon, 1983).

Developmental change is multiply determined. Lifespan developmental theorists (Baltes, 1979; Baltes, Reese, & Lipsitt, 1980; Lerner et al., 1983) distinguish three types of causal influences on developmental change: *age-graded normative events* (involving biological maturation and socialization in one's cultures within the lifespan), *history-graded normative events* (involving biological changes from one cohort to the next, such as a change in the gene pool due to nuclear radiation, and changes due to different interpretations of common experiences by different age groups or cohorts), and *nonnormative events* (involving biological causes unique to the individual, such as a physical accident or disease, and experiences unique to the individual, such as loss of job, divorce, etc.).

As part of this contextual/dialectic metamodel, these biological and environmental factors do not operate independently on the individual. They are part of the person-environment context that typifies this approach, with a reciprocal interaction between a changing individual in a changing environment.

A perceived reciprocal relationship exists between the perceiver and multilevel environmental forces along with any reciprocal relationships between the forces themselves. In this theoretical conception the multilevel forces and the psychological processes are inseparable, and relative to the perceived time and space of the moment. Life is a series of events that the individual constructs from a phenomenal world in which he or she is inseparable from the environment. In short, this is a dynamic person-environment system in which people, psychological processes, and multi-level forces are all inseparable and in a reciprocal relationship. They are all aspects of a momentary event; as aspects, they are defined in terms of each other.

In such a system, the activity represented in the event is predominant, for example, the activity of providing help. Individuals are derivatives in that one is a helper and is defined by the existence of a recipient; similarly, the recipient is defined in terms of the existence of a helper (Altman & Rogoff, 1987). In a subsequent event, the activity may shift, the people may be defined differently in terms of other complementary roles, and the impact of reciprocally interacting forces may be interpreted differently. Activity and change are intrinsic to the system. The direction of the change emerges out of perceived contradictions, inconsistencies, and conflicts between aspects of the system and the resolution of such conflicts. This system is an example of dialectical causality. However, the latter goes beyond mere resolution of conflicts to give priority to perceiving contradictions, conflicts, or inconsistencies to maintain disequilibrium. There is continual emerging of new directions of change as contradictions and resolutions continue, with no end point but continual change itself. As an open-ended system, novel directions of change may occur that are unpredictable, or they may be predictable because of similarities to past conditions.

Lifespan Developmental and Aging Psychology Perspective. In my view, there is also a lifespan developmental and aging psychology perspective. In such a perspective, aging is not only distinct from development, but development is part of aging (rather than aging being part of development as in the lifespan developmental psychology perspective). This position assumes that the individual is best represented by an organismic metamodel in early and late segments of the lifespan, and by a contextual/dialectic metamodel in the middle segment of the lifespan.

Both metamodels represent the individual as a system; a continually active individual who interprets or constructs his or her own world. However, the contextual/dialectic model represents the person and environment as an inseparable system; they exist together relative to time and space, and the individual's social constructions emerge from perceptions of a changing individual in a changing environmental setting. In contrast, the organismic model represents the person alone as a system, separable in time and space from the environment. Social constructions emerge from a changing individual and a relatively passive or nonactive environment. Also, the person as a system is made up of elements or components that can be defined independently of each other (rather than being aspects of a system that are defined in terms of each other, as in the contextual/dialectic approach). The reciprocal interaction of the system with the environment determines the interpretations or constructions of the individual in relation to the environment (but the individual is not necessarily part of or inseparable from the environment) (Altman & Rogoff, 1987; Overton & Reese, 1973).

In the organismic metamodel, the environment is secondary. The reciprocal interaction between the individual and the environment does not mean that equal weight is given to each. Rather, the environment is given less weight. The direction of change is determined within the individual while the environment merely facilitates or inhibits the rate of change. (If the rate of change is sufficiently slow, the environment may affect the ultimate level of development or aging.) The constructions of the world are determined from the reciprocal interaction of components within the individual (plus input from the environment), not from a system including the individual and the environment at a given time and place.

The fundamental difference between the contextual/dialectic and the organismic views is that the former is an open system and the latter is a closed system. Intrinsic to the organismic metamodel is the belief in the primacy of teleological causality, where the change in the individual over time is predetermined and has an end point.

If the organismic metamodel is applied to the early and late segments of the lifespan, I would argue that in the early formative years of life there is predetermined incremental change toward some end point of biological maturity in development, and in later life there is predetermined decremental change toward the end point of death.

Such a position assumes the importance of biological thresholds. In early life, biological maturation determines the direction of change with environmental forces facilitating or inhibiting the rate and possibly the level of development up to approximately 18 years of age. At this point a critical threshold is reached where certain factors in the genetic blueprint are "turned off," and genetic influence becomes minimal in determining further direction of change. The individual in the environmental context becomes an open system that is best represented by the contextual/dialectic model. I would also argue that another threshold is reached in late life with the activation of other genetic factors. At this stage of life, decremental change continues toward a predetermined end point of death. In this view, aging (as distinct from development) may be defined as decremental, deteriorative change in the individual, with decreasing potential over time to reverse such change, and with a concomitant decrease in adaptation to the environment. Reciprocal interaction with the environment continues, but the individual and environment no longer have equal status in determining the direction of change. Finally, as aging continues, individual differences tend to converge, with universality, unilinearity, unidirectionality, and irreversibility of decremental change.

One might argue that the above position concerns only biological development and aging, is preoccupied with survival, and has nothing to do with psychosocial aging (which focuses on adaptation of the individual within the environment and fulfillment of social roles). However, in the latter part of the lifespan (from approximately age 85 on), there is a relatively high correlation between biological and psychological decremental changes. We know now that there are limits to development, and empirical evidence indicates decline in almost every cognitive function in late adulthood. Second, the psychological decline occurs in elementary and pervasive functions (such as speed of cognitive processing) that in turn affect more complex or higher mental processes (such as problem solving).

Communication in Relation to
Lifespan Development and Aging

According to the contextual/dialectic view of development in earlier portions of adulthood, the quality of interactions and communications between individuals is of primary importance in determining the direction of developmental change (e.g., more effective decision making). In this sense the social construction paradigm of the communication theorist is consistent with the contextual/dialectic worldview.

However, with a shift to the organismic model in the latter part of the lifespan, and the concomitant mental decline in the older individual, the reduced quality of interaction/communication would lead to a predetermined direction of aging (e.g., less effective decision making). Although research findings are somewhat inconsistent, some evidence indicates aging changes in modes of communication themselves. Some decrements in speech production, linguistic knowledge, and processing occur even among "normal" elderly (Coupland, Nussbaum, & Coupland, 1991). These decrements include use of less complex syntactic structures, more syntactic errors, and poorer linguistic processing, as well as a tendency toward off-target verbosity unrelated to present contextual stimuli. The extent to which these communication deficits of the elderly are due to underlying cognitive decline of biological origin or to other motivational and contextual factors is not known as yet. Nevertheless, a view of elderly speakers as having an impaired ability to communicate is widely held.

In response to the perceived communicative deficits of elderly speakers, the younger member of the dyad may also overaccommodate (or underaccommodate) his or her own discourse to that of the older member. As a result, the younger member's communication to the older may be stereotyped or patronizing, overbearing or excessively directive, involving a limited repertoire of topics (Atkinson & Coupland, 1988; Coupland et al., 1988). When the older family member is dependent, it would seem that the overaccommodation would become more extreme.

In any event, as the older person declines mentally and in concomitant modes of communication, the younger person's discourse to the elderly changes in a reciprocal fashion, becoming patronizing, routinized, paternalistic, and so on (Atkinson & Coupland, 1988; Coupland et al., 1988; Giles, Williams, & Coupland, 1990; Kreps, 1990; Rook, 1990; Wiemann, Gravell, & Wiemann, 1990). The elderly, in turn, tend to develop "mindless" or passive patterns of responding (Kreps, 1990; Rook, 1990).

Communication in Dyadic Family
Caregiving Decision Making

Biological decline in an individual in late life reduces the aging individual's ability to make intelligent decisions, thereby necessitating some kind of caregiving by others. An adult child or other caregiver typically interacts and communicates with the elderly parent in making decisions regarding caregiving (Cicirelli, 1991). In dyadic decision making earlier in adult life, decisions made by dyad members emerge out of the discourse of decision making itself.

However, as age increases and decremental change continues, paternalistic decisions by an adult child (or other caregiver) would be expected to become more predominant, with the reciprocal interaction between parent and child becoming more repetitive and beliefs about who should make decisions for caregiving becoming more resistant to change.

In my present work, I am studying caregiving decisions made by elderly parent-adult child dyads. In the majority of family caregiving situations, one family member acts as a primary caregiver to an elderly parent. (Obviously, the degree of the elderly parent's illness and the extent of the caregiver's burden may have some effect on the whole family, with the larger family system having an effect on the type and amount of care provided, but in most families these effects will be minimal compared to the reciprocal influences within the caregiving dyad itself. In any event, understanding caregiving decision making within the dyadic caregiving unit is an important step in comprehending decision making in the larger family system.)

However, if caregiving decision making is to take place at all, a decision maker must be selected in some way, that is, a decision must be made on the decision maker as a prerequisite for making subsequent decisions on caregiving tasks. It is my position that dyadic decision making for selecting a caregiving decision maker goes beyond the immediate situation and involves concern with the ethical question of who should or ought to be the decision maker. Further, answering the ethical question involves psychological beliefs as to who *should* make such decisions, with the beliefs themselves a product of social construction developed out of previous interactions and reflections. Thus, on the psychological level, it is hypothesized that adults have developed certain ethical beliefs regarding the agent of caregiving decision making, and that in late life such beliefs become more resistant to change, exerting a stronger influence on the interaction/communication process of deciding on the decision maker.

Ethical Beliefs in Dyadic Family Caregiving Decision Making: The Meaning of Autonomy and Paternalism. Before continuing further, the identification and meaning of the relevant ethical beliefs will be discussed.

Autonomy refers to the capacity of the individual to make reasoned decisions freely and to carry them out in action (Collopy, 1986, 1988; Dworkin, 1988). Respect for autonomy is the belief that one should allow or promote another individual's autonomous decision making. It is justified by the ethical argument that it is intrinsic to a person's nature to reason if he or she is to be human, and to use that reasoning to make and execute decisions without external interference and regardless of personal consequences (Aristotle, 1925; Kant, 1964; Mill, 1926).

By contrast, *paternalism* is the imposition of one person's decision on another individual for the welfare of that individual (Collopy, 1986; Gert & Culver, 1979; Halper, 1980). An ethical belief in paternalism is to believe that one should make decisions for another, and that one has the moral right to go beyond persuasion even to using threats, deception, and force if necessary to impose a decision on the other individual. The ethical argument is that a person in authority or an expert knows what is best for another individual (e.g., a doctor dealing with a patient, a professor dealing with a student, a parent dealing with a child, or an adult child dealing with an incapacitated elderly parent), and if such a person is sincerely concerned about the welfare of another individual, then that person has a moral obligation to intervene. The welfare of the individual, as a member of society, has priority over that individual's freedom to make his or her own decisions, especially if the consequences may be personally harmful.

Although it is difficult to respect the autonomy of older people when their capacity to make informed and voluntary decisions and carry them out declines with increasing frailty and/or mental deterioration, it is also difficult to justify paternalism when older people retain some degree of capacity. The recent work of various ethicists (Collopy, 1986, 1988; Dworkin, 1988; Gillon, 1985; Young, 1986) has provided the basis for expanding the concept of autonomy to include various subtypes that help to avoid the dilemma. Partial autonomy is preserved in the face of the elder's declining decisional capacity by allowing another person to participate in the decision making in varying degrees. Also, paternalism is tempered when some decisional capacity remains by decreasing the degree of threats, deception, or force used to impose a decision or by decreasing the instances in which paternalism is applied.

In family caregiving, independent or direct autonomy occurs when the care receiver makes autonomous decisions for himself or herself, whereas partial autonomy is found in shared autonomy. The latter exists when both caregiver and care receiver participate in the decision to some degree. Shared decision making can occur in three ways: joint decisions, where parent and child reach a decision together; delegated decisions, where the parent requests the child to decide (under the assumption that the decision would be in keeping with the wishes and values of the parent); and surrogate decisions, where the child makes a decision when the parent is unable to do so, with the decision in keeping with the parent's wishes and values. (Delegated and surrogate autonomy in decision making will be considered later in this chapter.)

The Relationship of Beliefs About Autonomy and Paternalism to the Agent of Decision Making. Beliefs are subjective judgments that objects or ideas exist and have certain attributes (Fishbein & Ajzen, 1975); beliefs can have an important influence on behavior (Fincham & Wertheimer, 1985; Sigel, 1985).

Sigel's (1985) work provides support for the influence of beliefs on behavior. He found that when beliefs are "action oriented" they are strong predictors of behavior. The beliefs in respect for autonomy and paternalism are action oriented, because they express a belief in what an adult child should do in a caregiving decision situation. Reasoning by analogy from Sigel's findings, one would expect beliefs about autonomy and paternalism to predict whether the adult child makes paternalistic decisions, the elderly parent makes autonomous decisions, or parent and child participate together in shared decision making.

In earlier work (Cicirelli, 1991), I found that caregiving daughters' beliefs in respect for autonomy and paternalism were related to measures of autonomous and paternalistic decision making in caregiving; similar relationships were found for mothers' beliefs. Thus the beliefs of each member of the dyad may be important predictors of the agent of decision making. However, certain types of caregiver-care receiver dyads may exist, characterized by the particular combination of beliefs held by each member regarding paternalism and respect for the autonomy of the elder.

For example, considering paternalism alone, an adult child may have a strong belief in paternalism while the elderly parent has a weak belief in paternalism, or vice versa. A given combination of parent's and child's degree of belief in paternalism may influence communication and decision making outcome differently than other combinations of dyad members' beliefs.

Empirical Evidence. It might be best at this point to summarize my position. Ordinarily, one would expect a reciprocal interaction/communication involving dyad members' beliefs about the agent of decision making and the actual dyadic decision making in selecting the agent of decision making. Both the beliefs and the selected decision maker would undergo continuous change and modification through the reciprocal interaction/communication process (e.g., the dyad might shift from autonomous to shared to paternalistic decision making, with concomitant shifts in beliefs as to who should be the decision maker, relative to the changing context of the mother's need for care).

However, as time goes on and the elder's intellectual and decision-making abilities inevitably decline, the reciprocal interaction/communication between mother and daughter no longer leads to concomitant modification of both beliefs and decision making. At that point, as the organismic framework begins to apply to the elder, beliefs become more solidified regarding the agent of decision making in the caregiving context; both the communication patterns in the decision-making process and the actual decisions made as to the decision maker become relatively stable.

To provide some evidence for the position stated above, an exploratory study was carried out. (The evidence focuses on the stage of life when the mother is in decline, and thus is best represented by the organismic model.) The exploratory study dealt only with the paternalism beliefs of the dyad members and their relationship to paternalistic decision-making and communication patterns.

A group of 50 mother-daughter dyads from a medium-sized city in the American midwest was studied. The daughters ranged from

33-70 years in age (M = 54.90), and provided at least 10 hours of help weekly to their mothers (M = 31.42 hours). Their mothers ranged from 62-97 years in age (M = 82.34), and were judged by the interviewer and the daughter to have adequate cognitive functioning and sufficient physical health to be interviewed. The group was subdivided to form four approximately equal subgroups, using the medians of mothers' and daughters' paternalism belief scores as cutting points to form a two-way classification. (This was made possible by the fact that the correlation between mothers' and daughters' belief scores was only .09, indicating little consensus on belief.) The four groups were as follows:

Group 1. Daughter low and mother low (14 pairs)
Group 2. Daughter low and mother high (11 pairs)
Group 3. Daughter high and mother low (10 pairs)
Group 4. Daughter high and mother high (15 pairs)

When analysis of variance was used to compare the four groups on the number of caregiving task areas in which paternalistic decisions were made by the daughter, both the mothers' paternalism belief and the daughter's paternalism belief had significant main effects (p < .05). Group 4 daughters made paternalistic decisions in the most caregiving task areas (M = 8.20), followed by Group 3 (M = 5.70) and Group 2 (M = 5.44) daughters, with Group 1 daughters making paternalistic decisions in the fewest caregiving task areas (M = 2.13).

On the basis of the above data analysis, it appears that paternalistic decisions are most likely when both mother and daughter are high in paternalism beliefs (this is more likely to be the case among older mothers with some reduction in decision-making capacity) and least likely when both mother and daughter are low in paternalism beliefs. When beliefs differ, paternalistic decisions occur with intermediate frequency. One can conclude that beliefs of both mother and daughter contribute to the observed findings.

To explore the relationship between paternalistic beliefs and verbal communication in decision making, study participants were asked to respond to open-ended interview questions designed to elicit elderly mothers' and their caregiving daughters' retrospective comments regarding their communication in the decision-making situation. Comments were elicited with respect to a variety of caregiving decision areas: housekeeping, meals, shopping, transportation, personal care, health care, finances, and mediation for services. (It would have been desirable to observe and record the decision-making process itself, but we judged the likelihood of capturing actual caregiving decision making during a naturalistic observation period to be too low to make such an approach feasible. However, observations of dyadic decision making in response to hypothetical decision tasks are now being carried out in further work.)

Representative samples of mothers' and daughters' comments are presented in Table 10.1, with each set of comments made by a given mother-daughter pair. These comments can be classified on the basis of their content as indicating paternalistic decision making by the daughter, autonomous decision making by the mother, or shared decision making by the mother-daughter pair.

Where the comments of a pair indicate paternalistic decision making by the daughter, the mother's comment and the daughter's comment are complementary, with the daughter making a dominant comment (taking the leadership in the decision making) and the mother making a submissive comment. A few of the comments suggest that the mother has some feelings of resentment about the daughter's decision making. There is little indication of any extended discussion about the decision; both mother and daughter appear to take for granted the daughter's right to make the decision.

Where the comments of a pair indicate autonomous decision making by the mother, again the mother's and daughter's comments are complementary, with the mother making a dominant comment and the daughter making a submissive statement. As was the case with paternalistic decision making, there was little evidence of discussion about the decision. Many of the comments by the mothers reveal a confident assertion of their independent autonomy, and the daughters' comments indicate their respect for the mothers' right to make their own decisions (even when the daughters must go to extra effort to make it possible for them to do so).

When the comments of the pairs using shared decision making are examined, one is struck by the mutuality of the decision-making process that is revealed. Decisions appear to be discussed and negotiated by the dyad members; there is a sense of "we" and not just "I," of acting as team, and of making use of the abilities of both members of the dyad to reach decisions that are mutually agreeable. Even when daughters must make decisions for their mothers, they try to represent their mothers' views in the decision making. There appears to be more of an egalitarian relationship between mother and daughter than for those pairs reporting paternalistic or autonomous decisions, as mother and daughter communicate their views in relatively conscious and explicit ways so that mutual understanding or compromise to reach a decision can be achieved.

When measures of the paternalism beliefs of mothers and daughters were related to the type of decision making revealed by their comments, there was a statistically significant relationship. Those pairs high in paternalism beliefs also made more comments indicating paternalistic decision making by the daughter, while those low in paternalism beliefs made more comments indicating autonomous decision making by the mother.

Finally, the pairs were divided into two subgroups according to the mother's age. From the lifespan developmental and aging psychological theory discussed earlier in this chapter, one would expect that with increased age, elderly mothers would be less able to make intelligent decisions and thus there would be more paternalistic decision making by their daughters. As predicted, there were more comments indicating paternalistic decision making in the older group than in the younger, and fewer comments indicating autonomous decision making by the mother.

The empirical work provides some evidence in support of the organismic metamodel as applied to the elderly family member in a caregiving decision-making context. When there is physical and mental decline of an elderly family member, dyad members' beliefs in paternalistic decision making stabilize and influence the pattern of communication, leading to increased paternalistic decision making.

Promoting Autonomous Decision Making in Late Life

Although paternalistic decisions by caregivers are known to increase in late life, many practitioners working with the elderly have as an ethical ideal the aim of preserving some type or degree of autonomous decision making by the older person for as long as possible.

When faced with caregiving decisions for an aging family member no longer able to make independent decisions, family caregivers have three possible courses of action: to make decisions that they judge to be in the elders' best interest (paternalism), to accept delegation of authority from the elderly family member and make decisions in the way they judge that the elderly family member would make them (delegated autonomy), or to simply attempt to make decisions in the way that the elders would if able to do so (surrogate autonomy).

Communication Problems in Delegated Decision Making. Delegation of decision making to family caregivers is one way in which aging parents can preserve some degree of autonomy when it becomes too difficult for them to make and/or execute decisions independently. (Delegated autonomy is often confused with paternalism, because both involve someone making decisions for another person. In delegated autonomy, the elderly person accepts decisions made by others who have been previously delegated to make those decisions, whereas in paternalism, others make decisions for the elderly person without prior delegation and with expected submission to the decisions.) However, the communication of just what decisions are delegated and in what domains of activity may present additional difficulties. If an adult child extends delegated authority in one area into decisions about the parent's other activities, the elderly parent's direct autonomy may be eroded more than necessitated by his or her physical or mental impairments. Thus careful communication of delegated authority is essential.

Communication Problems in Surrogate Decision Making. The making of surrogate autonomous decisions by an adult child in behalf of a demented, comatose, or otherwise incapacitated elderly parent is one way to preserve the parent's autonomy. However, to be able to make such caregiving decisions for the elderly family member depends on the adult child's (or other surrogate's) knowledge of the parent's values and wishes regarding care, gained over the history of past parent-child discourse.

However, the adult child may not carry out autonomy-respecting surrogate decision making properly because prior communication regarding the parent's wishes for care in such an eventuality may have occurred only to a limited degree or not at all. Also, in earlier parent-child discourse, adult children may have misperceived, misinterpreted, or disagreed with their parents regarding the latter's wishes for future care should they become incapacitated.

There are few existing studies pertaining to family caregiving decision making. However, in studies concerned with agreement between caregiver and care receiver, elderly family members were more likely to report that they had the final say on decisions, while family caregivers were more likely to report the elderly family member "gave in" when there was any disagreement about decisions (Horowitz, Silverstone, & Reinhardt, 1991; Pratt, Jones, Shin, & Walker, 1989). In regard to hypothetical decision situations, Horowitz et al. found little congruence between elders' and caregivers' responses.

In my own work (Cicirelli, 1991), I found not only little congruence between elderly parents and their adult children regarding autonomy and paternalism beliefs, but relatively weak knowledge of their elderly parents' wishes in regard to care. Respondents were asked about the extent to which the child would know the parent's wishes for care in the event that the parent could no longer decide this for himself or herself. There was only moderate congruence ($r = .42$) between parents' and children's responses to the above question; 48% of the parents and 57% of the adult children reported that the child would know the parent's wishes "well" or "very well," while 47% of the parents and 36% of the adult children felt that the child would know the parent's wishes "somewhat" or "pretty well," and only 5% of the parents and 7% of the children indicated that the children would know the parent's wishes "not well at all" or "not too well."

Although their responses would seem to indicate that both parents and children felt that the adult children knew the parents' wishes reasonably well, when asked whether parent and child had ever discussed the parents wishes in regard to care, some 42% of the elderly parents and 20% of the adult children reported that the parent and child had never discussed the parent's wishes or that they had tried to discuss it but the other person would not talk about it. Another 25% of the parents and 28% of the children indicated that they had discussed some things but not all, and 33%

of the elderly parents and 52% of the adult children reported that they had discussed "most things" or had discussed the parent's wishes in great detail. Despite the fact that most parents and children indicated that the children knew the parents' wishes for care reasonably well, how can accuracy of communication between parent and child exist regarding the parent's wishes for care when there has been little or no discussion of these matters between the two? This paradox has yet to be resolved.

On the other hand, children's accurate knowledge of parents' wishes may not prevent some difficulties in surrogate decision making. Some parents may feel that their children understand their wishes but they prefer to conform to the children's wishes (High 1989a, 1989b; High & Turner, 1987). Similarly, some adult children may be accurate in interpreting their parents' wishes, but they plan to decide how care is to be given according to their own preferences rather than according to their parents' wishes. That is, they prefer paternalism to surrogate autonomy.

Existing studies of family members' predictions of elders' care preferences in regard to various medical treatment scenarios revealed that not only were family members unable to predict the elderly's care preferences in a substantial proportion of the cases, but the family members did not intend to decide in the way that the elderly person would even when they felt that they knew what the elderly person's wishes were (Tomlinson, Howe, Notman, & Rossmiller, 1990; Uhlmann, Pearlman, & Cain, 1988; Warren et al., 1986; Zweibel & Cassel, 1989). In such cases, there may be problems in maintaining a contemporary relationship between parent and child because there *is* accurate communication between them regarding the parent's wishes for future care in the event of incapacitation. In general, the question here is whether the caregiver has gained sufficiently accurate knowledge of an elder's views regarding care from their long history of interaction/communication together to be able to make surrogate autonomous decisions.

Concluding Remarks

In this chapter, I have provided some evidence to demonstrate that elderly parents' and adult children's ethical beliefs about autonomy and paternalism are not only related to their reports of caregiving decision-making discourse but are also related to the determination of the agent of decision making.

In general, the hypothesis that personality characteristics (e.g., beliefs) influence both the discourse of decision making and the decision itself applies to dyads where an elderly dyad member is beyond a certain biological threshold, activating a slow but gradual physical and mental decline, with a concomitant decrement in decision-making capacity. Under such conditions, social constructions regarding the agent of decision making emerging from reciprocal communication become stereotypic and unduly influenced by beliefs in paternalism. A second factor that facilitates this trend is that such family members have experienced a relationship over a long time period. After many years of discourse among family members who have a close or intimate relationship, there is an additional tendency for interactions to become repetitive and stereotyped, allowing personality characteristics such as ethical beliefs to gain weight as causal antecedents.

When a dependent elderly family member is no longer able to make decisions, ethical beliefs may determine whether the family caregiver will make paternalistic or autonomy-respecting decisions in behalf of the elder. Adult children's lack of knowledge of their elderly parents' needs and wishes for care suggests the need to promote effective communication among dyadic decision makers in family caregiving.

It is recognized that the tentative conclusions advanced here are based on limited evidence from existing research studies and on self-report data from a small sample of parent-child dyads in my own work. An observational study of communication patterns in actual decision-making interactions is needed to confirm the findings of the present work as well as to investigate new hypotheses.

Congruence of communication between parent and child needs to be understood within the context of effective decision making. Disagreement between parent and child about who should be the agent of decision making is one aspect of reduced decision-making effectiveness, since it can negatively affect the overall quality of the parent-child relationship. Inappropriate agreement between dyad members may also indicate ineffective decision making; for exam-

Table 10.1 Samples of Comments Made by Mother-Daughter Dyads About Caregiving Decisions in Various Areas of Caregiving

Mother's Comments	*Daughter's Comments*
PATERNALISM	
My daughter just takes me.	I decide when and where to take her.
She does what *she* wants.	I do what I think needs to be done.
She listens to my requests, but does what she wants.	I "listen" to her requests, but do what I think best.
She gets what she thinks I need.	I decide what she needs.
She decides and takes care of everything.	I do what I think best, pay the bills.
SHARED AUTONOMY	
My daughter asks me and makes sure she's available.	I tell mother when I'm free, and offer to take her.
We discuss it.	We discuss it and decide together.
We discuss what should be done.	We talk it over together and decide.
She helps me shop and find things.	I take her and help her shop.
She discusses things and teaches me.	I advise her and we discuss it.
AUTONOMY	
I decide and my daughter takes me.	If Mother asks, I take her.
She does what I ask.	Mother asks and I do it.
She gets foods I ask for.	If Mother requests a food, I get it.
She gets what I want, my list.	I get what mother describes or lists.
I decide and she carries it out.	I do what Mother asks.

ple, if the dyad members agree that the parent should be the agent of decision making when he or she no longer has the mental capacity to do so, the decision is unlikely to be effective for either parent or child.

In general, the role of communication in dyadic family caregiving decision making needs to be recognized as an important area for future study if an increasing number of frail elders in American society are to retain some degree of autonomy in caregiving decision making.

References

Altman, I., & Rogoff, B. (1987). World views in psychology: Trait, interactional, organismic, and transactional perspectives. In I. Stokols & I. Altman (Eds.), *Handbook of environmental psychology* (pp. 7-40). New York: John Wiley.

Aristotle. (1925). *Ethica Nicomachia* (W. D. Ross, Trans.). London: Oxford University Press.

Atkinson, K., & Coupland, N. (1988). Accommodation as ideology. *Language & Communication, 8,* 321-327.

Baltes, P. B. (1979, Summer). On the potential and limits of child development: Lifespan developmental perspectives. *Newsletter of the Society for Research in Child Development,* pp. 1-4.

Baltes, P. B., Reese, H. W., & Lipsitt, L. P. (1980). Life-span developmental psychology. *Annual Review of Psychology, 31,* 65-110.

Brody, E. M. (1978). The aging of the family. *The Annals of the American Academy, 438,* 13-27.

Brody, E. M. (1990). *Women in the middle: Their parent care years.* New York: Springer.

Cantor, M. H. (1975). Life space and the social support system of inner city elderly of New York. *The Gerontologist, 15,* 23-27.

Cantor, M. H. (1985). Families: A basic source of long-term care for the elderly. *Aging, 349,* 8-13.

Cicirelli, V. G. (1981). *Helping elderly parents: The role of adult children.* Boston: Auburn House.

Cicirelli, V. G. (1991). *Family caregiving: Autonomous and paternalistic decision-making.* Newbury Park, CA: Sage.

Collopy, B. J. (1986, December). *The conceptually problematic status of autonomy.* New York: Fordham University.

Collopy, B. J. (1988). Autonomy in long-term care: Some crucial distinctions. *The Gerontologist, 28*(Suppl.), 10-17.

Coupland, J., Nussbaum, J. F., & Coupland, N. (1991). The reproduction of aging and ageism in intergenerational talk. In N. Coupland, H. Giles, & J. M. Wiemann (Eds.), *Miscommunication and problematic talk* (pp. 85-102). Newbury Park, CA: Sage.

Coupland, N., Coupland, J., Giles, H., & Henwood, K. (1988). Accommodating the elderly: Invoking and extending a theory. *Language in Society, 17,* 1-41.

Coward, R. T., & Dwyer, J. W. (1990). The association of gender, sibling network composition, and patterns of parent care by adult children. *Research on Aging, 12,* 158-181.

Dworkin, G. (1988). *The theory and practice of autonomy.* New York: Cambridge University Press.

Fincham, J. E., & Wertheimer, A. I. (1985). Using the health belief model to predict drug therapy defaulting. *Social Science & Medicine, 20,* 101-105.

Fishbein, M., & Ajzen, I. (1975). *Belief, attitude, intention and behavior.* Reading, MA: Addison-Wesley.

Gert, B., & Culver, C. M. (1979). The justification of paternalism. In W. L. Robison & M. S. Pritchard (Eds.), *Medical responsibility* (pp. 1-14). Clifton, NJ: Humana Press.

Giles, H., Williams, A., & Coupland, N. (1990). Communication, health and the elderly: Frameworks, agenda, and a model. In H. Giles, N. Coupland, & J. M. Wiemann (Eds.), *Communication, health and the elderly* (pp. 1-28). London: Manchester University Press.

Gillon, R. (1985). Autonomy and consent. In M. Lockwood (Ed.), *Moral dilemmas in modern medicine* (pp. 111-125). New York: Oxford University Press.

Halper, R. (1980). The double-edged sword: Paternalism as a policy in the problems of aging. *Milbank Memorial Fund Quarterly/Health and Society, 58,* 472-499.

High, D. M. (1989a). Caring for decisionally incapacitated elderly. *Theoretical Medicine, 10,* 83-96.

High, D. M. (1989b). Standards for surrogate decision making: What the elderly want. *The Journal of Long-Term Care Administration, 17*(2), 8-13.

High, D. M., & Turner, H. B. (1987). Surrogate decision-making: The elderly's familial expectations. *Theoretical Medicine, 8,* 303-320.

Horowitz, A., & Dobrof, R. (1982, May). *The role of families in providing long-term care to the frail and chronically ill elderly living in the community.* New York: Brookdale Center on Aging of Hunter College.

Horowitz, A., Silverstone, B. M., & Reinhardt, J. P. (1991). A conceptual and empirical exploration of personal autonomy issues within family caregiving relationships. *The Gerontologist, 31,* 23-31.

Kant, I. (1964). Groundwork of the metaphysics of morals (H. Paton, Trans.). New York: Harper & Row.

Kenny, D. A., & Acitelli, L. K. (1989). The role of the relationship in marital decision making. In D. Brinberg & J. Jaccard (Eds.), *Dyadic decision making* (pp. 51-62). New York: Springer.

Kreps, G. L. (1990). A systematic analysis of health communication with the aged. In H. Giles, N. Coupland, & J. M. Wiemann (Eds.), *Communication. health and the elderly* (pp. 135-154). London: Manchester University Press.

Lerner, R. M., Hultsch, D. F., & Dixon, R. A. (1983). Contextualism and the character of developmental psychology in the 1970s. *Annals of the New York Academy of Sciences, 412,* 101-128.

Mill, J. S. (1926). *On liberty and other essays.* New York: Macmillan.

Noelker, L. S., & Townsend, A. L. (1987). The impact of parental impairment, community resources, and caregiver characteristics. In T. H. Brubaker (Ed.), *Aging, health and family: Long-term care* (pp. 58-79). Beverly Hills, CA: Sage.

Overton, W. F., & Reese, H. W. (1973). Models of development: Methodological implications. In J. R. Nesselroade & H. W. Reese (Eds.), *Life-span developmental methodology* (pp. 65-86). New York: Academic Press.

Poole, M. S., & Billingsley, J. (1989). The structuring of dyadic decisions. In D. Brinberg & J. Jaccard (Eds.), *Dyadic decision-making* (pp. 216-248). New York: Springer.

Pratt, C. C., Jones, L. L., Shin, H.-Y., & Walker, A. J. (1989). Autonomy and decision-making among single older women and their caregiving daughters. *The Gerontologist, 29,* 792-797.

Rook, K. S. (1990). Social networks as a source of social control in older adult's lives. In H. Giles, N. Coupland, & J. M. Wiemann (Eds.), *Communication, health and the elderly* (pp. 45-63). London: Manchester University Press.

Shanas, E. (1979). The family as a social support system in old age. *The Gerontologist, 19*, 169-174.

Sigel, I. E. (1985). A conceptual analysis of beliefs. In I. E. Sigel (Ed.), *Parental belief systems: The psychological consequences for children* (pp. 345-372). Hillsdale, NJ: Lawrence Erlbaum.

Sillars, A., & Kalbfleisch, P. J. (1989). Implicit and explicit decision-making styles in couples. In D. Brinberg & J. Jaccard (Eds.), *Dyadic decision-making* (pp. 179-201). New York: Springer.

Tomlinson, T., Howe, K., Notman, M., & Rossmiller, D. (1990). An empirical study of proxy consent for elderly persons. *The Gerontologist, 30*, 54-64.

Uhlmann, R. F., Pearlman, R. A., & Cain, K. C. (1988). Physicians' and spouses' predictions of elderly patients resuscitation preferences. *Journal of Gerontology: Medical Sciences, 43*, M115-M121.

Warren, J. W., Sobal, J., Tenney, J. H., Hoopes, J. M., Damron, D., Levenson, S., DeForge, B. R., & Muncie, H. L., Jr. (1986). Informed consent by proxy: An issue in research with elderly patients. *The New England Journal of Medicine, 315*, 1124-1128.

Wiemann, J. M., Gravell, R., & Wiemann, M. C. (1990). Communication with the elderly: Implications for health care and social support. In H. Giles, N. Coupland, & J. M. Wiemann (Eds.), *Communication, health and the elderly* (pp. 229-242). London: Manchester University Press.

Young, R. (1986). *Personal autonomy: Beyond negative and positive liberty.* New York: St. Martin's.

Zweibel, N. R., & Cassel, C. K. (1989). Treatment choices at the end of life: Comparison of decisions by older patients and their physician-selected proxies. *The Gerontologist, 29*, 615-621.

CHAPTER ELEVEN

Investigations of Marital Communication and Lifespan Development

ALAN L. SILLARS
PAUL H. ZIETLOW

After "keeping house" together for many years, couples may find, to no one's surprise, that their relationship has changed. Many changes are dramatically obvious, for example the erosion of prenuptial misconceptions in early marriage, the shift from couple-oriented to family-oriented activities during child rearing, stress and readjustment due to career change or relocation. These changes are clear to us because they are identified with discernible life stage events and phases. Superimposed on this roller coaster are more subtle, evolutionary changes, which may pass without notice. Couples may gradually acquire new forms of interdependence, such as shared memories, unstated assumptions, and a more unified and coherent joint identity (or conversely, a more clearly and rigidly articulated separate identity). Along with increased interdependence, there potentially comes a different value perspective. Flexibility and problem-solving skill may be the preeminent concerns when identities and roles are in flux, but more static values such as security, loyalty, and "survivorship" sometimes take

AUTHORS' NOTE: The research reported in this chapter was assisted by a grant from the University of Montana small grant program.

precedence late in marriage (Johnson, 1988; Stinnet, Carter, & Montgomery, 1972).

From a certain perspective these relationship changes are synonymous with changes in couple communication. As many authors have emphasized, communication patterns continuously reveal implicit characteristics of relationships (e.g., Berger & Kellner, 1964; Watzlawick, Beavin, & Jackson, 1967). For example, couples may show their interdependence through shared stories, private codes, and predictable interaction patterns. Value orientations may be revealed by statements affirmed and topics pursued or avoided in conversation. Relationship change is accomplished by modifying these conversational practices. Thus couples may experience lifespan change as a succession of events (e.g., marriage, childbirth, "empty nest," retirement); however, it also involves subtle transformation from one type of communication system to another.

In this chapter we consider how marital communication might evolve over the family lifespan, drawing primarily on an observational study (Zietlow, 1986) and several subsequent analyses of these data. The results of this work provide a broad profile of communication within young, mid-life, and elderly couples, encompassing such processes as interpersonal perceptions, conflict patterns, self-disclosure, linguistic elaboration, and conversational themes. These aspects of communication appear to reflect the cumulative-experiences and developmental tasks of couples at different phases of life. A potential concern is that, after several thousand interactions, marriages might show signs of rigidity, loss of intimacy, and boredom. Although some research seems to support this view, the overall picture is more balanced. Essentially, we find greater passivity and less disclosure in later life stages, but also an increased focus on the dyad and less concern for interpersonal conflicts. These differences appear to reflect greater differentiation of individual identities and greater relationship stress in early phases of marriage, rather than reduced intimacy or interdependence thereafter.

General Rationale

Elsewhere (Sillars & Wilmot, 1989; Zietlow & Sillars, 1988) we have described three factors potentially affecting couple communication over the lifespan: (a) intrinsic developmental processes, (b) life stage experiences and developmental tasks, and (c) cohort-related values and experiences. The first two of these categories are truly developmental influences; that is, they describe changes in relationships over time. The third category is static; it refers to expressivity norms and marital ideologies that are carried forth from an earlier point in life. Since the 1950s, popular culture in the United States has shifted from a role-bound view of the ideal relationship, emphasizing discreet and tactful communication, to a process-oriented model anchored by such themes as openness, expressivity, honesty, and communication as "work" (Katriel & Phillipsen, 1981; Kidd, 1975). Thus expressivity is generally valued more highly by young spouses than by those middle-aged and older (Dobson, 1983; Fengler, 1973; Thurnher, 1976).

Intrinsic developmental processes include the development of shared meaning and modes of conduct over time. For example, couples may acquire an increasingly sophisticated view of one another's psychological dispositions; an increasing store of insider knowledge (e.g., common background experiences and shared constructs); a more congruent outlook; and more efficient, implicit, and idiosyncratic forms of communication (e.g., Altman & Taylor, 1973; Bell, Buerkel-Rothfuss, & Gore, 1987; Knapp, 1984). These changes are natural consequences of the intense bonding and sharing of personal information that normally accompanies the development of intimacy. Sillars and Wilmot (1989; see also Sillars & Kalbfleisch, 1989) speculate that couples continue to be affected by the accumulation of shared background experiences over the lifespan. Consequently, interactions might take on a more "implicit" or cryptic character with time, reflecting an increased emphasis of unstated expectations and taken-for-granted meanings versus fully elaborated requests and disclosures. Interactions might also be expected to show less differentiation of individual perspectives and personalities with time, reflecting greater integration of separate identities (i.e., an enhanced sense of "we-ness").

The developmental tasks associated with each life stage potentially shape the functions and characteristics of messages. Young couples have many instrumental concerns to reconcile (e.g., housing, careers, finances, household responsibilities) with little precedent for how to proceed. Pregnancy and childbirth bring about an additional stressful reorganization, as children require time, energy, and attention and they increase geometrically the number of family issues and conflicts that arise. Consequently, the conversations of young couples and families may be absorbed by instrumental functions, that is, decision making, role negotiation, conflict management, and adaptation to environmental stressors.

Although marriages may take many different paths, there is often an increased sense of intimacy and companionship among couples after parental obligations subside (Blieszner, 1988; Troll, Miller, & Atchley, 1979). Late in life, spouses may be especially reliant on one another, given their increased vulnerability to social isolation and physical disability. Consequently, older couples tend to value emotional security, loyalty, obligation, and companionship over other important characteristics of marriage (Johnson, 1988; Stinnet et al., 1972). Communication may primarily serve a companionate function in these relationships, in contrast to early marriage where instrumental coordination and negotiation of relationship rules are often more pressing concerns.

Each of the above factors leads us to expect that young couples will tend to exhibit a style of communication that is more expressive, intense, direct, and individualistic than mid-life and elderly couples. We now turn to the research where we consider these comparisons in detail.

Details of the Study

Couples were recruited at a Lutheran church in suburban Milwaukee through a notice in church bulletins over a 3-month period. A total of 77 couples participated in some capacity, although some couples did not complete all parts of the study.[1] The participants ranged in age from 23 to 83 years and had been married from 1 to 56 years. In direct contrast to the usual case in marital research, young couples were somewhat underrepresented, probably because the recruitment letter stressed the need for older couples and young couples were relatively inactive at the church. There were 12 couples from early family stages (without children or with children under age 13), 11 adolescence stage couples (with teenage children aged

13-20), 12 "launching" couples (with children 21 or older living at home), 12 empty nest couples (with no children still living at home), and 30 retired couples (both spouses retired).

Although we employed standardized questionnaires and a structured discussion task, we tried to naturalize the research environment somewhat by having couples complete the procedures at home without direct supervision. An instruction sheet asked participants to work separately in responding to the questionnaires, to refrain from sharing information, and to seal the completed surveys within separate envelopes when completed. Then, the couples were asked to discuss with one another several areas of conflict that are common to marriage, including affection, communication, household tasks, housing, irritability, leisure activities, money, and time spent together.

The discussions were recorded by the couples. Instructions asked the couples to consider each topic one at a time and to discuss the extent to which each area of conflict had come up in their marriage. Couples were told to skip topics that they felt uncomfortable discussing, otherwise they were simply asked to discuss each topic until they had nothing further to say. They later returned tapes and questionnaires to a designated location.

Individual and Interpersonal Perceptions

The questionnaires measured a number of perceptions of marriage. Some of these are individual perceptions, for example, marital satisfaction, sex role identification, and reported self-disclosure. Others are "interpersonal perceptions," borrowing the phrase of Laing, Phillipson, and Lee (1966). Interpersonal perceptions involve the interplay of "direct perspectives" (i.e., one's own belief's, evaluations, etc.) and "meta-perspectives" (i.e., perceptions of the spouse's beliefs, evaluations, etc.). Whereas individual perceptions reflect the subjective impacts of life stage experiences on each spouse, interpersonal perceptions reflect cognitive interdependence between spouses, particularly their consensus and understanding toward each other.

Marital Stress and Satisfaction

The single area where there is a concentration of relevant research is the study of marital satisfaction and adjustment over the lifespan. Although our research does not provide as definitive a picture of marital satisfaction as larger, probability-based samples, the results reveal important characteristics of the sample. It is helpful to compare our results with past studies to see whether our sample behaved in the manner typically reported.

Past studies have identified a "U-shaped" trend in marital satisfaction (Anderson, Russell, & Schumm, 1983; Medling & McCarrey, 1981; Miller, 1976; Rollins & Cannon, 1974) and a linear decrease in negative tensions over the family lifespan (Johnson et al., 1986). Early in marriage, couples enjoy companionship and the novelty of romance. The birth and development of children introduces stressors and time-demands that detract noticeably from marital satisfaction. Marital quality may subsequently increase during later life stages, peaking in retirement, due to freedom from child-rearing tensions, increased companionship, and reduced marital discord (Schumm & Bugaighis, 1986; Sporakowski & Hughston, 1978).

In our study, marital satisfaction was measured using the 10-item satisfaction subscale of Spanier's (1976) Dyadic Adjustment Scale. We looked for trends in satisfaction across five life stages (early family stages, adolescent, launching, empty nest, and retirement stages). Although we found no significant life stage trends in satisfaction, a curvilinear pattern was closest to fitting the data (Zietlow, 1986).

Consistent with previous research, retired couples in our sample reported the highest marital satisfaction of the life stage groups. In addition, couples rated the salience of eight sources of conflict.[2] These were the same problem areas that provided the focus of the taped conversations. When all the ratings were summed to form a single measure, there was a significant linear decrease in problem salience over the eight life stages. Thus the results are roughly in line with the picture provided by other samples. This picture is one of decreased tension and increased satisfaction later in the family lifespan.

Sex Role Identification

Some research finds a softening of traditional sex-typed behavior subsequent to retirement, particularly among husbands (see Dobson, 1983). There is less normative pressure to do either masculine or feminine things subsequent to parenting and retirement, so males may become more reflective, dependent, and affiliative and females more assertive. Though this potential change is of interest in and of itself, it is also of interest because of the implications for interpersonal perception. Identity changes late in life threaten consensus about implicit role expectations. These expectations include not only who will wash the car and take out the trash but also subtle roles, such as how spouses provide emotional support or how analytically they approach major purchases. Couples may adjust to the change by establishing a new consensus around revised roles. Alternatively, the weight of prior experience might be so heavy and existing expectations so entrenched that spouses become impervious to subtle changes in the partner. In the latter case we would expect to find declining consensus as a function of identity change.

Our results confirmed a shift in gender identity for husbands but not wives. Bem's (1974) sex-role inventory, which measures "masculine" and "feminine" trait attributions (e.g., "assertive," "analytical," and "athletic" versus "sympathetic," "cheerful," and "yielding"), was used to measure the traits attributed to self and to the partner. There was little difference in traits attributed to wives across life cycle stages. However, femininity attributed to husbands by both husbands and wives followed a significant U-shaped trend over the lifespan. Husbands' own assessments of their femininity took a notable dip from the early family stage to adolescent child period and then rebounded sharply in the retirement period. Conversely, perceived masculinity rose sharply among husbands with adolescent children and then dropped again among retired husbands; however, this trend was not statistically significant. If husbands did undergo an identity shift, it appears that wives were cognizant of it, because wives' attributions about husbands generally duplicated the life stage pattern of husbands' self-attributions. This supports the interpretation that there is a mutual readjustment of role perceptions late in marriage.

Reported Self-Disclosure

Previous studies have identified a decline in reported self-disclosure late in marriage (Eskew, 1978; Jourard, 1971; Swensen, Eskew, & Kolhepp, 1981) and an increase in unexpressed feelings during every phase subsequent to the newlywed period (Swensen et al., 1981). In our research three dimensions of reported self-disclosure were investigated: the overall amount of disclosure, depth or intimacy of disclosure, and valence of disclosure (Wheeless, 1976). With respect to the last dimension, some marriage research has suggested that mates become more negative or critical over the duration of marriage (Pineo, 1961). However, we did not find any differences in the valence of disclosure across the life cycle groups.

Consistent with earlier research, retired spouses were noticeably lower in amount and depth of disclosure than other life stage groups. However, the effect was mainly for wives. Wives in the earliest life stages reported relatively high levels of disclosure. However, there was a significant linear decrease in both amount and depth of disclosure for wives across the life stage categories. Disclosure levels for husbands, on the other hand, began relatively low and remained stable across the lifespan.

Attitude Agreement and Understanding

Swensen et al. (1981) speculated that some elderly spouses might gradually lose the ability to predict the partner's attitudes, thoughts and feelings because of low self-disclosure. One might also presume the opposite, that elderly spouses are more able to anticipate the partner's perspective because of the longevity of the relationship. It appears, however, that elderly spouses are generally no better or worse at predicting the partner's perspective than their younger counterparts. Evidence for the above conclusion comes from the couples' responses to a survey of marital attitudes. In this portion of the questionnaire, the couples were presented with 40 statements about marriage (e.g., "Families should spend less time watching television." "In a good marriage people are always honest with one another."). Spouses first reported their own agreement with each statement (on 5-point Likert scales) and then predicted how their partner would respond to the same items. Understanding scores were computed using a partial correlation procedure, which compensates for the natural advantage that similar partners have in predicting a mate's responses.[3] Although spouses in the earliest life stages had somewhat higher understanding scores than the rest of the sample, there was no overall effect of life stage on understanding. Retired spouses were about average in predicting their partner's attitudes. Similarly, there was no effect of life stage on attitude agreement (calculated as a correlation between attitudes of each spouse). Intuitively, one might expect years of repeated interactions to gradually fuse the attitudes of marriage partners. Instead it appears that a certain level of agreement and understanding is achieved early in marriage and is generally maintained through subsequent phases.

Overall, the perceptual data indicated that couples maintained a similar level of satisfaction, consensus, and understanding across the lifespan categories, in spite of apparent changes in gender identity among husbands and lower reported disclosure among wives. These results lead us to believe that the lower disclosure levels sometimes observed among older couples reflect different values and developmental tasks in later life stages, rather than gradual disengagement from the spouse.

Conflict Management

The questionnaire results indicated that marital conflicts decreased in salience over the family lifespan. The next set of results allows us to look more directly at how actively the couples engaged in management of conflict. Here we coded transcripts and tapes of the conversations using an interaction analysis scheme that identifies conflict styles and patterns. Complete details of the coding are provided by Zietlow and Sillars (1988). For the purpose of this and other interaction analyses, the life stage categories were collapsed into three stages: young couples (childless couples and couples with school-age children), mid-life couples (preretired couples with adult children), and retired, aging couples (both spouses retired). The codes were analyzed using log linear analysis, which is a method appropriate to multivariate cross-classification tables.

The results revealed rather strong differences in communication patterns across the life stage groups. Three main findings are of interest. First, overall differences between life stage groups confirmed our speculations about young couples; that a primary function of their communication is explicit negotiation of conflict. Young couples were generally most engaging and direct when discussing marital problems. Of the three life stage groups, they had the highest percentage of "irreverent" (i.e., humorous), "analytic," and "confrontive" remarks and the lowest percentage of "denial and equivocation," "topic management," and "noncommittal" remarks. The analytic and confrontive codes refer respectively to informational and verbally competitive statements. These codes represent engagement styles of conflict. In contrast, denial and equivocation (i.e., denial of conflict or evasive replies), topic management (evasive topic shifts), and noncommittal remarks (low risk, low disclosure comments that neither confirm or deny conflict) represent nonengagement or conflict avoidant conflict styles. In contrast to young couples, mid-life couples had a relatively high percentage of denial and equivocation, topic management, and noncommittal codes and a low percentage of irreverent and confrontive codes. Curiously, retired couples had the highest percentage of noncommittal codes but they also had a comparatively high percentage of confrontive codes. Additional findings help us to make sense of this unexpected blend of passivity and aggression.

The second result has to do with the salience of discussion topics. We naturally assumed that couples might respond more assertively or defensively to discussion topics that were salient areas of conflict. Consequently, we identified issues that were salient to each couple from the questionnaire ratings (see Note 2) and compared interactions on these topics with nonsalient topics. Predictably, the salience of the issue had an effect on the conflict codes. More important, the effect of salience was different within each life stage group. Retired and middle-aged couples were more dramatically affected here than young couples. Retired couples were surprisingly confrontive when issues were salient (40% of the codes were confrontation), and extremely congenial when topics were nonsalient (only 3% of the codes were confrontation). Mid-life couples, on the other hand, shifted from a passive style on nonsalient topics (only 13% analytic remarks) to constructive engagement on salient topics (39% analytic remarks).

The third result has to do with sequences of interaction. Overall, there was a strong tendency for spouses to match or reciprocate the immediately preceding remark by the partner (e.g., denial elicited denial, confrontation elicited confrontation). However, reciprocity varied among the life stage groups. Specifically, retired couples had a much stronger tendency to reciprocate confrontive remarks by the partner (88% reciprocation) than either young (57%) or mid-life (31%) couples. Thus, when confrontive remarks were introduced into the discussions, retired couples were apt to chain out on these remarks, thereby constructing escalation sequences.

In effect, retired couples invoked one of two extreme patterns. Much of the time, the conversations of retired couples were calm, characterized by pleasant digressions and reminiscing (i.e., the noncommittal style), and contained little or no acknowledgment of conflict in the marriage. Exceptions mainly involved a small number of dissatisfied retired couples who bickered throughout the discussions. Evidently, these were couples whose long-simmering conflicts had never been successfully addressed. Troll et al. (1979) note that some elderly couples remain together in a sort of "armed truce" due to cohort-related stigmas and prohibitions against divorce. These couples accounted for the highly predictable confrontation sequences observed when conflict issues were salient. The results thus illustrate something about both the strengths and weaknesses of the older marriages we observed. A strength demonstrated by many of the couples was their overall compatibility and harmony. The weakness demonstrated was an impoverished communication repertoire among elderly couples whose conflicts remained unresolved.

Young couples seemed better practiced at conflict. They acknowledged conflict most consistently but also counterbalanced different forms of engagement, giving the discussions a dynamic and flexible quality. Mid-life couples, on the other hand, were somewhere between the passivity of most retired couples and the intense style of young couples. Like the retired couples, mid-life couples were often nonconflictive and noncommital in their discussions, but they became analytic when marital conflicts were salient. The direct but subdued quality of these interactions suggests that adjustments in the relationship were still being made but fundamental issues (e.g., those concerning identity, warmth, regard, dominance, and trust) had been resolved or put aside.

Language and Disclosure Styles

We next consider whether the relatively inexpressive conflict style of most older couples was a consequence of limited conflict only, or whether these couples were also less expressive in other ways. Several other aspects of discourse pertain to the directness or explicitness of marital communication. Couples may differ generally in the extent to which they make information about their subjective experiences and observations explicit. For example, some authors have observed that traditional relationships require relatively less articulation of individual experiences, due to the stabilizing influence of shared traditional ideologies (Ellis & Hamilton, 1985; Fitzpatrick, 1988). Internalized relationship norms may, in this case, become a largely unarticulated, taken-for-granted component of marital communication; consequently, there is "less need to talk" and "the interaction that does occur does more 'work' " (Ellis & Hamilton, 1985, p. 274). Similarly we might expect couples who have interacted over many years to establish efficient communication systems richly colored by implicit insider meaning. Thus their conversations might be fairly brief and to the point, contain few explicit references to individual experiences (i.e., self-disclosure), and contain frequent statements presuming a shared frame of reference.

The discussion transcripts were coded using a set of procedures devised by Stiles (1978) to identify self-disclosure patterns and general conversational styles. Stile's Taxonomy of Verbal Response Modes classifies utterances into eight categories according to their form and intent. The categories are: "disclosure" (statements about the speaker's internal experience), "interpretation" (statements about the other's experience or behavior), "confirmation" (statements about mutual experiences), "question" (requests for information or guidance), "edification" (statements presumed to express objective information), "advisement" (advice, commands, instructions, permission, and prohibition), "reflection" (restating, summarizing, clarifying), and "acknowledgment" (utterances showing reception of communication, such as "oh," "mm-hm"). We coded the first 40 utterances in each discussion and calculated the percentage of codes that fell into each category.

Consistent with the self-report responses, young couples were the most disclosive of the life stage groups, although the differences in disclosure codes were not strong: 22% of the statements made by young couples were coded as disclosure, in comparison to 17% for mid-life couples and 16% for retired couples. The differences in disclosure codes were not statistically significant (according to an F test). The one area where there was a clear difference between the groups was in the use of the confirmation code. There was a significant linear increase in use of this code across the life stage groups. Young couples made the fewest confirmation statements (17%), by comparison with mid-life (28%), and retired couples (33%). This result supports the idea that couples might acquire an increased focus on their shared frame of reference during later phases of marriage (i.e., increased we-ness). Confirmation statements use the internal viewpoints of both speaker and other, either through reference to agreements and similarities or to disagreements and dissimilarities (Stiles, 1978). Some examples include: "We both feel the same way." "We disagree about that." "You and I make a good team." The strikingly heavy reliance on this code by retired couples (i.e., one out of every three utterances), suggests that these couples were accustomed to speaking for one another.

Some additional specific discourse features were coded on the same transcript segments to extend and clarify the above results. To determine whether the couples had a more or less elaborated linguistic style, we computed the number of words spoken per discussion topic covered (with *topic* referring to the eight discussion issues), mean utterance length (average words per sentence), nouns (including gerunds) and adjectives (excluding definite or indefinite articles and possessive pronouns), and instances of "meta-talk," defined as recursive talk directing or organizing the conversation, (e.g., "I'll put it this way . . . " "The point is . . . " "Listen to this . . . "). To determine whether spouses linguistically differentiated their own experience from their partner's experience, we distinguished "I" and "you" versus "we" pronouns and computed an index of linguistic "cross-referencing" (i.e., the percentage of nouns and adjectives that were used jointly by both spouses). Finally, to determine whether spouses demonstrated uncertainty about the partner's perspective through linguistic expressions, we coded instances of "qualifiers" (e.g., "it seems to me," "maybe," "I guess") and "disclaimers" ("I'm not sure." "I'm not an expert but . . . " "I could be mistaken but . . . ") (see Hewitt & Stokes, 1975).

The results from this extensive analysis of linguistic features were humbling but instructive. No indicators of elaboration or uncertainty were related to life stage. The one item that varied across the life stage groups (again, according to an F test) was the frequency of "we" pronouns (e.g., "we," "ours," "each other"), computed as a percentage of total words uttered by either spouse. The use of "we" pronouns essentially mirrored the effect for confirmation codes; young couples used the fewest "we" pronouns and retired couples used the most.

Although we speculated that older couples might use a less elaborated linguistic code than young couples, we found no clear evidence to this effect. The groups did not differ in terms of the elaboration or complexity of their communication. Rather, the main discriminating feature was the tendency of older couples to assume a shared frame of reference, indicated by their frequent use of confirmation statements and "we" pronouns and somewhat less frequent use of self-disclosure statements. These results are consistent with the idea that couples develop a more integrated shared identity later in the lifespan.

Relationship Themes

The results of the previous section point to an important aspect of couple communication, but they only scratch the surface. In the final section we consider, in greater detail, how shared definitions of relationships might be reproduced in the content and structure of conversations. Here, the conversations were viewed as jointly authored "accounts" (see Gergen & Gergen, 1987) that turn on certain key elements (e.g., the husband's father, the wife's forgetfulness, the couple's love for their children). We refer to these elements as "relationship themes." Our attention was drawn to two aspects of relationship themes (see Sillars, Burggraf, Yost, & Zietlow, 1991, for details).

First, we were interested in the particular view of marriage suggested by various themes, particularly the contrast between certain themes that focus on joint or interdependent attributes of the marriage (what we refer to as "communal" themes) and other themes that emphasize the autonomy of spouses (i.e., "individual" themes). Naturally, we expect couples to use varied themes in their conversations, but the overall emphasis given to specific themes may reveal different ontological perspectives (e.g., marriage as a cooperative effort versus a pooling of distinct individual personalities). To consider this possibility, we identified types of themes in the discussions, based on an analytic scheme developed in earlier research (Sillars, Weisberg, Burggraf, & Wilson, 1987). Examples of communal and individual themes are given in Table 11.1. The analytic scheme also includes a third main category, "impersonal" themes, which is not relevant here.

Results showed that the young couples often focused their conversations on individual differences and separate identities, whereas retired couples focused extensively on shared activities, common interests and beliefs, similarities, communication together, and similar communal themes. Mid-life couples generally fell in between the individualism of young couples and the strong communal focus of retired couples. Retired couples had the highest percentage of themes coded as "togetherness" (15% versus 10% and 9% for mid-life and young couples) and "communication" (14% versus 9% and 7% for mid-life and young couples). Retired couples also had very few "separateness" themes (5%) by comparison to mid-life (11%) or young (10%) couples. Young couples, on the other hand, had a high percentage of "personality" themes (26% versus 17% and 16% for mid-life and retired couples). The effects of life stage on togetherness, communication, personality, and separateness themes were all statistically significant and linear.

Table 11.1   Illustrations of Relationship Themes

I. *Communal Themes:* Marriage is seen as the product of joint or interdependent qualities of the couple.

  A. *Togetherness*

    "We enjoy the same things."

    "We don't take enough time to do things."

    "We enjoy doing chores together."

  B. *Cooperation*

    "We talk out disagreements so that we don't confuse the children."

    "We work together in paying things."

    "I don't have the right to be irritable with you and vice-versa."

  C. *Communication*

    "We talk all the time."

    "I feel better if I get it off my chest."

  D. *Romanticism*

    "If two people don't show affection, chances are they're not in love."

    "Lack of affections stems from people marrying for the wrong reasons."

  E. *Interdependence*

    "It's hard to be depressed when someone else is not."

    "If you're irritable and I'm feeling irritable, that makes it worse."

II. *Individual themes*

  F. *Separateness*

    "You have your friends, and I have mine."

    "Individual decisions are made individually."

    "I need to be left alone sometimes."

  G. *Personality*

    "You bitch all the time."

    "I've never been a person to do a lot of touching."

    "I'm not good at communicating."

    "You're just a conscientious person."

  H. *Role*

    "I get mad when you don't get something done."

    "You have your things to do and I have my things to do."

    "You're never home to discipline the kids."

A *second* way of inferring interdependence or autonomy is to consider the integration of individual perspectives within conversations. In more interdependent marriages, we expect spouses to coordinate their remarks with each other to achieve a coherent, mutually authored description of the relationship. Increasing interdependence is suggested as conversations approach the degree of coherence found in individual accounts and narratives. On the other hand, autonomous marriages may produce something more like "his and her" accounts (Mansfield & Collard, 1988). Integration may be achieved through the chaining of themes by successive speakers (a property we refer to as *continuity*) as well as the expression of abstract themes encompassing and reconciling lower order themes (referred to as *hierarchy*). With respect to continuity, Bormann (1986) suggests that the chaining out of discussion themes establishes a shared base of symbolic experience and a referent for collective identity. These chains may be subsequently reenacted and embellished as part of ongoing relationship maintenance and development. With respect of hierarchy, Hess and Handel (1959) suggest that family members maintain a sense of connectedness by mutually orienting to abstract, higher order themes (e.g., escaping the insecurity of the partners' youth). Such themes transcend specific issues, activities, and family members.

We proceeded in our analysis of integration by first identifying segments of conversation where there was a chaining out of several or more related themes. This screening process utilized a quantitative analysis of interact sequences (two contiguous statements).[4] We then described qualitative features of each discussion segment selected. From the qualitative analysis we eventually discerned three basic clusters of similar interaction segments, labeled "blending," "differentiating," and "balancing" chains.

As the term *blending* suggests, the conversational segments in the first cluster presented an undifferentiated couple identity. This was accomplished through mutually confirming and overlapping talk about shared rules, interpretations, activities, backgrounds, and experiences. Mostly these sequences were produced by couples who were elderly or middle-aged (80%), and above the median in satisfaction (90%). The content of statements within the blending cluster often expressly referred to the theme of togetherness or sameness (e.g., " . . . after 19 years of marriage we've probably blended together as far as our beliefs, ideas, and activities, friends and lifestyles."). These images were reinforced structurally as speakers affirmed, repeated, paraphrased, extended, and completed one another's statements (i.e., high continuity). Blending chains were also typically anchored by central themes (e.g., spirituality, age, family background, widowhood) that provided a central explanation for various facets of the marriage and were frequently reiterated throughout the discussions. One couple referred to their Christian beliefs to explain other facets of the relationship:

> Any marriage that involves just two people is headed for trouble. It takes three . . . as each of the two draw closer to Christ, they inevitably draw closer to one another.

Couples within this cluster seemed to experience little difficulty producing a simple and uniform account, thus suggesting a thoroughly integrated couple identity.

In contrast, differentiating chains identified the marriage as a union of distinctively separate, unintegrated husband-wife identities. These chains were largely composed of personality and separateness themes, and were characterized by a lack of continuity from speaker to speaker. There were few instances where speakers directly disagreed with one another. However, they often disconfirmed each other through topic shifts, countercomplaints, leading questions, evasive replies, and "attributional conflicts" (Orvis, Kelley, & Butler, 1976), where a certain behavior was relabeled and reinterpreted on successive speaking turns. For example, one wife described her husband as "too reclusive," while the husband stated that he gets "channeled" and too "keyed up" to "shift gears." Similarly, a wife stated that, "You just do not communicate." The husband responded that, " . . . some of the things in my everyday life, the work I'm in, are not communicable ideas." Predictably, these chains were mostly enacted by couples who were below the median in marital satisfaction (73%) and a majority (53%) were produced by young couples. However, a third of the differentiating chains were enacted by retired couples, bringing to mind the conflict escalation sequences observed among some of these couples in an earlier analysis.

Whereas blending and differentiating chains expressed either undifferentiated identities or separate personalities, balancing chains provided a bridge between these extremes. In balancing chains, speakers commented on individual characteristics that were linked by superordinate themes. For example, several of the couples pictured themselves as having a complementary relationship (i.e., one in which opposite tendencies balance one another; such as a "carefree" wife and a "conservative" husband) and complementarity sometimes provided a central integrating theme (e.g., "We correct each other." "Opposites attract."). In other excerpts, communication processes or abstract cooperative principles were used to integrate individual differences (e.g., " . . . if I think you ought to change in an area . . . I have told you." " . . . a way of communication is knowing where we are emotionally."). These sequences, which suggested balanced interdependence and autonomy, were mainly enacted by young couples (67%) with variable marriage satisfaction (56% at or above the median).

Our analysis of relationship themes suggested that the oldest couples in the sample typically showed the greatest degree of interdependence, both through their overall emphasis of communal themes and through uniform, highly integrated conversational accounts. Young couples focused much more on individualistic constructs, in some cases achieving overall coherence through higher order relationship themes that acknowledged and reconciled individual differences. Both younger and older couples occasionally lapsed into highly individualistic and competitive sequences, but this was more commonly the case among young couples, reflecting their greater emphasis of individual differences generally.

Conclusions

Most studies of marital communication are primarily studies of young couples. This is a period of marriage when demands for explicit communication are high. Aside from the adjustments and decisions that first accompany marriage, major life changes (e.g., initiation of careers, relocation, birth of children, beginning of school) are often densely packed into the early years. Young couples also have the intangible task of blending separate personalities and achieving a common sense of purpose and identity. Researchers have given much of their attention to the factors needed to sustain couples through such a volatile period of change, such as self-disclosure, understanding, and conflict management. These variables are undoubtedly important to marriage at any point in the life cycle, yet they are particularly significant during the initial integration of personalities and subsequent periods of stressful change. Well-seasoned marriages might reflect somewhat different developmental priorities.

An illustration is the "passively congenial" interaction style of some elderly couples (Troll, 1982; Zietlow & Sillars, 1988). The oldest couples in our research generally took a noncommital stance during discussion of potential conflict issues and they showed limited self-disclosure. It is tempting to conclude that these couples may have lost their vitality; that they have stopped addressing problems directly and ceased checking to see where the other person's thoughts are. Yet, couples often put a favorable gloss on marriage late in life, as indicated by the relatively high satisfaction ratings of older couples in this and other research. Further, agreement and understanding remained fairly stable across the lifespan groups, rather than declining with life stage as we would expect if spouses were disengaging from each other. In some respects the retired couples demonstrated enhanced interdependence, for example, they frequently expressed communal themes, adopted a common frame of reference (i.e., "we" pronouns and confirmation statements), and produced highly integrated joint accounts (i.e., blending chains). These interaction characteristics suggest less concern for marital conflicts and greater integration of identities than at early stages of marriage.

In contrast to the general trend, some retired couples enacted highly predictable confrontive sequences and highly individualistic thematic chains (i.e., differentiating chains). This raises the possibility that the developmental path established earlier in marriage might culminate in rigid and extreme forms of interaction later on. That is, couples who fail to manage fundamental conflicts successfully at earlier stages might eventually become embittered and entrenched in unproductive patterns of interaction. Young couples showed greater variety in their response to conflict than retired couples, presumably because frequent conflict is a normal consequence of this family stage. Mid-life couples shared some interaction characteristics with both young couples and retired couples. Mid-life couples discussed salient conflict issues directly but without the contentiousness and emotionality often demonstrated by young couples. The direct but subdued quality of these interactions suggests that adjustments in the relationship were still being made but fundamental issues (e.g., basic issues of warmth, regard, dominance, or trust) had been resolved or put aside.

An obvious limitation of our research is the cross-sectional nature of the design. It goes without saying that differences between the life stage groups might represent cohort effects (e.g., generational attitudes about disclosure and conflict in marriage) as well as developmental changes. However, the fact that many differences between life stage groups were linear supports the interpretation of gradual developmental change. In several areas, young couples and retired couples formed two ends of a continuum, with mid-life couples occupying the middle ground. This was true with respect to problem salience, self-disclosure, conflict engagement, confirmation statements, "we" pronouns, and relationship themes, including "togetherness," "communication," "personality," and "separateness" themes. If the differences in communication were purely a function of cohort rather than developmental change, we would not expect to find such a regular life stage pattern.

Finally, the research identified some aspects of relationship development that may not continue over the lifespan. Sillars and Wilmot (1989) speculated that interactions might become increasingly "implicit" over the lifespan, as couples achieve more taken-for-granted consensus and acquire increasingly efficient forms of communication. However, there was no evidence that older couples talked any less than young couples or that they spoke in a cryptic code. Although it is still possible that communication decreases or becomes more efficient in the initial year or so of marriage (Huston, McHale, & Crouter, 1986), it appears that any such change levels off quickly. In part, this might be because explicit conversation retains a vital function late in marriage, even when instrumental issues and conflicts are subdued. For some older couples, conversations with the spouse appear to serve a companionate function primarily, as their conversations are largely devoted to sharing of similar experiences rather than negotiation of conflicts and roles.

Notes

1. All couples provided questionnaire responses. However, only 54 couples also completed the discussion task, which is the basis of several analyses. One tape was inaudible. In addition, four retired and remarried couples were excluded from the analyses performed by Zietlow (1986) and Zietlow and Sillars (1988) in order to make the elderly group more homogeneous. These four couples were included in later analyses of observed disclosure patterns, language, and relationship themes.

2. Spouses separately indicated the extent to which each problem was present in the marriage on 5-point scales ranging from "not at all" to "very large extent." Individual's scores were combined to form couple's scores. We used these scores to determine the prominence of various conflicts over the lifespan and also to identify salient areas of conflict from among the discussion topics. Topics were considered salient if the combined husband and wife rating equaled 4 or greater.

3. As in other studies (Sillars, Weisberg, Burggraf, & Zietlow, 1990), understanding was calculated as the correlation between predicted attitudes of the partner and the partner's self-ratings, with the self-ratings of the predicting spouse partialed out. This method eliminates confounding of understanding and agreement scores that otherwise occurs in research on understanding.

4. We reasoned that if there are recurring chains of relationship themes, these should produce statistical dependencies between contiguous codes (e.g., separateness themes followed by personality themes). There were 22 interact sequences that occurred more often than expected by chance. We used these 22 sequences to identify extended chains, where several statistically related themes occurred in succession. Extended chains that lasted at least six utterances were then analyzed for qualitative features, with no more than two chains coming from a given couple. In this manner, 41 discussion excerpts from 21 couples were selected for the qualitative analysis.

References

Altman, I., & Taylor, D. A. (1973). *Social penetration: The development of interpersonal relationships*. New York: Holt, Rinehart & Winston.

Anderson, S. A., Russell, C. S., & Schumm, W. R. (1983). Perceived marital quality and family life-cycle categories: A further analysis. *Journal of Marriage and the Family, 45,* 127-139.

Bell, R. A., Buerkel-Rothfuss, N. L., & Gore, K. E. (1987). "Did you bring the yarmulke for the cabbage patch kid?": The idiomatic communication of young lovers. *Human Communication Research, 14,* 47-67.

Bem, S. L. (1974). The measurement of psychological androgyny. *Journal of Consulting and Clinical Psychology, 42,* 155-162.

Berger, P., & Kellner, H. (1964). Marriage and the construction of reality. *Diogenes, 46*, 1-24.

Bormann, E. G. (1986). Symbolic convergence theory and communication in group decision-making. In R. Y. Hirokawa & M. S. Poole (Eds.), *Communication and group decision-making* (pp. 219-236). Beverly Hills, CA: Sage.

Blieszner, R. (1988). Individual development and intimate relationships in middle and late adulthood. In R. M. Milardo (Ed.), *Families and social networks* (pp. 147-167). Newbury Park, CA: Sage.

Dobson, C. (1983). Sex-role and marital-role expectations. In T. H. Brubaker (Ed.), *Family relationships in later life* (pp. 109-126). Beverly Hills, CA: Sage.

Ellis, D., & Hamilton, M. (1985). Syntactic and pragmatic code choice in interpersonal communication. *Communication Monographs, 52*, 264-268.

Eskew, R. W. (1978). *An investigation of cohort differences in the marriage relationships of older couples.* Unpublished doctoral dissertation, Purdue University.

Fengler, A. P. (1973). The effects of age and education on marital ideology. *Journal of Marriage and the Family, 35*, 264-271.

Fitzpatrick, M. A. (1988). *Between husbands and wives: Communication in marriage.* Newbury Park, CA: Sage.

Gergen, K. J., & Gergen, M. M. (1987). Narratives of relationship. In R. Burnett, P. McGhee, & D. D. Clarke (Eds.), *Accounting for relationships: Explanation, representation and knowledge* (pp. 269-288). London: Methuen.

Hess, R., & Handel, G. (1959). *Family worlds.* Chicago: University of Chicago Press.

Hewitt, J. P., & Stokes, R. (1975). Disclaimers. *American Sociological Review, 40*, 1-11.

Huston, T. L., McHale, S. M., & Crouter, A. C. (1986). When the honeymoon's over: Changes in the marriage relationship over the first year. In R. Gilmour & S. Duck (Eds.), *The emerging field of personal relationships* (pp. 109-132). Hillsdale, NJ: Lawrence Erlbaum.

Johnson, C. L. (1988). Relationships among family members and friends in later life. In R. M. Milardo (Ed.), *Families and social networks* (pp. 168-169). Newbury Park, CA: Sage.

Johnson, D. R., White, L. K., Edwards, J. N., & Booth, A. (1986). Dimensions of marital quality: Toward methodological and conceptual refinement. *Journal of Family Issues, 7*, 31-49.

Jourard, S. M. (1971). *Self-disclosure: An experimental analysis of the transparent self.* New York: John Wiley.

Katriel, T., & Phillipsen, G. (1981). "What we need is communication": "Communication" as a cultural category in some American speech. *Communication Monographs, 48*, 301-317.

Kidd, V. (1975). Happily ever after and other relationship styles: Advice on interpersonal relations in popular magazines, 1951-1973. *Quarterly Journal of Speech, 61*, 31-39.

Knapp, M. L. (1984). *Interpersonal communication and human relationships.* Boston: Allyn & Bacon.

Laing, R. D., Phillipson, H., & Lee, A. R. (1966). *Interpersonal perception.* New York: Springer.

Mansfield, P., & Collard, J. (1988). *The beginning of the rest of our life: A portrait of newly-wed marriage.* London: Macmillan.

Medling, J. M., & McCarrey, M. (1981). Marital adjustment over segments of the family life cycle: The issue of spouses' value similarity. *Journal of Marriage and the Family, 43,* 195-203.

Miller, B. C. (1976). A multivariate developmental model of marital satisfaction. *Journal of Marriage and the Family, 38,* 643-657.

Orvis, B. R., Kelley, H. H., & Butler, D. (1976). Attributional conflicts in young couples. In J. H. Harvey, W. J. Ickes, & R. F. Kidd (Eds.), *New directions in attribution research* (Vol. 1, pp. 353-386). Hillsdale, NJ: Lawrence Erlbaum.

Pineo, P. C. (1961). Disenchantment in the later years of marriage. *Marriage and Family Living, 23,* 3-11.

Rollins, B. C., & Cannon, K. L. (1974). Marital satisfaction over the family life cycle: A reevaluation. *Journal of Marriage and the Family, 30,* 271-282.

Schumm, W. R., & Bugaighis, M. A. (1986). Marital quality over the marital career: Alternative explanations. *Journal of Marriage and the Family, 48,* 165-168.

Sillars, A. L., Burggraf, C. S., Yost, S., & Zietlow, P. H. (1991). *Conversational themes and marital relationship definitions.* Unpublished manuscript, University of Montana.

Sillars, A. L., & Kalbfleisch, P. J. (1989). Implicit and explicit decision-making styles in couples. In D. Brinberg & J. Jaccard (Eds.), *Dyadic decision-making* (pp. 179-215). New York: Springer.

Sillars, A. L., Weisberg, J., Burggraf, C. S., & Wilson, E. A. (1987). Content themes in marital conversations. *Human Communication Research, 13,* 495-528.

Sillars, A. L., Weisberg, J., Burggraf, C. S., & Zietlow, P. H. (1990). Communication and understanding revisited: Married couples' understanding and recall of conversations. *Communication Research, 17,* 500-522.

Sillars, A. L., & Wilmot, W. W. (1989). Marital communication across the life-span. In J. F. Nussbaum (Ed.), *Life-span communication: Normative processes* (pp. 225-253). Hillsdale, NJ: Lawrence Erlbaum.

Spanier, G. B. (1976). Measuring dyadic adjustment: New scales for assessing the quality of marriage and similar dyads. *Journal of Marriage and the Family, 38,* 15-28.

Sporakowski, M. J., & Hughston, G. A. (1978). Prescriptions for happy marriage: Adjustments and satisfactions of couples married for 50 or more years. *The Family Coordinator, 27,* 321-328.

Stiles, W. B. (1978). Verbal response modes and dimensions of interpersonal roles. *Journal of Personality and Social Psychology, 36,* 693-703.

Stinnet, N., Carter, L. M., & Montgomery, J. E. (1972). Older persons' perceptions of their marriages. *Journal of Marriage and the Family, 42,* 825-839.

Swensen, C. H., Eskew, R. W., & Kolhepp, K. A. (1981). Stage of family life cycle, ego development, and the marriage relationship. *Journal of Marriage and the Family, 48,* 841-853.

Thurnher, M. (1976). Midlife marriage: Sex differences in evaluation and perspectives. *International Journal of Aging and Human Development, 7,* 129-135.

Troll, L. E. (1982). *Continuations: Adult development and aging.* Monterey, CA: Brooks-Cole.

Troll, L. E., Miller, S. J., & Atchley, R. C. (1979). *Families in later life*. Belmont, CA: Wadsworth.

Watzlawick, P., Beavin, J., & Jackson, D. D. (1967). *Pragmatics of human communication: A study of interactional patterns, pathologies and paradoxes*. New York: Norton.

Wheeless, L. R. (1976). Self-disclosure and interpersonal solidarity: Measurement, validation, and relationships. *Human Communication Research, 3,* 47-61.

Zietlow, P. H. (1986). *An analysis of the communication behaviors, understanding, self-disclosure, sex-roles, and marital satisfaction of elderly couples and couples in earlier life stages*. Unpublished doctoral dissertation, Ohio State University.

Zietlow, P. H., & Sillars, A. L. (1988). Life stage differences in communication during marital conflicts. *Journal of Social and Personal Relationships, 5,* 223-245.

CHAPTER TWELVE

Couples and Change: Intervention Through Discourse and Images

WILLIAM W. WILMOT

JOYCE L. HOCKER

Each couple is a unique culture. The discourse embedded within the couple relationship both shapes and reflects the relationship definition (Wilmot, 1987). Once the patterns of the culture become established, this relationship definition molds the emergent discourse. When the members of a couple see themselves, for example, as "partners in raising children" their discourse will both reflect and reinforce this co-parenting reality. The couple's discourse can become, then, the entry point for altering the structure, function, and guiding image or myth that is the overall conveyance within which the relationship moves through time.

This chapter highlights the change process experienced by couples through the lifespan, examining the congruence of discourse episodes and the guiding myth or image the two people use to make sense of their committed relationship. Although recent work on "turning points" (Baxter & Bullis, 1986; Conville, 1988) has presented snapshots of relationship shifts, this perspective lacks discourse data to illuminate the richness and complexity of change in long-term relationships. Abundant research has been completed on the macro features of relationship changes (such as divorce) (cf. Sillars & Zietlow, this volume), but it has not fully addressed the intricate processes of change per se that integrate a couple's discourse, guiding myths and definitions, and the inter-relationships between them. An earlier call for "full-scale studies of the symbolic and metaphoric processes by which individuals make sense of their relationships" (Wilmot & Sillars, 1989) pre-dates the current project.

One can enter the couple's culture through their discourse, both for the purpose of understanding the current relationship defini-tion and to provide grounded data for later intervention as they make modifications in the relationship. This is the level of working with the "interpretive milieu" of the relationship; the explanation formed by the couple themselves. The intervener or researcher be-comes a qualitative researcher, anthropologically seeking to under-stand what happens in the interpretive frame of the relationship culture. Specifically we will explore how recognition and analysis of (1) the couple's discourse and (2) the couple's guiding images or metaphors that emerge from the discourse can be used to generate change within a couple. Our theoretical framework is an outgrowth of previous data-based studies, academic study of conflict and discourse (Hocker & Wilmot, 1991; Wilmot, 1987), and applied work with couples in the middle of major changes in therapy and divorce. In our applied roles we serve couples as a family mediator and therapist respectively and our data come from helping more than 80 couples navigate changes in their relationships.

As both analysts and practitioners in the area of couple commu-nication, our approach to discourse analysis is dictated by prag-matic concerns, such as what particular clients can relate to in their talk, and what we find works with a given couple. In addition, pragmatic considerations led us to varied procedures of data gathering, including taping a few sessions and, at other times, making notes during sessions or making participant observation notes immediately after sessions. The time of the data collection spans 5 years.

We have observed and facilitated redefinitions of relationships, intervening to reduce toxic and unproductive interactions and helping couples move their relationships into new dynamics. Un-derlying all our interventions is an attempt to honor the idiosyn-cracies of each couple culture as we assist, nudge, follow, and "go with" the change rather than imposing it from outside. We will review the challenges of change for couples, explicate the role of the intervention agent, examine the various entry points for relationship modifications, and conclude with theoretical propositions of effective change.

Change in Personal Relationships

An inescapable element in all personal relationships is change. In intimate couple relationships, even when the partners' "objective" relationship definition is stable (e.g., cohabiting, married), there is a constant ebb and flow within the parameters of this definition. To call a couple "married," for example, is to apply a static social definition to a vastly more complex microculture created by the two people.

Couples who stay together under the umbrella of a constant definition face many problems, especially as they try to stay together over many years. With longer lives, the young married couple may be making a 50 to 60 year commitment to a life of communicating with each other. Any understanding of couple relationships must assume a great deal of change in their lives. The couple in their twenties may be establishing two careers, with all the pulls of work and home life, relocation, and risky career choices that time may bring. The thirties may be largely involved with child raising, adapting to less income and role change between spouses as they adapt to parenting. The forties bring, for many, reentry into the job market, adapting to the needs of older children who come and go, career reassessment, and, for many, continued parenting of younger children. Mid-life brings reassessment and a new focus to questions of meaning, such as time priorities, the way couples spend their money, how they find purpose beyond career-building and child raising, and ethical and religious concerns. The fifties often bring expansion into avocational interests as primary orientations toward children and career fade. The sixties present challenges of changes in health, possible partial or total retirement, a change in the standard of living, and critical problems of aging parents. The seventies and eighties bring challenges of loss of friends and health, often a new-found desire to give back to society part of what one has been given, and ultimately, facing one's spouse's death as well as one's own.

For many people, the scenario of change is intensified beyond "mere" aging. Separations, divorces, remarriages, and entering into roles as step-parents bring further strain for people. Fluctuations between various relationship constellations (Wilmot & Sillars, 1989) are often experienced without adequate support structures for hope and renewal for couples. For example, many couples conceptualize divorce as a fight or war, often taking the children as hostages in the never-ending small-scale sorties. Even the new modes of divorce mediation, effective as they are with couples who choose to cooperate in their redefinition, must be chosen within a cultural expectation that divorce is win-lose.

Whatever the specific challenge, with intracouple change over the lifespan and changes in and out of relationships, people who set sail in the waters of couple relationships have to deal with storms and rough waters as part of the voyage (Wilmot & Stevens, in press). In the process of negotiating change, they often turn to third parties to help in charting their course for the journey.

The Role of the Change Agent

The person who guides a couple in the change process, whether as a mediator or therapist, works with a set of skills that enables the negotiation of a new meaning in the couple's culture. First, the change agent observes the couple, listening and watching and noting the couple's discourse and nonverbal communication. Couples enact their structural dynamics, their usual patterns of discourse, and their embedded stories in the unfolding discourse. The third party must be able to describe nonjudgmentally a pattern; for instance, noting "looks like weekends are pretty predictable—you look forward to being together, then by Sunday both of you are disappointed and angry about the way the weekend has gone." The third party elicits observations about the pattern as described, for example, "tell me how it goes, half day by half day, until the fight on Sunday night," or "talk to each other about what happens during a typical weekend." Then the function of the pattern is discussed, usually frequently and at length with the couple, for example, "when tensions rise on Sunday afternoon you each take off and get some time alone, is that right?" Then satisfaction level with the pattern is determined, for instance, "How does that work out? Do you get to do what you really want to, Carolyn, or do you end up being disappointed about what you do alone?"

Nonevaluative description grounds any discussion of patterns. One couple presented a recurring pattern of the wife wanting more help with housekeeping and child-raising tasks, and the husband wanting more time for himself, and time off. As we listened to the description of task allocation, daily routine, and how decisions are made, the husband's voice became softer and softer. Several times we had to ask him to "speak up so we could hear him." When the therapist noted that the man's voice was getting lost in the discussion so that he could almost literally not be heard, the man said, "Yeah, I guess that's the way it is at home, too." After a long period of silence, he said, "I want to have a say in what I do. I'm eager to share the tasks (this was a non-traditional couple) but I need to have a say." The productive work that followed centered around both people "having a say" in the decision making. The wife dropped her defeatist nonverbal tone of voice when they negotiated a process that led each to state clearly what they wanted and what they expected. Accurate description of what is happening right now provides a cornerstone for building a new structure of discourse. In addition, the third party gains data by taking seriously everything stated, by remembering discourse sequences and bringing them back when needed, and by looking for discourse patterns that might need to change to reach the couple's stated goals, whether the goal is to negotiate pension funds for a divorcing couple or to help a newly married couple separate from their families of origin and build their own new family rituals. High-level discourse skills of the third party are taken for granted in intervention: listening, modeling, coaching, asking open-ended questions, clarifying without adding new ideas, restating and paraphrasing, noting differences, summarizing, and helping balance over- and underexpressive partners. Even though these skills are sometimes taught in basic communication classes, we have found that much of mediation and negotiation training depends on fine-tuning the third party's ability to perform these discourse tasks, which are also part of how we would prefer couples to communicate.

Assessing the couple on several dimensions helps the change agent decide which skills to teach, which structures to change, and when to intervene with conversation involving metaphorical characterizations. We have found that the most helpful kind of assessment combines checklists of various kinds keyed to the kind of intervention desired, along with observational assessment. The emotional climate of the couple must be assessed. Guerin, Fay, and Burden (1987) present an excellent system for assessing the couple climate as a basis for designing intervention. They suggest that climate can be described in terms of "safety, temperature, and turbulence." In the safest relationship, couples experience little threat of loss of control by self or other, or so much reactivity that discourse is nonproductive. Temperature can be gauged from very cold to superheated (indeed this is one of the most common metaphors employed by couples to describe their relationship). Coldness embodies distance and separation, or overintellectualization. Warmth leads to either closeness and empathy or, at the overheated end of the spectrum, to explosiveness and loss of control. Turbulence refers to the present conflict level. In a turbulent relationship, stabilization has to occur before relational work of any kind can take place (Guerin et al., 1987). Often the mediator or therapist helps to stabilize the discourse. We have found that asking directly about climate often elicits helpful information from the couple, and leads immediately into metaphoric-level talk. Couples often report "the calm before the storm," "partly cloudy," "fog rolling in," "the sun came out," or other common climate-based metaphors. At the least, intervention must address issues of stabilization and safety before productive work can occur. The discourse "warms up" in marital couples in a positive way when the couple becomes more immediate, responsive to the other's content and process and when couples initiate talk about positive attributes of the other or pleasant times. Seldom can talk be "warmed up" in the positive rather than explosive sense if the couple is in deep distress.

Stages of marital conflict must be accurately assessed (Guerin et al., 1987; Hocker & Wilmot, 1991). The continuum from disengagement to engagement provides myriad possibilities for intervention styles, which range from getting the couple engaged enough to talk with each other to the other extreme of prevention of violence between couples. A couple's behavior, cognition, and affect determine where they are on this continuum. The Dyadic Adjustment Scale (Spanier, 1976) and the Conflict Tactics Scale (Straus, 1979) assess level of verbal or physical reactivity and violence. The Guerin et al. (1987) system asks the third party to decide whether the couple falls into Level 1-4 of conflict, based on system dynamics such as triangles, intensity, level of self- or other focus, ability to engage productively, and use of outside authorities such as attorneys or therapists, or other legal system involvement. Each level of conflict suggests different kinds of intervention. For instance, a highly distressed and reactive dissatisfied couple will not be able to use written instructions, self-help directions for use at home, or reading about productive communication to improve their interaction style, while more highly satisfied, engaged, and nonreactive couples will be able to improve their basic communication with such training (Hocker, 1985).

Couples who fall in the mid-range of conflict involvement should be most able to use creative collaboration strategies, because they are engaged enough to communicate effectively and safe and nonturbulent enough to monitor their potentially destructive discourse (Hocker & Wilmot, 1991). Using pleasant satisfaction-enhancing interventions with a highly conflicted couple in the divorce process would be unproductive, while using highly structured negotiation with a reasonably engaged, satisfied couple would be perceived as simply in the way of a free flow of discourse. We have consistently found that mid-range couples, no matter what their goals, can use metaphoric intervention much more successfully than couples at either end of the spectrum. This is not to suggest that angry, disappointed, and self-focused couples cannot benefit from metaphoric techniques in their separation process and work well with new images, as will be discussed.

The change agent also carries the role of negotiating meaning, both current and any new thread of meaning, with the couple. This role remains embedded in cultural, philosophical and even depth-psychology orientations. In the postmodern world, the change agent does not correct a faultily functioning "patient," but instead views the "problem" as only being a problem because of one's participation in multiple relationships. According to Gergen (1991):

> The challenge to the (therapist) is thus to facilitate renegotiation of the meaning system within which "the problem" exists. The therapist actively enters into discourse with those who maintain the problem definition, not as a clairvoyant, but as a co-participant in the construction of the new realities. The emphasis may be placed on new narratives and metaphors for understanding one's life and improving skills for negotiating meaning. (p. 151)

To enact this relativistic, nonhierarchical role of third-party helper, the change agent becomes artistic rather than formulaic, listening at multiple levels, and directing conversation to multiple levels. By artistic, we mean that the change agent intentionally constructs metaphoric statements relating to the couple's discourse. The metaphor is a new statement that serves to encode the discourse style of the couple. Clients of therapists who intentionally used metaphors during sessions recalled more of those sessions than they could in sessions in which metaphors were not used. Clients were noted to gain more emotional and conceptual understanding of their talk when metaphors were used and rated the therapeutic alliance more highly than when metaphors were not used (Martin, Cummings, & Hallbert, 1992). New meaning is negotiated by insertion of a new metaphor, which is then accepted into the discourse by the couple. The image becomes a touchstone that can be held throughout the process of change. Only occasionally does the third party suggest an entirely new image, metaphor, or story that does not arise from the discourse of the couple.

Entry Points for Change

Modifications are activated in relationships at three different levels: (1) the micro level of discourse expressions, (2) the structural level of overall dynamics, and (3) the guiding image, story, or metaphor. Previous research and intervention traditions have elucidated parts of the change puzzle; we will illustrate how each level can be an entry point for generating relationship alterations.

Altering Discourse at the Micro Level

Behavioral Marital Therapy (BMT) began in the early 1970s with the first systematic micro-analyses of observed couple discursive behavior (Weiss, Hops, & Patterson, 1973). An extensive literature developed focusing on the characteristics of satisfied and dissatisfied couples, specifically highlighting their observable discourse (Filsinger, 1983). Researchers consistently found that couples who engage in productive conflict remain more satisfied in the long run than do couples who avoid conflict or engage in destructive conflict (Gottman & Krokoff, 1989; Hocker & Wilmot, 1991). Almost universally, in the BMT and communication skills intervention literature, the approach is to teach couples to problem-solve, negotiate, do active listening, speak without blaming or complaining, and express feelings accurately and effectively. The BMT researchers refer to communication skills at a micro level. Such a group of skills remains the set piece of a satisfied couple's repertoire. Distressed couples are typically taught to minimize distorting comments, slow down complaints, and to show more positive affect (Baucom, Epstein, Sayers, & Sher, 1989; Gottman & Krokoff, 1989).

Although the utility of discourse skills training has been demonstrated, three main hindrances remain: (1) The personality orientations of the individuals that limit their flexibility in adapting to each other, (2) the marital satisfaction level of couples when they are taught the skills, and (3) the couples' relational images of "who they are together." These factors limit behavioral change options. Because general personality orientations, such as psychopathologies or toxic early family life are beyond the scope of this chapter, we will address the second two couple factors—the marital satisfaction level of the couples and their ability to engage in conversation about their own relationship.

The more highly satisfied couples are, the more likely they are to use discourse skills taught in a behavioral training program (Hocker, 1985). Couples in the most distress are often the recipients of communication skills programs offered through clinics. Yet, paradoxically, the more the couple needs the skills, the less they are able to utilize them successfully. Moderately satisfied couples are the ones who are best able to use the skills for relationship improvement, yet unless they happen to be involved in a couple enrichment program, it is unlikely they will be taught the necessary discourse skills.

Another limitation of the discourse skills approach is that it is not unique in generating change. Both insight-oriented therapy and BMT appear to be about equally effective in creating lasting change in couple relationships (Snyder & Wills, 1989). Few studies have assessed the relationship change occurring when both approaches are used; that is, when content (parenting, money, sex, family, leisure time) is negotiated along with discussion of "what does this new agreement mean?" We suggest that joining specific behavioral change with insight-oriented discourse about what the change means to the couple will enhance the effectiveness of change programs.

Couples bring to therapy or mediation images of who they are together and separately. Many times, these two images are in conflict with each other. In addition, some of the mediation and therapy solutions offered by a third party are not consonant with the couples' images or guiding metaphors, thus assuring that change will be short-lived, if it occurs at all.

Structural Observation and Intervention

Structural analysis, especially as championed by systems theorists, provides a rich mine of dialogical data long known to communication theorists. The 25 years following the publication of *Pragmatics of Human Communication* (Watzlawick, Beavin, & Jackson, 1967) has brought deep and broad development of the heuristic structural analysis concepts begun in the 1960s. Most communication theorists and therapists use systems concepts routinely. Structural change in relationships precedes change in the participants' meaning systems. Both must occur for change to be lasting in the couple's way of talking. Readjustment occurs in triangulation so that direct two-person talk becomes possible instead of one passing messages through another or forming a coalition with another to gain power. For example, dad and son plan leisure time activities that exclude mom. Mom withdraws support for them doing the activities. Mom and dad don't resolve their disagreement about how to spend family and couple leisure time . . . . Power is rebalanced toward equality, if possible, by describing interdependence and the best interests of each. Description of underlying rules governing talk (to whom, when, about what, in what circumstance) provides possibilities for change. Micro-events (small episodes of discourse that result in predictable, unsatisfactory outcomes) are studied and different options are practiced. Many couples enact pursue/flee dynamics and changes in these habitual patterns emerge in the intervention.

The late 1980s and 1990s have brought serious challenges to the standard fare of systems theory. Feminist critics have begun the process of deconstructionist analysis that brings into sharp focus areas of power imbalance and gender differences in accommodation and dominance. Given our assumption that effective intervention (1) *balances power* and (2) *effects synchronization,* a look at representative critiques is in order.

Feminist postmodern theory assumes that discourse is both the medium and the product of human activities, and is the way in which a certain cultural perspective is maintained. The dominant discourse in a culture appears "natural" to most members of the society (Hare-Mustin, 1991), unfortunately often including the change agent. Therefore, any attempt to balance power must include an understanding of how such power is perceived, distributed, maintained, and changed. For instance, many therapists have realized that although the husband/father might talk infrequently with family members about crucial decisions, his attitudes often become family law (Hare-Mustin, 1991). In one couple in which the wife was depressed and the husband came to therapy to support her, she spent most of the early sessions complaining about her own failures and lack of communication skills, while the husband appeared benign, supportive, and concerned. He did not have to state his perspective—his wife had completely assumed her husband's (supposed) view of her behavior. While she criticized herself for not communicating and including him, he gently reminded her of the ways he had suggested she might solve her problems and said he was willing to wait for her to feel better. When the therapist pointed out that his solutions had not, in fact, worked to solve his wife's problem, the wife attacked the therapist for not understanding how hard the husband had tried to help. Power balancing remained many sessions away for this couple who enacted an extreme form of the view that rational, thoughtful solutions would work and "being emotional" would not.

Even basic discourse skill training has to come under the scrutiny of post-structuralist critiques. Gottman and Levenson (1986) reported that 78% of husbands' negative affect in couple discourse was anger and contempt whereas 93% of the wife's negative affect was fear, complaining, and sadness. The researchers regarded the fact that wives often respond with fear to husbands' anger as illustrative of the way in which power relationships are maintained. Many woman maintain a "state of conscious preoccupation with perpetual self-surveillance" (Bartky, 1988). Such a woman is far more likely than is a man to offer change in her behavior and to criticize herself. Thus our intervention goals of power balancing and synchronization of meaning may well come at the expense of the woman's accommodation and refusal to challenge her husband's behavior openly and angrily.

Finally, any conversational, dialogic mode of initiating intervention must take into constant account that both the content and process of conversation is tied to the dominant discourse of society. Conversation has relationship implications, notably dominance and submission (Hare-Mustin, 1991; Watzlawick et al., 1967). Although the subordinate person in a dyad is not completely powerless, it is strange to "regard her power as equal to his" as so many strategic theorists do. Though a complete analysis and set of suggestions for remediation of this imbalance lies beyond the scope of this chapter, we can make some suggestions for the change agent. The third party can discuss with the couple the function of certain patterns, how they began, and what would happen if they were to change. Stated *satisfaction* should be explored along with stated or obvious dissatisfaction. Change strategies that were tried to no effect in the past should be examined. Belief systems should be discussed, especially about roles of women and men, appropriate behavior for each, and responsibility for relationship enhancement or problem solving. Innovative research from theorists such as Surrey (1987), Stiver (1985), Miller (1986), and Surrey and Miller (1991) from the Stone Center at Wellesley is important in redefining gender roles in relationship empowerment issues.

Changes in Guiding Images, Metaphors, and Stories

Several theoretical approaches advocate, as we are doing, the use of metaphoric, narrative, and story-level communication to effect couple change. Detailed, helpful training is offered by Coombs and Freedman (1990) who present material on how to think metaphorically, how to design and use symbols, and how to find stories and narratives. Helpful as their approach to teaching imaginal thinking is, their goal is primarily to train the third party to recognize and present helpful, change-oriented metaphors. We advocate using the *couple's discourse* as a source for change strategies based on their own, spontaneously occurring symbolic speech. Likewise, Eriksonian and Batesonian schools of intervention focus more on the therapist as storyteller. These are useful approaches more suited to therapy than to mediation and conciliation.

Metaphoric communication provides a framework in which to analyze couples' current discourse. Likewise, metaphors can stimulate change in dysfunctional communication by providing an alternative meaning system to make sense of the suggested changes. Metaphoric communication provides an opportunity to analyze couples' current discourse styles. An effective metaphor, Hobson (1985) argues, "points a way towards a new creation with a resolution of contradiction and conflict" (p. 82). This process of analysis of metaphors involves a kind of artistic creation that is similar to literature, drama, music, or painting (Hobson, 1985). Changes in metaphors can lead toward changes in the meaning system of the couple, which can then provide new options for discourse, thus changing the relationship in a positive direction. If a divorcing couple has envisioned themselves as "boxers," as evidenced by talk of "round three," "needing a referee," "bloodied but not bowed," "going down for the count," and "battering me (with words)," they envision only a win-lose solution to their property and custody decisions.

Metaphoric discourse can be viewed as an elementary structure of thought. We are not simply given our world, we "construct" it through individual perception, relational interpretation, and categories of thought (Lakoff, 1987; Lakoff & Johnson, 1980; Lakoff & Turner, 1989). Langer (1948), in her seminal *Philosophy in a New Key*, held that the main way humans develop new ideas is through metaphors, which create a new, or "third" thing, after comparing two unlike objects or categories.

General cultural attitudes about divorce assume that the couple will go from "lovers" to "enemies," with little imagined in the way of metamorphosis of their formerly intimate relationship. Instead, many couples remain intimately involved, but in an enmeshed conflict rather than a loving relationship. Helping them find a new image for their relationship, preferably one that emerges from their stated goals for the future, provides sense-making for a new relationship. Screaming at an enemy makes sense; screaming at one's "business partner" (in raising the children) makes little sense. Using manipulative tactics such as surprise legal documents sent by one's attorney makes sense if one person is "mounting an attack" on a dangerous enemy. Such tactics make little sense if one is dealing with "a co-parent."

We continue to find that working with metaphoric discourse provides an avenue out of a former blind alley. Often in our work with couples, we feel as hopeless for a while as does the couple. After all, they have tried many different change strategies through the years to little avail. At the conclusion of divorce mediation, one couple said, "If we had been able to communicate this clearly earlier in our marriage, maybe this divorce never would have happened." By that time, their hope and satisfaction level, key elements that must be present for change to occur, had dropped so low that they could not envision change that would keep them together, and had experienced so much mistrust and hurt that they were unable to interpret neutral (as perceived by the other) actions as anything other than negative.

The concreteness of metaphor engages our feeling and thinking as abstractions never can. A woman who called her marriage "a valley of dry bones" made a viscerally felt point that would not have been felt had she simply noted that the life had gone out of her marriage (which is a less vibrant metaphor). The therapist or change agent helps the unit not stay stuck in a story that provides an unacceptable ending. One couple changed from a view of their marriage as a "whodunit," complete with the search for the killer, the victim, the sleuth, and the murder weapon, to an adventure story. This new story emerged from conversation about what they wanted in the future. One example of the change from whodunit to adventure novel emerged from their shared value of "excitement and intrigue." Gradually the new story emerged. Change in the story requires flexibility, careful analysis of current structure and function, noting of functional and dysfunctional communication patterns (judged by the couple's standards weighed against power-balancing and synchronization). They can't dance if they aren't hearing the same song. The person crouched into submission eventually goes away or stands up, furious or injured. High power people often remain lonely. Thus change helps people move to the next stage of life instead of staying stuck in a spiral.

Metaphoric Transformations

Several processes have emerged from our work with more than 80 couples thus far. Although not yet systematized, the following categories appear to be the most common in couple intervention.

Away With the Old, In With the New. Often a couple, with third-party help, identifies an old guiding image that limits or hurts them in some way. They then participate in basic discourse skill training, structural change, and then do or do not find a new image to guide them to their next phase. One such couple, Shelly and Tom, presented a pattern of him blowing up with angry, loud words, her defending herself, his recovery, and her continuing hurt. As is so often the case, this conflict structure worsened in intensity after the birth of a child. Both agreed that they felt like debaters "going at each other." Then Shelley said her feeling was more like being "on trial," and that she felt the stakes were higher than in a debate. They talked together about which image captured their feelings and the outcomes best. They discussed their couple belief system, which was a desire to be objective and keep their wits "razor sharp." As they talked, they realized that their verbal tactics of attack and defense were appropriate for their previous philosophical debates, but that the individual hurts were escalating. They realized that their earlier "debater/colleague" image had transformed into a "prosecutor/defense" image that inevitably ended with someone being guilty of a crime and having to serve a time of punishment. She discovered that her tendency to assign him the role of "standard bearer" had changed into a less benign image of her husband as "judge." The function that had emerged was one of her needing to form an elaborate defense, which took much of her time and emotional energy. Their intimacy suffered. They agreed that this image had to go and they went to work on structural and discourse changes. The limiting image provided the framework for their work, and gave them a new sense of meaning, searching for a new story that told about who they were now and wanted to become.

Two People in Search of an Image. This process, searching for an image that each can or does adopt, takes at least two forms. In one aspect, the couple talks together about their image—what it is, should be, is not, how it has changed historically, or something similar. Less satisfied or consensually based couples compete, either directly or by indirect means such as ignoring the other, over the guiding image for their relationship.

Characteristic of the latter, less satisfied, couple is a noticeable lack of talk that picks up and extends each other's imaginal speech. One highly dissatisfied couple, considering divorce, came into therapy. Their climate was cold, safety level was acceptable, and their turbulence was low. They were a mid-range conflict couple, with long, silent periods of time between overt conflict episodes. Referring to his ethnic background, the husband called himself "one of God's frozen people," and she agreed that they were in a "cold war." Both agreed that they had withdrawn to keep the peace, that they seldom communicated about important things, and that they used "spies" (the children) to inform them about the moods of the other. The husband spoke wistfully about the two of them "warming up again." As the therapist attempted to extend the "cold war" metaphor, the wife began to add her own images. She said it was like "speaking two languages." The therapist tried again to extend the metaphor to a "different languages between countries in a cold war" theme, but the image was dropped and never referred to again. The husband tried out "being on the same team" as an image. The wife responded with death images, such as the "valley of dry bones" we referenced above. The husband later said, advancing a machine metaphor, "we just don't click." With no response from the wife, he said he "was drifting in the ocean." By this time, so was the therapist! All attempts to work with these various images failed, as did homework designed to remedy discourse skills and structural problems. Finally the husband said he was "drowning," and they ended treatment for a year. When they came back, he reported that the relationship was "stagnant," still pursuing the watery theme, and the wife simply said "it's just all dead," indeed effectively killing all relational work. The couple then moved toward separation, never having found an image even to communicate their distress effectively.

In contrast to the above couple, the following exchange was produced by a couple where the two people had more of a basic agreement in their view of the relationship:

> **Fred:** We're just looking for something to pull us through, you know . . .
>
> **Jackie:** . . . something to hitch on to when we're out of steam.
>
> **Fred:** Our marriage needs to be more spirited, more adventurous, like Wow!, kayaking down the Alberton gorge or something.
>
> **Jackie:** Something to carry us along.

Six sessions later when describing a fight over the weekend, Jackie said, "We survived the waterfall," picking up on the earlier "flow" image. This provided the chance for the following intervention.

> **Therapist:** Nice to know you could survive the plunge, I'll bet.
>
> **Fred:** You bet.
>
> **Therapist:** Sounds like you two need more control over the speed and route of these adventures.
>
> **Jackie:** Yeah, I'm getting battered around.

This couple attained some commonality in their search for a guiding metaphor to characterize their relationship. When a couple fails to find a metaphor, the third party may actively be involved in constructing it. When that is the case, mediators are more likely than therapists to suggest a new image, because the couple has acknowledged a breakdown of their couple relationship, and often come to mediation eager for some way to make sense of their situation. One couple was stuck in mediation because of their devitalization. One would say, "Well, we do want to get a divorce, don't we?" and the other would respond, "I guess so." Only when the husband said he wanted to "be a family the way we should be" was the mediator able to suggest an image of a family that lived in separate houses but still considered themselves family. The parents could have scheduling sessions and planning sessions about the children. They could "sit at the table" as families should. Although the man was saddened, he was able to transcend his old image of "what a family should be" when given new activities for a divorced family that he could use to make sense of their situation.

Images That Metamorphose. Some couples enter therapy with images that both accept, but that no longer work well for them. They then work with the old image, noticing how it changes as they clarify their goals and change their basic discourse. The Dukes spoke of the fact that they had been "more willing to roll" in previous years. He had been the "head," or the clear thinker and direction giver, and she the "gut," or the emotive, soft side of the couple. They wanted their relationship to be one characterized by "unbridled joy," which advanced a notion of a wild, free horseback ride. Both wanted more support. They said they did not know how to disagree and still be one unit. When offered a version of Plato's round, androgynous original human being as an image to describe how they had been, they agreed that was them, "on a roll," until professional and family responsibilities interfered. Now they felt separated from their other half, sad, and incomplete, and sometimes angry. He advanced the image of "guiding the ship together," and talked about the joy of flying over the water (like in a horseback ride). She agreed that this sounded good, and that "no one should have to be in steerage while the other one charts the course." Then the relational work shifted to "charting the course," meaning working with schedules, decisions, child-raising issues, and data from the environment such as money, pressures, weather disturbances, and supplies. This effective couple stayed on in therapy only a short while, needing only a new image to help them make sense of their life transition from "a couple on a roll," to "co-captains of a great ship." They changed to an image more appropriate, perhaps, to their child-raising, professionally demanding thirties.

Some communicatively competent couples can identify several guiding metaphors that limit their interaction, and discuss together how to change the image. Bill and Karen both agreed that their marriage was arranged to "put Karen on the hook." Bill, rescuing Karen early in the marriage, had "gotten Karen off the hook." Their repetitive pattern had developed such that Karen would get in a bind and Bill would help her. But both were aware of the limits of this image, while not knowing what else to do to stay close. Bill said he wanted someone to "ride along with him." In a burst of enthusiasm, Karen said, "We can be the New Riders of the Purple Sage" (a North American folk singing group) and get in the car and go when they want to be together. They played with the Western theme and even agreed that they could take turns being the sidekick. Additionally, their car and their "Riders" image gave them a sense of privacy, of intimacy, and of fun. Toward the end of therapy, Karen said that "being on the hook" had been a lot like getting hung from a tree, and Bill said he was tired of being the good guy all the time and wanted to try being an outlaw. The humor helped heal an old, outworn pattern.

We continue to find that couples can transcend what appear to be intractable problems by discovering whether the thread of meaning has frayed and can be repaired or whether a new design is in order. One of the gratifying results of this work is the lighthearted "aha!" that so often results when meaning is restored. People have more strategies than we communication researchers and therapists often think, but they need a system of meaning to engage and energize their potential strategies.

A Theory of Flexible Change

The continuing successful transformation of personal relationships throughout the lifespan is a difficult process. Past work attempting to ferret out change strategies has tended to look at specific communication or discourse skills, or the overall structure of the relationship without placing those interventions within a cultural, relational context. As Gergen notes, "The emphasis may be placed on new narratives and metaphors for understanding one's life and improving skills for negotiating meaning" (Gergen, 1991, p. 151).

We suggest a theory of "embedded discourse" from which one can help couples manage changes by affecting (1) the specific discourse skills within the context of their relationship image, (2) change in their power and synchronization dynamics, and (3) change in their guiding image as a way to "reframe" how they generate new discourse with the other. Based on our applied work as mediator and therapist with couples, we suggest the following propositions:

1. Congruence between a couple's relationship image and discourse patterns results in relational satisfaction.

2. When an image breaks down at a time of crisis (or is outmoded), the specific discourse behaviors become even more important—the discourse becomes an important index of the relationship. The more fundamental building blocks (discourse patterns and exchanges) become the mode of generating a new negotiated meaning.

3. An image can only be successfully imported from the outside if it is congruent with the couple's own relationship definition. One cannot "force" or "give" a definition to a couple; rather, one can only offer options for their consideration.

4. Discourse changes are enduring only if they fit the couple's new image for the relationship. The image and discourse must be congruent AND believed by the couple to be effective.

5. Communication with the third party is one important medium for transformation, thus discourse between the two people and with an outsider is the bedrock of change. An outside perspective helps add meaning to the couple's relationship.

6. Change can be generated by teaching couples to create content out of their relationship. The "relationship talk" allows them to shift between content and process and is essential to relationship adaptation and change over time. Meta-talk about process and about the relationship allows a new perspective to generate change.

7. Change necessarily involves altering the image system the couple uses to "make sense" out of their relationship. Most couples having difficulties in their relationships find it difficult to change their definition, so they stay stuck in an old image. New images create collaborative options.

In this chapter we have advocated an "artistic" approach to intervention with couples, using multiple entry points based on a couple's particular discourse. With the approach of using a couple's guiding image, metaphor, or story as the basis for their relational definition, the outside helper can effect change in basic discourse patterns, structural dynamics, and the guiding image or metaphors themselves. Change at the metaphoric level interacts in a particular, noncausal fashion with change in communication patterns and dynamics. As a couple negotiates new patterns of meaning with the third party, entirely new ways to make sense of their relationship emerge, which then lead, in an optimistic sense, to more productive discourse. The riches of effective intervention techniques can be mined in the backyard of the couple's own territory—their discourse, shared with and observed by someone from another country.

References

Bartky, S. L. (1988). Foucault, femininity, and the modernization of patriarchal power. In I. Diamond & L. Quinby (Eds.), *Feminism and Foucault: Reflections on resistance* (pp. 61-86). Boston: Northeastern University Press.

Baucom, D. H., Epstein, N., Sayers, S., & Sher, T. G. (1989). The role of cognitions in marital relationships: Definitional, methodological, and conceptual issues. *Journal of Consulting and Clinical Psychology, 57*(1), 1-13.

Baxter, L. A., & Bullis, C. (1986). Turning points in developing romantic relationships. *Human Communication Research, 12,* 469-494.

Conville, R. L. (1988). Relational transitions: An inquiry into their structure and function. *Journal of Social and Personal Relationships, 5*(4), 423-437.

Coombs, G., & Freedman, J. (1990). *Symbol, story and ceremony.* New York: Norton.

Filsinger, E. E. (Ed.). (1983). *A sourcebook of marriage and family assessment.* Beverly Hills, CA: Sage.

Gergen, K. J. (1991). *The saturated self: Dilemmas of identity in contemporary life.* New York: Basic Books.

Gottman, J. M., & Krokoff, L. J. (1989). Marital interaction and satisfaction: A longitudinal view. *Journal of Consulting and Clinical Psychology, 57,* 47-52.

Gottman, J. M., & Levenson, R. W. (1986). Assessing the role of emotion in marriage. *Behavioral Assessment, 8,* 31-48.

Guerin, P. J., Jr., Fay, L. F., & Burden, S. G. (1987). *The evaluation and treatment of marital conflict: A four-stage approach.* New York: Basic Books.

Hare-Mustin, R. T. (1991). Sex, lies and headaches: The problem is power. In T. J. Goodrich (Ed.), *Women and power: Perspectives for family therapy* (pp. 21-39). New York: Norton.

Hobson, R. F. (1985). *Forms of feeling: The heart of psychotherapy.* London: Tavistock.

Hocker, J. L. (1985). *Change in marital satisfaction and positive communication behavior in enrichment couples using a self-help manual: A multiple baseline study.* Unpublished doctoral dissertation, University of Montana.

Hocker, J. L., & Wilmot, W. W. (1991). *Interpersonal conflict.* Dubuque, IA: William C. Brown.

Lakoff, G. (1987). *Women, fire and dangerous things: What categories reveal about the mind.* Chicago: University of Chicago Press.

Lakoff, G., & Johnson, M. (1980). *Metaphors we live by.* Chicago: Chicago University Press.

Lakoff, G., & Turner, M. (1989). *More than cool reason: A field guide to poetic metaphor.* Chicago: University of Chicago Press.

Langer, S. K. (1948). *Philosophy in a new key: A study of the symbolism of reason, rite and art.* New York: Mentor.

Martin, J., Cummings, A. L., & Hallbert, T. (1992). Therapist's intentional use of metaphor: Memorability, clinical impact, and possible epistemic/motivational functions. *Journal of Consulting and Clinical Psychology, 60*(1), 143-145.

Miller, J. B. (1986). *What do we mean by relationships?* (Work in Progress, No. 22). Wellesley, MA: Stone Center Working Papers Series.

Snyder, D. K., & Wills, R. M. (1989). Behavioral versus insight-oriented marital therapy: Effects on individual and interspousal functioning. *Journal of Consulting and Clinical Psychology, 57*(1), 39-46.

Spanier, G. B. (1976). Measuring dyadic adjustment: New scales for assessing the quality of marriage and similar dyads. *Journal of Marriage and the Family, 38,* 15-28.

Stiver, I. (1985). *The meanings of dependency in female-male relationships* (Work in Progress, No. 11). Wellesley, MA: Stone Center Working Paper Series.

Straus, M. A. (1979). Measuring intrafamily conflict and violence: The conflict tactics (CT) scales. *Journal of Marriage and the Family, 41,* 75-88.

Surrey, J. (1987). *Relationship and empowerment* (Work in Progress, No. 30). Wellesley, MA: Stone Center Working Paper Series.

Surrey, J., & Miller, J. B. (1991). *Revisioning women's anger: The personal and the global* (Work in Progress, No. 43). Wellesley, MA: Stone Center Working Paper Series.

Watzlawick, P., Beavin, J. H., & Jackson, D. D. (1967). *Pragmatics of human communication.* New York: Norton.

Weiss, R. L., Hops, H., & Patterson, G. R. (1973). A framework for conceptualizing marital conflict: A technology for altering it, some data for evaluating it. In L. A. Hammerlynck, L. C. Handy, & E. J. Mash (Eds.), *Behaviour change: Methodology, concepts and practice* (The Fourth Banff International Conference on Behaviour Modification) (pp. 83-99). Champaign, IL: Research Press.

Wilmot, W. W. (1987). *Dyadic communication* (3rd ed.). New York: McGraw-Hill.

Wilmot, W. W., & Sillars, A. L. (1989). Developmental issues in personal relationships. In J. F. Nussbaum (Ed.), *Life-span communication: Normative processes* (pp. 119-135). Hillsdale, NJ: Lawrence Erlbaum.

Wilmot, W. W., & Stevens, D. (in press). Relationship rejuvenation. Accepted for publication in R. Conville (Ed.), *Communication Structure.* Norwood, NJ: Ablex.

Epilogue: Future Prospects in Lifespan Sociolinguistics

NIKOLAS COUPLAND

JUSTINE COUPLAND

JON F. NUSSBAUM

It is worth reviewing the original context in which this book came to be produced. First, and most basically, there is growing recognition of the need for a lifespan perspective in social research generally. This is not least because of the clear overrepresentation of young adults in research designs. But also, the lifespan approach can usefully recontextualize research on apparently discrete populations such as children, young adults, mid-life-adults, and the elderly. There already exists an important body of theory that specifies priorities for lifespan research generally (cf. Abeles, 1987; Baltes, 1979; Cicirelli, this volume; Sorensen, Weinert, & Sherrod, 1986), but these priorities have not been consistently followed outside lifespan psychology itself.

Second, in the sorts of interdisciplinary literatures on selfhood and identity that we examined in the Introduction—which are themselves central to contemporary *social* theory generally—there are new imperatives for considering the lifespan. Aging and the lifespan very clearly inform many aspects of how we experience our social lives, and our selves in relation to them. Following the arguments of Woodward (1991) and Cole (1986) we might even say that, until recently, aging has been a theme that we have not only ignored, as researchers and as people, but in fact actively *repressed*.

Third, what is very loosely characterized as "the linguistic turn in the social sciences" is producing a new consensus on the priorities for social research. Ethnomethodologists' concerns to expose the means by which our interpretations of social circumstances and events are reached are being taken up in conversation analysts' explorations of how interaction is experienced by, and so made meaningful to, participants in social encounters. Social psychologists have largely accepted the value of qualitative, text-based accounts of language and interaction and of the value of reinterpreting their literatures on social attitudes, social categorization, and identity in these terms. Sociolinguistics (which we take to be the best superordinate term for this interdisciplinary research activity) has for decades been drawing approaches to language description and theory increasingly away from decontextualized accounts of language structure and has led the search for associations between language and social context (Giles & Coupland, 1991). Yet *all* of these overlapping disciplines have as yet failed to take up the challenge of lifespan studies with any real impetus.

As we initially conceived of it, the book could valuably address a wide array of sociolinguistic aspects of lifespan identity. And at least the majority of these have been explored by some means, though of course by no means exhaustively, in the principal chapters of the volume. We reproduce the subheadings and keywords that were our starting point for this project below, because they may trigger associations, or even future research plans, for other researchers. Any one study would no doubt span several of the major and minor headings in these keyword summaries. The notes added after each section are again oriented to future questions that, in our view, could profitably be addressed.

Age categories in text and discourse. Age self-presentations and generational alignments. Age-salience in character descriptions. Satisfaction/dissatisfaction with life-position occupancy. The identity consequences of cross-generational talk (e.g., children's experiences of social control; patterns of generational self-disclosure).

Referring back to Hadden and Lester's review of discursive categorizing processes (discussed in the Introduction), lifespan research needs to develop a heuristic model for exploring specifically *developmental* categorizing processes in discourse. This is arguably the *central* task to be accomplished within the remit of discursive lifespan studies, accounting for the sociolinguistic construction of aging. The taxonomy of age-identifying discourse strategies and markers in intergenerational talk (that we discussed in the Introduction, summarized here as Table 13.1) could be developed further, in particular applications, for these purposes.

This taxonomy of strategies was developed to account for a very specific corpus of conversational data and will of course need elaboration to capture discourse processes operative elsewhere. Also, in future studies, it will be important to overlay it with a framework that recognizes multiple dimensions of social and individual change. For example, Coupland, Coupland, and Giles (1991, p. 5ff) noted three (theoretically) alternative interpretations of "elderly" attributes. First, *"inherent causes"*: for example, voice quality changes in late life might be attributable to degenerative processes affecting the larynx as an "inevitable" or at least predictable consequence of biological aging. Second, *"historical causes"*: for example, some older speakers may continue to use vocabularies or pronunciation styles that were learned in earlier times, so that using these features in late life marks the speaker as "elderly." Third, *"environmental causes"*: for example, after retiring from full-time work, some older people might be cut off from domains of talk that were important to them in their working lives. Cicirelli (this volume) refers to an overlapping perspective from lifespan developmental psychology that distinguishes *age-graded normative events, history-graded normative events*, and *nonnormative events*. Sillars and Zietlow (this volume) similarly, but in the context of the development of *relationships*, distinguish *intrinsic developmental processes, life-stage experiences and developmental tasks*, and *cohort-related values and experiences*.

In Table 13.1, several of the discourse processes listed refer to intra-individual circumstances and change, such as the telling of personal frailty. Yet within this, there is clearly scope for people to tell their personal circumstances in ways that project them as "normative" (probabilistically associated with "all" people of that age) or as nonnormative (the result of unique experiences or personal ill-fortune). Other strategies locate aging in cohort experiences, such as talking about past experiences (including remi-

Table A.1   A Taxonomy of Age-Identification Strategies in Discourse

---

A. Age-Categorization Processes
   1. Disclosure of chronological age
   2. Age-related category or role reference
   3. Age-identity in relation to health, decrement, and death

B. Temporal Framing Processes
   4. Adding time-past perspective to current or recent-past states or topics
   5. Self-association with the past
   6. Recognizing historical, cultural, or social change

---

niscing) with others who share them. Again, aging can be cast as living in a changing world, and specifically in a world that changes for everyone, independent of a person's own age and history.

For discourse analysis, there is a challenge here—to explore the ways in which lifespan experiences are textualized through these various formats, and with what impact on local goals and achieved identities. Appeals to normativity might, for some people, be the means to defuse the threat of highly personalized interpretations of experience. Locating "aging" in cohort terms seems to offer potential for social support, from adolescence through mid-life into old age. A discourse of "individual development" may well work to oppose a discourse of "alienation from contemporary values," and so on. It may well be valuable to document lifespan representations of the self as a negotiative arena in which competing and multidimensional formulations of personal and social experiences are set in opposition and worked through.

Age-salience in character descriptions refers to, for example, journalistic practices of "age-tagging" in sketching demographic and personal characteristics of protagonists in news reporting (e.g., "Soldier, 19, killed in Belfast"). Issues relevant to this practice are how, in particular respects, the fact of referencing age colors readers' interpretations of such stories, inviting them to orient to them in lifespan frameworks. (Is a death at age 19 inherently more tragic, or news-worthy, than a death at 29, or 59?) Whereas media analyses relevant to the lifespan have typically been content analyses of the representation of different age-groups in the media (e.g., Atkins, Jenkins, & Perkins, 1990), there has been far less work done to unpackage the textual significance of age-references and age-portrayals. Harwood and Giles (1992) show the value of a highly contextualized approach in their analysis of age-related humor in the television comedy series, *The Golden Girls.*

Issues of "satisfaction" could very valuably come up for reconsideration in a discursively more sensitive framework. To take one widely cited instance, Bultena and Powers (1976) argued that the "surprisingly" high levels of morale that they found being espoused in old age, in their quantitative research, could be attributed to the lower expectations elderly people themselves have for their well-being. They wrote that the "detrimental" circumstances of the "aged" "may be defined as normative by the aged, and hence may not precipitate the demoralization that is otherwise anticipated" (p. 177; see also Riley & Foner, 1968, for related reviews).

Certainly there appear to be formulaic *discourse* equivalents to this line of interpretation. In a study of our own (Coupland, Coupland, & Robinson, 1992), we found that older people commonly appraised their own circumstances (in answer to a *How are you?* opening in interviews) in expressions such as "not too bad considering . . . ," "mustn't grumble . . . ," and often by self-appraising in relation to their age. This *relativization of experience* in formulations of "how one is" is of course not limited to elderly people's talk, and could be explored across lifespan populations. The importance of an interpretive, discourse analytic approach is that we need not take these responses prima facie as "reports" of life conditions, following the model of Bultena and Powers. It is important to understand how such reports are strategically produced *in local contexts*, for example in the service of face and other identity needs. The *negotiative* quality of self-reports of all sorts is all too easily lost in the drive to aggregate data within coding frames.

Discourse and lifespan moments and boundaries. **Lifespan language socialization. Achieving transition. Boundary-marking in ritual discourse events, but also in desultory conversation. Sociolinguistic experiences of childhood, studentship, parenthood, marriage, grandparenthood, and so forth. Relational development through talk.**

The potential for sociolinguistic research under many of the above subheadings is quite well demonstrated throughout this book. But there are important exceptions. Interactional research has given us very illuminating accounts of "micro" rituals marking rites of passage—greetings and leave-takings at the fringes of everyday conversations (Laver, 1974; Schegloff & Sacks, 1973; see also Coupland et al., in press, for a review). But it has not yet matched anthropologists' traditional concerns with "macro" or culturally consolidated rituals—such as weddings, funerals, birthdays, retirements, and so on. Yet these are par excellence the means by which, very differently across cultures, lifespan identities and lifespan rites of passage are given public form and social significance. Elsewhere (Coupland, Coupland, & Giles, 1989), we have noted the existence of lifespan "calendar-marking" discourse traditions in our own cultural contexts, for example involving the exchange of flippant, though undoubtedly ageist, greetings cards and personal jokes at decade boundaries. Within this subcategory are many of the routine discursive resources available to particular communities for confirming assumptions about aging and human development. But we have not systematically explored their range or their local significance.

Age-appropriate behavior. **How (when and why) is age-appropriateness implied or inculcated prescriptively ("act your age"), such as in relation to moral responsibility, health, sexuality, appearance, social control, maturation, achievement? Age in accounting, and blaming, strategies.**

Aronsson and Evaldsson, and Prusank (this volume) have both addressed the issue of social control through talk, though from different perspectives. This work connects to a central though enduringly controversial area of sociolinguistic research— Bernstein's (e.g., 1974) hypotheses about sociolinguistic coding orientations in the achievement of social control. To take one aspect of this work, Bernstein argued that social control of children in families is achieved by a variety of means, including simple "imperative" strategies but also "positional" and (alternatively) "personal" appeals. These were never adequately documented in Bernstein's work (and hence much of the controversy over the strengths of Bernstein's claims in relation to his data). But what he called positional appeals were supposedly framings of social control in terms of the rights and obligations obtaining within particular families and adhering to certain established family roles—parenthood versus childhood. This work has been superseded in many ways by far more differentiated and subtle sociolinguistic research on how, in family settings, children are discursively positioned. They can be constituted variously, for example, as adult-equivalents or as subordinates in relation to different strategies and themes of talk, and differently across cultures (Blum-Kulka, 1990). A rich seam of future work could take this interpretive line into many other intergenerational relationships and settings.

Also, Cicirelli (this volume) has developed a challenging thesis on how moral concerns relate to discourse practices (to do with decision making) in families where an elderly person is very frail. The issue of appropriateness is again central here. But it is useful to approach the analysis of discourse events with the view that *all* human behavior is subject to evaluation in terms of its age-appropriateness, however ageist this might be. Children in their peer-groups develop an acute sense of the rights and obligations attaching to conduct and talk at particular ages; however we designate "mid-life," it is no doubt partly in terms of encounters we feel (or at we feel others feel) we can and cannot legitimately take part in. Perceived legitimacy could be usefully diagnostic, then, as a researchable dimension of people's talk about age-linked behavior.

The rhetorical functioning of time. **The surfacing and social functioning of life-narratives (in bureaucratic and lay contexts). Implications for development. Discourses of change and stability (framing the present in terms of the past, and the projected future). Life-position appraisals. The identity functions of reminiscence.**

The management of time-perspectives in discourse across the lifespan has only been examined fitfully. In the Introduction we referred to important exploratory work by Boden and Bielby on how the past can serve in many ways as a resource for older speakers. This theme is taken up in our taxonomy of age-identifying markers in talk (Table 13.1, above), and of course in literatures on autobiography and reminiscence (see Buchanan & Middleton, Gergen & Gergen, Van Langenhove & Harré, this volume).

Gubrium's *Time, Roles and Self in Old Age* (1976) serves as an important introduction to this field. Discourse studies could build on and refine Durkheim's view that the function of time is "pragmatic" in that it is "determined by the rhythmic ordering of cultural life" (Hendricks & Hendricks, 1976, p. 27). For example, a person's individually perceived life-prognosis can radically influence her or his orientation to social relationships, day-to-day decisions, and of course to medical care (Coupland & Coupland, in press; Elias, 1985). We have argued elsewhere (Coupland, Coupland, Giles, Henwood, & Wiemann, 1988) that physical mobility and change (travel, socializing, meetings, etc.) constitute a major resource for small talk. Therefore it seems likely that some problems attributed to talk between younger and older adults can in fact be traced to the absence of mobility and change in some elderly people's lives. Other related questions arise. For example, in what ways does the discourse of adolescents articulate values premised on "living for the present"? Contrary to this, how is the conception of a finite lifespan used strategically—in humor (e.g., the aphorism, "Life is hard . . . then you die") or in advertising (e.g., promoting sports goods with the slogan "Life is short, play hard")?

Discourse and ageism. **Textual representations and social stereotypes of age-groups and human development. Intergeneration and intergender consonance and conflict through talk. Educational, medical, scientific, literary, institutional, and lay settings.**

Since Butler's introduction of the term *age-ism* (1969, 1975), there have been only a few attempts (e.g., Coupland, Nussbaum, & Coupland, 1991) to develop sociolinguistic accounts of ageism, contrasting with the extensive studies now available of sexist language and racist discourse. But the issue of moral justifiability lies close to the surface in many of the chapters of this book. It seems fair to say that the very concept of ageism has yet to become clearly established in many Western contexts, so that even blatant age-discriminatory practices (e.g., precisely specifying age limits in job advertisements in British newspapers) sometimes go unseen and unchallenged. Perhaps it is also true that academic social science has failed to recognize the many ways in which ageism organizes and motivates so many dimensions of social practice. In the same way that feminist sociolinguistics made a sharp contribution to early feminist literatures, it should prove useful to give language-based accounts of our routinely ageist Western societies.

On the other hand, conceptualizing ageism in discourse terms can contribute to much-needed *theoretical* understanding of social aging itself. One way forward is to argue (cf. Coupland & Coupland, in press) that a basic discourse of ageism, recognizing that there is a discriminatory social force operative in Western contexts, is at least beginning to be sustained. (Admittedly, it is far better established in the United States than in the United Kingdom). Then, in opposition to perceived age-related inequalities and prejudices, an anti-ageist discourse is developing, in "defense" of the old. It is probably dominant, at present, in the social services domain, and is becoming more widely heard in professional social science. However, there are some important ambiguities that need to be teased out. The anti-ageist discourse may be interpreted to be building on the same basic assumptions that give rise to ageist practices, to the extent that it argues that older people are dependent, vulnerable, and ill treated.

Another manifestation of anti-ageist (but still in a sense ageist) discourse that we have considered is in the realm of geriatric medicine (Coupland & Coupland, in press). Here, correct assumptions that old age is not inherently a time of decrement and failing health appear to be leading medical practitioners into denying the age-salience of older people's medical problems. Arguably, this in turn cuts off one avenue of self-legitimation for older patients, who may in fact derive comfort from attributing their ill health to their aging ("Old age doesn't come alone"). These and other complexities can be the substance of future research on societal ageism, its discourse origins and implications.

References

Abeles, R. P. (1987). *Life-span perspectives and social psychology*. Hillsdale, NJ: Lawrence Erlbaum.

Atkins, T. V., Jenkins, M. C., & Perkins, M. H. (1990). Portrayal of persons in television commercials age 50 and over. *Psychology, a Journal of Human Behavior, 27*, 30-37.

Baltes, P. B. (1979). Life-span developmental psychology: Some converging observations on history and theory. In P. B. Baltes & O. G. Brim (Eds.), *Life-span development and behavior* (Vol. 2, pp. 255-279). New York: Academic Press.

Bernstein, B. (1974). *Class, codes and control* (Vol. 1). London: Routledge & Kegan Paul.

Blum-Kulka, S. (1990). "You don't touch the lettuce with your fingers": Parental politeness in family discourse. *Journal of Pragmatics, 14,* 259-288.

Bultena, G., & Powers, E. (1976). Effects of age-grade comparisons on adjustment in later life. In J. F. Gubrium (Ed.), *Time, roles and self in old age* (pp. 13-49). New York: Human Sciences Press.

Butler, R. N. (1969). Age-ism: Another form of bigotry. *The Gerontologist, 9,* 243-246.

Butler, R. N. (1975). *Why survive? Being old in America.* New York: Harper & Row.

Cole, T. R. (1986). The "enlightened" view of aging: Victorian morality in a new key. In T. R. Cole & S. A. Gadow (Eds.), *What does it mean to grow old?: Reflections from the humanities* (pp. 117-130). Durham, NC: Duke University Press.

Coupland, J., Coupland, N., & Robinson, J. (1992). "How are *you?*": Negotiating phatic communion. *Language in Society, 21,* 207-230.

Coupland, J., Nussbaum, J. F., & Coupland, N. (1991). The reproduction of aging and ageism in intergenerational talk. In N. Coupland, H. Giles, & J. Weimann (Eds.), *Miscommunication and problematic talk* (pp. 85-102). Beverly Hills, CA: Sage.

Coupland, N., & Coupland, J. (in press). Age-identity and health-identity in geriatric medical discourse. In *Health Care Encounters and Culture* [Proceedings of the 1992 Summer University of Stockholm Seminar, Botkyrka, Sweden].

Coupland, N., & Coupland, J. (in presss). Discourses of ageism. *Journal of Aging Studies.*

Coupland, N., Coupland, J., & Giles, H. (1989). Telling age in later life: Identity and face implications. *Text, 9*(2), 129-151.

Coupland, N., Coupland, J., & Giles, H. (1991). *Language, society and the elderly: Discourse, identity and ageing.* Oxford: Basil Blackwell.

Coupland, N., Coupland, J., Giles, H., Henwood, K., & Wiemann, J. (1988). Elderly self-disclosure: Interactional and intergroup issues. *Language and Communication, 8*(2), 109-133.

Elias, N. (1985). *The loneliness of the dying.* Oxford: Basil Blackwell.

Giles, H., & Coupland, N. (1991). *Language: Contexts and consequences.* London: Open University Press.

Gubrium, J. F. (Ed.). (1976). *Time, roles and self in old age.* New York: Human Sciences Press.

Harwood, J. T., & Giles, H. (in press). "Don't make me laugh": Representations of age in a humorous context. *Discourse and Society.*

Hendricks, C. D., & Hendricks, J. (1976). Concepts of time and the aged. In J. F. Gubrium (Ed.), *Time, roles and self in old age* (pp. 13-49). New York: Human Sciences Press.

Laver, J. (1974). Communicative functions of phatic communion. *Work in Progress, No. 7,* pp. 1-18. Edinburgh: University of Edinburgh, Department of Linguistics.

Riley, M. W., & Foner, A. (1968). *Aging and society: Vol. 1. An inventory of research findings.* New York: Russell Sage Foundation.

Schegloff, E. G., & Sacks, H. (1973). Opening up closings. *Semiotica, 8*(4), 289-327.

Sorensen, A. B., Weinert, F. E., & Sherrod, L. R. (Eds.). (1986). *Human development and the life course.* Hillsdale, NJ: Lawrence Erlbaum.

Woodward, K. (1991). *Aging and its discontents: Freud and other fictions.* Bloomington: Indiana University Press.

Author Index

Abeles, R. P., 197, 284
Abelman, R., 133, 134
AbuEleileh, M. T., 56
Acitelli, L. K., 215
Adams, Ansel, 34, 35, 47
Ainley, S. C., xiv
Ajzen, I., 224
Aldous, J., 194
Alinder, M. A., 34
Altman, I., 217, 219, 239
Anderson, S. A., 242
Apter, T., 201
Aristotle, 223
Aronsson, K., xix, 101, 104, 105, 124,
    125, 289
Atchley, R. C., 176, 177, 240, 247
Atkins, T. V., 288
Atkinson, J. M., 78n3
Atkinson, P., 129n1, 211n1
Atkinson, K., 215, 221

Baez, J., 38, 42, 49
Baines, S., 56
Bakhtin, M. M., 1, 8, 12, 12, 15, 17, 18,
    24n10, 25n12, 25n14, 25n15,
    25n17, 52n2
Ballow, J. W., 201
Baltes, P. B., 217, 284
Baranowski, M. D., 174
Barnett, R. C., 197
Barrow, S. B., 44
Barky, S. L., 273

Bart, P., 201
Baruch, G., 197
Bateson, M. C., 5
Baucom, D. H., 270
Baum, W., 175
Baurind, D., 133
Baxter, L. A., 262
Bazeman, C., 15
Beavin, J., 238
Beavin, J. H., 271, 273
Bell, R. A., 239
Bem, S. L., 243
Bender, M. P., 56
Benedek, T., 198, 200
Bengston, V. L., 195
Benjamin, J., 201
Berger, P., 238
Berkowitz, L., 92
Bernstein, B., 103, 105, 106, 120, 126,
    127, 128, 129n1, 133, 289
Berti, B., 197
Bielby, D., xxiv
Billig, M., 1, 12, 13, 14, 16, 18, 63, 74
Billingsley, J., 215
Blieszner, R., 240
Blum-Kulka, S., 290
Boden, D., xxiv
Bodo, Peter, 36
Booth, A., 242
Bordo, S., 51
Bormann, E. G., 253
Bornat, J., 56
Bourdieu, P., xxv

Boyd, C. J., 197
Brody, E. M., 215
Brodzki, Bella, 32
Bronfenbrenner, U., 169
Bromley, D., 96
Brown, P., xxi, 110
Brown, R., 104, 124
Bruner, J., 29
Bruss, E., 52n3
Buchanan, K., xx, 3, 56, 57, 72, 75, 102, 290
Buerkel-rothfuss, N. L., 239
Buhaighis, M. A., 242
Bullis, C., 262
Bultena, G., 288
Burden, S. G., 267, 268
Burggraf, C. S., 251, 258n3
Butler, D., 254
Butler, R. N., xxvi, 56, 57, 58, 63, 72

Cain, K. C., 231
Calvert, B., 154
Campbell, J., 32
Cannon, K. L., 242
Cantor, M. H., 215
Carter, D., 133
Carter, L. M., 238, 240
Cassel, C. K., 231
Cederborg, A. C., 124
Cheng, Nien, 42, 43, 49, 50
Chodorow, N., 199, 200, 202, 39
Cicirelli, V. G., xix, 187, 188, 215, 222, 224, 230, 284, 286, 290
Cicourel, A., xxii
Clark, K., 17
Cole, T. R., 284
Coleman, P. G., 56, 63
Collard, J., 253
Colopy, B. J., 223
Condor, S., 12, 13, 14, 74
Conville, R. L., 262
Conway, M., 91
Coombs, G., 274
Cooper, A. E., 56
Coughlan, xvii, xix, 187

Coupland, J., xi, xvii, xxi, xxiii, xxv, xxvi, 104, 125, 177, 215, 221, 286, 288, 289, 291, 292
Coupland, N., xi, xvii, xx, xxi, xxiii, xxv, xxvi, 104, 125, 177, 215, 221, 285, 286, 288, 289, 291, 292
Coward, R. T.,
Crouter, A. C., 257
Culver, C. M., 223
Cummings, A. L., 269

Damron, D., 23
Davies, B., 83, 94
DeForge, B. R., 231
DeMan, P., 30
Derrida, J., 15
Deutsch, H., 198, 200
DeWaele, J. P., 96
Dinnerstein, D., 39
Dixon, R. A., 217
Dobrof, R., 215
Dobson, C., 239, 243
DuBois, B., 192
Duelli-Klein, R., 203
Dworkin, G., 223
Dwyer, J. W., 215

Eakin, P. J., 21, 32
Edwards, D., 12, 13, 14, 74, 81
Edwards, D. E., 59
Edwards, J., xii
Edwards, J. C., 24n4
Edwards, J. N., 242
Ehlert, K., 56
Ehrhardt, A. A., 28
Eichenbaum, L., 201
Einarsson, J., 116
Elias, N., 291
Ellis, D., 248
Ellerbee, L., 43, 44
Emerson, C., 13, 24n10
Engles, F., 24n7
Epstein, N., 270
Eskew, R. W., 244

Evaldsson, A. C., xix, 101, 106, 107, 127, 128, 289
Exley, H., 173
Exley, R., 173

Falk, J. M., 71
Fallot, R. D., 56
Fanshel, D., 114
Farrell, T. B., 174
Fay, L. F., 267, 268
Featherstone, M., xviii, 58
Fengler, A. P., 239
Feyerabend, P., 192
Filsinger, E. E., 270
Fincham, J. W., 224
Fischer, L., 197
Fishbein, M., 224
Fishman, J. A., xxi
Fitzpatrick, M. A., 248
Flax, J., 39, 200
Foner, A., 288
Foucault, M., 15
Frankel, J., 56, 58, 63
Freedman, J., 274
Freeman, M., 58
Friday, N., 191
Friedman, M., 21
Frye, 52n4

Gallie, W. B., 25n11
Gane, M., 12, 13, 14, 74
Garfinkel, H., 135, 138, 140, 147
Gergen, K. J., xiv, xx, xxv, 1, 2, 3, 5, 8, 10, 16, 19, 20, 24n3, 52, 52n5, 52n1, 58, 92, 93, 192, 251, 269, 280, 281, 290
Gergen, M. M., xiv, xx, 2, 3, 32, 52n5, 58, 92, 93, 251, 290
Geertz, C., xxiv
Gert, B., 223
Getty, J. P., 40, 41, 46, 50
Gibson, F. G., 56, 58, 63
Giddens, A., xiv, xv, xvi, xvii, xviii, xx, xxii, xxv, 1, 5, 6, 16, 19, 20, 188

Giles, H., xi, xix, xxi, xxiii, 104, 125, 177, 215, 221, 285, 286, 288, 289, 291
Gillon, R., 223
Gilman, A. 104, 124
Glaser, B. G., 156
Godberg, M., 175
Goffman, E., xvii, xxii, 70, 82, 104, 105, 116
Goodwin, C., xxiv
Gore, K. E., 239
Gottman, J. M., 270, 273
Gravell, R., 221
Griffith, A. I., 202, 203
Greenwald, A. G., 91
Gubrium, J. F., xvii, xviii, 76, 77, 290
Guerin, P. J., 267, 268

Hadden, S. C., xxii, xxiii, 285
Halbert, T., 269
Hall, S., 20
Halliday, M. A. K., xxi
Halper, R., 223
Hancock, R., 201
Handel, Gl, 253
Handler, R., 175
Hamilton, M., 248
Hammersley, M., 211n1
Harding, S., 192, 204
Hare-Mustin, R. T., 272, 273
Harré, R., xiv, xx, 1, 2, 11, 24n5, 81, 83, 84, 94, 95, 96, 290
Harwood, J., xix, 288
Havasy, S., 56, 58, 63
Heath, S. B., 104, 106
Held, D., 20
Hendenquist, J. A., 116
Hendricks, C. D., 291
Hendricks, J., 291
Henwood, K., xvii, xix, xxiii, 177, 187, 215, 221, 291
Hepworth, M., xviii, 58
Heritage, J., 59, 78n3, 136, 141, 143, 147, 152
Hermans, H. J. M., 97

Hess, R., 253
Hewitt, J. P., 250
High, P. M., 231
Hobbs, A., 56
Hocker, J., xvii, xix, xx, 188, 263, 267, 268, 270, 274
Hollway, W., 83, 204
Holmes, J., xxi
Holquist, M., 17
Hoopes, J. M., 231
Hops, H., 270
Horowitz, A., 215, 230
Howe, A., 56
Howe, K., 231
Hoyer, W. J., 173
Hughston, G. A., 242
Hultman, T., 116
Hultsch, D. F., 217
Huston, T. L., 257
Huyck, M. H., 173

Iacocca, L., 37

Jacklin, C., 28
Jackson, D. D., 238, 271, 273
Jackson, P. W., 110
James, L., 36
Jelinek, E. C., 31
Jenkins, M. C., 288
Johnson, C. L., 193, 238, 240
Johnson, D. R., 242
Johnson, G. M., 170
Johnson, M., 274
Jones, L. L., 230
Jourard, S. M., 244
Jouve, N. W., 29

Kalbfleisch, P. J., 215, 239
Kahana, B., 178
Kahana, E., 178
Katriel, T., 239
Kallos, D., 103
Kant, I., 223

Kelley, H. H., 254
Kellner, H., 238
Kenny, D. A., 215
Kidd, V., 239
Kiernat, J. M., 56, 58, 63
Kirkland, G., 35, 45
Kitzinger, C., 192
Knapp, M. L., 239
Kolhepp, K. A., 244
Kreps, G. L., 221
Krokoff, L. J., 270
Kulis, S., 194

Labov, W., 114
Laing, R. D., 22, 23, 241
Lakoff, G., 274
Landry, P. H., 195
Langer, S. K., 274
Lasch, C., 19
Laver, J., 289
Lawrence, G., 35
Lazarus, L. W., 56, 58, 63
Lee, A. R., 241
Lejeune, P., 31
Lerner, R. M., 217
Lesser, J., 56, 58, 63
Lester, M., xxii, xxiii, 285
Levenson, R. W., 273
Levenson, S., 231
Levinson, D. J., 96
Levinson, S. C., xxi, 73n3, 110
Lewis, C., 56, 57, 58, 63, 72, 76
Lieberman, M. A., 57, 71
Linderman, L., 38
Lipsitt, L. P., 217
Logan, R. D., 86
Luchmannn, T., xvii

Maccoby, E., 28
MacIntyre, A., 8, 12, 23
Macke, A., 198
Magrab, P., 199
Mahler, M., 199
Mangern, D. J., 195

Manheim, K., xv
Mansfield, P., 253
Markus, H., 91
Martin, J., 269
Marx, K., 24n7
Mason, M. G., 32
Mbiti, J. S., 87
McCarrey, M., 242
McDermott, R. P., 128
McHale, S. M., 257
McKay, xvii, xx, 102
McMahon, A. W., 56, 57, 58, 63, 72, 76
Meacham, J. A., 56
Mead, G. H., xiv
Mead, M., 174, 175
Measor, L., 196
Medling, J. M., 24-2
Mehan, H., 1 57
Mercer, K., 20, 21
Meryman, R., 35
Meyrowitz, J., 24-n2
Michaels, S., 106
Middleton, D., xx, 3, 56, 57, 63, 72, 74, 75, 81, 102, 290
Mill, J. S., 223
Miller, B. C., 242
Miller, J. B., 273
Millers, S. J., 240, 247
Mills, C. W., 22
Money, J., 28
Montgomery, J. I., 238, 240
Morgan, W., 198
Morson, G. S., 13, 24n10
Morss, J., 29
Mortimer, E., 58
Moscovici, S., 95
Muhlhauser, P., 81, 84, 94
Muncie, H. L., Jr, 231

Navratilova, M., 35, 37, 49
Noblit, G. W., 160
Noelker, L. S., 194, 215
Norris, A. D., 56, 58, 63
Notman, M., 231
Novak, W., 37, 44
Nussbaum, J. F., xx, 173, 221, 291

Oakley, A., 196
Ochs, E., xxiv, xxv, 104, 105, 107, 125, 127
O'Connor, P., 195, 196
Olney, J., 31
Ong, W. J., 86, 87, 175
Orbach, S, 201
Orvis, B. R., 254
Overton, W. F., 219

Parlee, M. B., 192
Pascal, R., 31
Patterson, G. R., 270
Pearlman, R.A., 231
Perkins, M. H., 288
Perrotta, P., 56
Petre, P., 53
Phillipsen, G., 239
Phillipson, H., 241
Piaget, J., 178
Pickens, T. B. , Jr. 34, 36
Pillemer, K., 194
Pineo, P. C., 244
Pomerantz, A., 64, 78n3
Poole, M. S., 215
Postman, N., 90
Potter, J., xii, 59, 204
Powers, 288
Pratt, C. C., 230
Prusank, D, T., xvii, xix, 101, 102, 289

Rabuzzi, K. A., 52n3
Radley, R., 12, 13, 14, 74
Raphael-Leff, J., 210
Rashad, A., 36, 41
Redfoot, D. L., xiv
Reese, H. W., 217, 219
Reinhardt, J. P., 230
Revere, V., 71
Rhudick, P. J., 56, 57, 58, 63, 72, 76
Rich, A., 51, 52n4, 191, 210
Ricover, P., xvii, 175
Riley, M. W., 288
Rivers, J., 35, 45
Roberts, E. L., 195

Robinson, J. D., xx, xxv, 288, 289
Rogoff, B., 217, 219
Rollins, B. C., 242
Rollins, J., 198
Romaniuk, J. G., 71
Romaniuk, M., 71
Rook, K. S., 221
Ross, M., 91
Rossmiller, D., 231
Rundstrom, B., 124
Russ, J., 52n3
Russell, C. S., 242
Ryan, E. B., xxi
Ryden, M. B., 56, 58, 63

Sacks, H. xxii, 73n3, 289
Sampson, E. E. 9
Sarbin, T. R. 92
Sayers, J. 201
Sayers, S. 270
Saxby, P. 56
Schegloff, E. G. 289
Schenck, C., 32
Schenkein, J., 108
Schieffelin, B. B, xxiv, xxv, 104, 105,
    107, 125, 127
Schummn, W. R., 242
Schutz, A., xvii
Schwartx, T., 36
Shanas, E., 215
Sheehy, G., 5, 19
Sher, T. G., 270
Shin, H. Y., 230
Shotter, J., xiv, xx, 1, 2, 6, 8, 11, 16,
    25n11, 52n1, 82, 188, 189, 192
Sigel, I. E., 224
Sillars, A. L., xvii, 188, 215, 238, 239,
    245, 251, 256, 257, 258n1, 258n3,
    262, 263, 265, 286
Sills, Beverly, 38, 43, 48
Silverman, D., 129n1
Silverstone, B. M., 230
Slevin, K., 198
Smith, D., 192
Smith, D. E., 202, 203
Smith, R., xxiv

Snyder, D. K., 271
Sobal, J., 231
Sorensen, A. B., 284
Spainer, G. B., 242, 267
Spodek, B., 157
Sporakowski, M. J. 242
Sprinker, M., 52n3
Stam, H., 15
Staton, A. Q., xvii, xix, 102, 155, 170,
    171n1
Steinmetz, S. K., 133, 194
Stern, D., 201
Stevens, D., 265
Stiles, W. B., 248, 249
Stinnet, N., 238, 240
Stiver, I., 273
Stokes, R., 250
Straus, M. A., 267
Strauss, A. L., 156
Strong, P. M., 105
Suitor, J., 194
Surrey, J., 273
Sussman, M. B., 195
Suurmond, J., 56
Swenson, C. H., 244

Taylor, C., xiv, xxiii, xxiv, 1, 8, 10, 16
Taylor, D. A., 239
Tenny, J. H., 23
Thompson, T., xx
Thurnher, M., 239
Tobin, S. S., 57, 71
Tomlinson, T., 231
Torode, B., 129n1
Townsend, A. L., 194, 215
Tracy, K., xxi
Troll, L. W., 240, 247, 256
Trump, D., 36, 39
Turner, H. B., 231
Turner, M., 274
Tylbor, H., 128

Uhlmann, R. F., 231
Urban, G., 88
Urwin, C., 202

Vallacher, R. R., 96
van Gennep, A., 155
Van Langenhove, L, xiv, xx, 2, 83, 90, 290
Vecsey, George, 35
Volosinov, V. N., 8, 12, 21, 24n10, 25n13, 25n17

Walker, A. J., 230
Walkerdine, V., 29
Wallace, J. B., 76, 77
Warren, J. W., 231
Watson, T., Jr., 53, 47, 48
Watzalwick, P., 238, 271, 273
Weedon, C., 203
Wegner, D. M., 96
Weider, D. L., 136, 147
Weinhert, F. E., 284
Weintraub, K. J., 31
Weisberg, J., 251, 258n3
Weiss, R. L., 270
Welch, D., 133
Wertheimer, A. I., 224
Wetherell, M., xii, 59, 204
Wheeless, L. R., 244
White, L. K., 242
White, P., 198
Widdecombe, S., 70

Wiemann, J. M., 125, 177, 221, 291
Wiemann, M. C., 221
Wilkinson, D. Y., 195
Williams, A., 221
Williams. B. A. O., 82
Wills, R. M., 271
Wilmot, W. W., xvii, xix, xx, 186, 238, 239, 257, 262, 265, 267, 268, 270
Wilmott, M., 194, 195
Wilson, E. A., 251
Wingrove, C. R., 198
Winnicott, D., 199
Wittgenstein, L., 1, 7, 9, 11, 12, 14, 24n4
Woodward, K., 284
Wooffitt, R. C., 70
Woolgar, S., 192
Wurf, E., 91

Yeager, C., 36, 40, 41, 42, 46, 50
Yost, S., 251
Young, P., 194, 195
Young, R., 223

Zietlow, P. H., xvii, 188, 238, 242, 245, 251, 256, 258n1, 258n3, 262, 286
Zweibel, N. R., 231

Subject Index

Academic domain, 157, 161, 164
Accounting/accountability, 8, 62, 67, 74, 77, 81, 101, 132, 134, 136, 251, 255
Adolescent, 160, 163, 170
Affective proximity, 124
Age-appropriate behavior, 289
Age-categorization processes, xxiii, 285, 287
Age-graded normative events, 217, 286
Ageism, xxvi, 291
Age-salience, 287
Analogies, 60
Anaphora, 88
Androcentric bias, 191
Anti-ageist discourse, 292
Architectonics, 17
Attachment, 195
Attitude agreement and understanding, 244
Autobiography, 30, 31, 81
Autonomy, 223, 228, 232
Autonomy/paternalism and decision making, 224, 232, 252

Balancing chains, 254
Behavioral marital therapy, 270
Benefitance, 91
Biological threshold, 219
Blending chains, 253
Boundaries, 116, 125, 127, 288

Career genres, 8

Change agent, 265
Chomsky, 14
Closeness, 204
Cognitive bias, 91
Cohort-related values and experiences, 239, 286
Communal themes, 251
Compliant child, 156, 158
Conflict, 187, 194, 199
Conflict management, 240, 245, 256, 270
Conservatism, 92
Contemporary social theory, 284
Contextual/dialectic models, 217, 220
Continuity, 174, 176, 253
Conversation analysis, xxii
Criterial rules, 105
Cross generational talk, 285
Cultural identity, 81
Culture, xxiv, 19

Deconstructive, 15
Deconstructionist analysis, 273
Decontextualized accounts, 285
Defense mechanism, 58
Delegated decision making, 229
Desolates, xviii
Developmental change, 216
Developmental-functionalist, 57
Dialectic, 11, 12, 72, 73, 217, 273
Dialectical causality, 218
Dialogue pedagogy, 103
Differentiating chains, 254

Direct perspective, 241
Discipline, 13, 138, 151
Discourse and ageism, 291
Disengagement, 143
Dispreferred, 64, 67, 70
Dominance, 273
Dramaturgical analysis, 104
Dyadic decision making, 215, 2333

Ecological transition, 169
Egocentricity, 91
Elderly parent-adult child, 215
Embedded discourse theory, 281
Embodied selves, 33, 39, 50
Environmental causes, 286
Escalation sequences, 247
Et cetera clauses, 139, 151
Ethical beliefs, 223
Ethnography, 105, 107
Ethnolinguistic identity, xxi
Ethnomethodology, xxii, 107, 132, 135,
     140, 285
Exchange value, 71
External continuity, 178

Family caregiving, 215, 221
Feminist theory, 187, 191, 192, 196, 203
Figures of speech, 60
Formative power, 22

Gendered narrative, 33
Genealogy, 181
Generational alignment, 285
Generational boundaries, 116
Generational self-disclosure, 285
Genre, 20, 22, 48
Greetings, 143

Hegemony, 20
Hierarchical rules, 105
Hierarchy, 253
Historical causes, 286
History-graded normative events, 286
Horizontal distance, 104, 124

Identification, xiv

Identity, 6, 65
Idiographic, 81
Implicit communication, 257
Indexicality, 88
Individualism, xviii
Individualistic themes, 251
Inherent causes, 286
Insight-oriented therapy, 271
Interdependence, 237, 252
Intergenerational alignment, 125
Intergenerational dyadic caregiving,
     216
Intergenerational family relationships,
     193
Intergenerational solidarity, 187, 195
Internal continuity, 178
Intervention, 188
Intimacy, 195, 240
Intrinsic developmental processes,
     239, 286
Intrinsic value, 70
Isolates, xviii

Kinship, 194

Launching couples, 241
Legitimate information, 113
Lifespan development and aging, 218-
     220
Lifespan developmental and psycho-
     logical perspective, 216
Lifespan identity, xiv
Lifespan language socialization, 288
Lifespan psychology, 216
Life stage experiences, 239, 286
Life stories, 32
Literacy, 85
Locating, xxii

Marital communication, 238
Marital conflict, 242, 247, 267
Marital satisfaction, 241, 242, 270, 277
Marital stress, 242
Mental deterioration, 63
Metamorphose images, 279
Meta-perspective, 241
Metaphoric discourse, 274

Metaphoric transformations, 276
Metaphors, 60, 89, 267, 269, 274
Meta-talk, 250
Micro rituals, 289
Modernism, 8
Monomyth, 32
Multiaccented, 21

Narrative, 30, 86, 87, 174, 274
Narratology, 92
Nonevaluative description, 266
Nonnormative events, 217, 286
Normative events, 217

Objectivism, 10
Oral cultures, 87, 94
Orality, 85
Ordinary theorizing, 77
Organismic meta-model, 219

Particularize, 63
Passively congenial interaction style, 256
Paternalistic/paternalism, 188, 221,
    223, 227, 232
Pedagogies, 105, 126, 128
Personal identity, 82
Perspicuous representation, 7
Plasticity, 216
Positioning theory, 83
Power, 124, 272
Pragmatics, 59
Preferred, 67, 75
Prospecting, xxiii
Prospective views, 136
Proximity, 128
Psychobiography, 86, 96
Psychodynamics, 86
Psycholinguistics, x, xi
Psychological development, 198
Psychosexual, 198
Psychotherapy, 200

Reciprocal interaction, 225
Reconstitution, 143
Relational power, 22
Relationship change, 264

Relationship constellations, 265
Relationship themes, 251
Reminiscence, xx
Retrospective views, 136
Rhetorical functioning of time, 290
Rhetorical-responsive, 7, 12
Romanticism, 8, 10
Rule-governed, 147

Satisfaction, 288
Saussurian, 14
Self-actualization, 175
Self-disclosure, 125, 241, 244, 248, 256
Self-esteem, 175
Self-other, 10, 65
Sequencing rules, 105
Sex role identification, 241, 243
Sharing time settings, 106
Social constructionism, xxii, 6, 7, 10,
    58, 187, 192, 196, 202
Social domain, 157
Social exchange, 70, 71
Social identity, xxiv, 17, 20, 81, 125
Social learning theory, 198
Social objects relations, 198, 199
Social positioning, 57
Social representation, 95
Sociolinguistics, 83, 285, 288, 289
Solidarity, 124
Speech act theory, 124
Status domain, 161, 164
Status passage, 155, 162, 165, 166, 169
Structural analysis, 271
Subjectivism, 10
Submissiveness, 273
Surrogate autonomy, 229
Surrogate decision making, 229
Systems theory, 271

Temporal change, 197
Temporal framing processes, xxiv, 287
Triangulation, 271
Topoi, 21
Turning points, 262

Verbal response modes, 248
Vertical distance, 104, 124

About the Contributors

Karin Aronsson (Ph.D., University of Lund, 1978) is Professor at the Department of Child Studies at the University of Linköping. She has published widely in the field of language and social interaction, especially language and social identity in institutional settings. Current publications center on the participant status of children in adult-child interactions such as pediatric consultations and everyday family life.

Kevin Buchanan is a lecturer in Social Psychology at Nene College, Northampton, in the School of Social and Behavioural Sciences. His research interests are focused on the application of discourse analysis to psychological topics. He is a member of the Loughborough Discourse and Rhetoric Group (DARG).

Victor G. Cicirelli is Professor of Developmental and Aging Psychology at Purdue University, holding Ph.D.s from the University of Michigan and Michigan State University. He is a Fellow of the American Psychological Association and of the Gerontological Society of America. His research interests include dyadic caregiving decision making and family relationships in later life. He is the author of *Family Caregiving: Autonomous and Paternalistic Decision Making* as well as numerous articles and book chapters.

Geraldine Coughlan qualified as a registered general nurse at St. Bartholomew's College of Nursing and Midwifery in 1989. She is interested in women's health, cultural approaches to sickness, and psychological development in adulthood. She is currently studying for a B.S. in psychology at Brunel University.

Justine Coupland is lecturer in Sociolinguistics in the School of English and Communication at the University of Wales in Cardiff. She is coauthor of *Language, Society and the Elderly*, and coeditor (with Jon F. Nussbaum) of the forthcoming *Handbook of Communication and Aging Research*.

Nikolas Coupland is Reader in Sociolinguistics and Director of the Centre for Language and Communication Research at the University of Wales in Cardiff. For the session 1989/1990 he was Fulbright Scholar and Visiting Associate Professor at the Department of Communication, University of California, Santa Barbara. He has previously published nine books and three journal special issues on topics in sociolinguistics, discourse analysis and interpersonal/intergroup communication. These include *Dialect in Use*, *Language: Contexts and Consequences* (with Howard Giles), and *Language, Society and the Elderly: Discourse, Identity and Ageing* (with Justine Coupland and Howard Giles). Proceedings of an International Colloquium on *Communication, Health and the Elderly*, under his coeditorship, appear in the Fulbright Colloquia series.

Ann-Carita Evaldsson (Ph.D., University of Linköping, June 1993) is a researcher at the Department of Communication Studies, Linköping University, Sweden. Her interest is in children's everyday social life, and the relationships between language socialization and local notions of action and self.

Kenneth J. Gergen is Professor of Psychology at Swarthmore College. He is the author of *Toward Transformation in Social Knowledge* and *The Saturated Self*, and is currently completing a volume titled *Realities and Relationships*. Along with John Shotter, he edits a series on social construction for Sage, and is coeditor with him of *Texts of Identity*.

Mary M. Gergen is Associate Professor of Psychology and affiliated with the Women's Studies Program at Pennsylvania State

University, the Delaware County Campus in Media, PA. In 1988 she edited *Feminist Thought and the Structure of Knowledge,* and is currently writing a book on social constructionism and feminist psychology. She is interested in gender relations and their impact on narrative forms, particularly autobiography.

Alan Grossman teaches in the English Department at the University of Cardiff, Wales. He is currently working on a Ph.D. in the area of the discursive construction of cultural identity and colonial discourse theory.

Rom Harré is a Fellow of Linacre College, Oxford and Professor of Psychology, Georgetown University, Washington, D.C. His publications include *Personal Being* (1983), *Varieties of Realism* (1987), *Physical Being* (1991), *Social Being* (new edition, 1993), and many others. His main field of research is discursive psychology.

Karen Henwood (Ph.D., University of Bristol, 1987) was employed for 4 years on a collaborative research project between social psychologists and applied linguists, investigating the social construction of aging in interaction and talk. Her current research on adult mother-daughter relationships fuses her interests in feminist scholarship, gender identity, and qualitative research. She has lectured at Brunel University since 1989.

Joyce L. Hocker received her Ph.D. in Speech Communication from the University of Texas-Austin in 1974, and in Psychology from the University of Montana in 1985. She is coauthor of *Interpersonal Conflict* and taught in the communication departments of the Universities of Colorado and Montana for 15 years. In 1985 she left her full professor position to enter private practice as a Clinical Psychologist in Missoula, MT.

Valerie Cryer McKay (Ph.D., University of Oklahoma, 1988) is an Associate Professor at California State University, Long Beach. Her primary research areas are intergenerational and family communication with a focus on grandparents and grandchildren; she is currently investigating multicultural aspects of this relationship.

David J. Middleton (Ph.D., Nottingham University) has lectured in the Department of Human Sciences at Loughborough University since 1979. His research interests center on social remembering in a variety of organized and institutional settings. He is a member of the Loughborough Discourse and Rhetoric Group (DARG), coauthor of *Ideological Dilemmas: A Social Psychology of Everyday Thinking,* and coeditor of *Collective Remembering.*

Jon F. Nussbaum (Ph.D., Purdue University) is Professor of Communication at the University of Oklahoma. He is coauthor of *Communication and Aging,* editor of *Life-Span Communication: Normative Processes,* and is currently coediting *Interpersonal Communication and Older Adulthood: Interdisciplinary Research* and *The Handbook of Communication and Aging Research.* He has published more than 50 journal articles and book chapters including recent articles within *Ageing and Society, The International Journal of Aging and Human Development,* and *Communication Education.* He was named a Fulbright Research Scholar for the 1991-1992 academic year and was appointed a visiting professor at the University of Wales, College of Cardiff to study interpersonal communication and successful adaptation to the aging process. His current research interests include the study of friendship across the lifespan and intergenerational relationships. In addition to research, he is involved in establishing the Oklahoma Center for Aging at the University of Oklahoma Health Sciences Center.

Diane T. Prusank (Ph.D., University of Oklahoma, 1989) is an Assistant Professor of Communication at the University of Hartford. Her research interests include family interaction, the politicalization of the family, and magazine portrayals of intimate relationships.

John Shotter is Professor of Interpersonal Relations at the Department of Communication, University of New Hampshire. His long-term concern is with the social conditions conducive to the development of autonomous personhood, social identities, and responsible action. His latest book is *Cultural Politics of Everyday Life: Social Constructionism, Rhetoric, and Knowing of the Third Kind.*

Alan L. Sillars (Ph.D., University of Wisconsin, 1980) is Professor of Communication Studies at the University of Montana. He teaches and conducts research in the areas of communication, conflict, and family relations.

Ann Q. Staton (Ph.D., University of Texas, 1977) is Professor of Speech Communication at the University of Washington. She has published in the area of instructional communication, focusing on teacher communication concern, teacher socialization, and student socialization. Her book, *Communication and Student Socialization*, explores in more depth the student transitions described in her chapter in this volume.

William W. Wilmot is Professor of Communication Studies at the University of Montana. He is author and coauthor of five books, the most recent *Interpersonal Conflict*, *Dyadic Communication*, and *Mediation at Work*. He has an active consultation, facilitation, and mediation practice and is a Senior Associate with the Yarbrough Group, a consulting firm located in Boulder, CO.

Luk Van Langenhove holds a master's degree in criminology and a Ph.D. in psychology. Since 1981 he has worked as a researcher and lecturer at the Vrije Universiteit, Brussels (VUB). His main research interests are personality assessment and several applied fields of psychology, including the psychological study of science and technology. He currently is coordinator of the "Science Technology Assessment Management" group at the VUB and holds the post of Vice-Chief of Cabinet of the Belgium Minister of Science Policy.

Paul H. Zietlow (Ph.D. in Communication, Ohio State University, 1986) is currently an Assistant Professor of Communication, Adjunct Professor of Family Studies, and Director of Communication at Concordia University. Formerly, he served as an ordained Lutheran minister and Assistant Professor of Communication at Ripon College. He is currently completing an 8-year longitudinal study of marital communication behavior among aging couples.